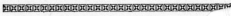

Americans from Norway

BY

LEOLA NELSON BERGMANN

THE
PEOPLES
OF AMERICA
SERIES

Edited by Louis Adamic

J. B. LIPPINCOTT COMPANY

PHILADELPHIA   NEW YORK

Acknowledgments

I AM INDEBTED to numerous libraries and historical societies, particularly to the Norwegian-American Historical Association whose archives at St. Olaf College, Northfield, Minnesota, were for me a house of treasure. From the association I received permission to quote unpublished material from the collected correspondence of the late Kristian Prestgard, editor of *Decorah-posten*, of the late Olaf Ray, Chicago attorney, and of Nicolay Grevstad, one-time United States Minister to Uruguay and Paraguay; the association also gave me permission to reprint the ballad "Oleana," translated by Theodore C. Blegen and published in *Studies and Records*, and to quote widely from its numerous publications. From the Minnesota Historical Society I received permission to quote from an unpublished manuscript by Andrew A. Veblen and from a letter among the A. A. Veblen Papers. The library of Montana State University granted me permission to use material from "The Contribution of the Scandinavian and Germanic People to the Development of Montana," an unpublished master's thesis by O. M. Grimsby. The following publishers permitted me to quote from the books listed: Alfred A. Knopf, Inc., *Not So Wild a Dream* by Eric Sevareid and *Kristin Lavransdatter* by Sigrid Undset; E. P. Dutton & Co., *Seventy Years of Life and Labor* by Samuel Gompers; Doubleday & Co., Inc., *Woodrow Wilson, Life and Letters* by Ray Stannard Baker.

Among the many individuals to whom I am indebted for information through conversation, letters, and through documents which they have permitted me to use I should like to thank the Grant Anderson family, Little Sister Bay, Wisconsin; Louis Nyhammer, St. Louis, Missouri; James Berdahl, Sioux Falls, South Dakota; O. O. Enestvedt, Sacred Heart, Minnesota; and Jarle Leirfallom, St. Paul, Minnesota. To Dr. Olaf Trygvason of Iowa City I am indebted for a thorough scrutiny of the manuscript. Beyond measure is my gratitude to Gustav Bergmann who, as a philosopher and logician, relentlessly forced me to clarify my thought, sharpen my expression, and polish my style; who, as my husband, was ever patient, generous with his encouragement, warmly interested, and proudly considers himself the only American

5

from Vienna who likes *lutefisk* and knows how many Norwegians live in North Dakota.

L. N. R.

Contents

THE BACKGROUND

THE SPREAD

PRAIRIE SOCIETY

8 CONTENTS

THE CITIES

SAILORS

OUTSTANDING INDIVIDUALS

Foreword

THE GREAT NORWEGIAN novelist, Arne Garborg, once wrote of his people, "They are a strong, stubborn folk who dig their way through a life of brooding and care, putter with the soil and search the Scriptures, force a little corn from the earth and hopes from their dreams, put their faith in the penny and trust in God."

Over a million of these people came to America between 1825 and 1925. Not long ago the writer of a Norwegian newsletter which is sent to American readers commented, "For twenty years I have looked for a person—man or woman in Norway—who does not have some kind of relatives 'over there,' and I am still looking." The story of the fortunes of these "strong, stubborn folk" in the New World has been preserved in letters that were treasured by families in Norway and later collected by historians; in reminiscences of the pioneers who, in the dreamy days of old age, recalled their youthful conquest of the new earth; in Norwegian newspapers published in the large Midwest, the East and the West of America; in pamphlets and books which traced the history of local churches, schools, towns, and societies organized and built by the immigrants.

From such records has emerged the story of Norwegian migration, settlement and life on the frontier, in small towns, and young cities, highlighted by the deeds of its leaders, many of them clergymen. Much of all this, told frequently and well, I have repeated. Some I have not. A tale told too often breeds, if not contempt, at least boredom. Because the majority of the intellectuals, in other words, those who did the writing, were either Lutheran clergymen or closely affiliated with the church, it is only natural that the church looms large in the written record; one easily gets the impression that very little Norwegian life existed outside its pale.

This is a lopsided picture, for there was another life, a significant minority. Only in recent years have historians brought this other life into view and treated it with the respect it deserves. I, too, have tried to add to that picture and, consequently, have drawn to the center of the stage figures who have too frequently been kept in the background be-

9

cause they did not fit the prevailing pattern. Others who have long been in the spotlight I have treated as scarcely more than names; others, still, may not appear at all. The story of Americans from Norway has not yet been fully recorded. As it unfolds in the years to come we shall know more intimately their life in the coastal states, on the western ranges, and their part in the labor movement, as well as we now know them as farmers, clergymen, and politicians in the Middle West.

AMERICANS FROM NORWAY

THE BACKGROUND

1

These Came Early

THE STORY OF the coming of the people from the land of Thor to the American forests and plains has more than one beginning. One could start with an autumn day in 1825 when a pint-sized sloop, the *Restaurationen,* docked in the New York harbor and unloaded half a hundred bewildered passengers. A newspaper reporter recorded their arrival and commented on the coarse dress of those from farms, the calicos and gay shawls of the townfolk. Few Americans with Norwegian ancestors can trace their American roots further back than to this event. Yet there were Norwegians scattered here and there on the eastern seaboard all through the early history of our country. For another beginning we could go to New Amsterdam in the year 1630, almost to the same spot where the sloop folk landed, and watch *de Eendracht* anchor off the bank of an island, at the tip of which a fort, a few houses, and a windmill gave sign of settlement, and see a few Norwegian families step off the boat with their Dutch friends. But even that is too late for our history to start. We must turn back to the days of the Norse vikings and the sagas to find the story of the first Norwegian family and the birth of the first white child on American soil. Even then, sometime in the 1020's it is thought, the landing site may have been in the general region of that of the 1630 and the 1825 Norwegians. Perhaps one would have seen, coming up the Sound between the sandy shores of a cape and an island of meadowland and trees, a wide-bottomed vessel with a square scarlet sail bellied to the breeze, a dragon-headed prow pointing its way through the waters. A small boat is lowered and rows toward the beach. One of the men springs ashore and walks to the grasses' edge to taste the sweet dew undried by the new day's sun. This is Thorfinn Karlsefni and his party. They have come to Vinland, discovered a few years earlier by one of their own Greenlanders, Leif Erikson, who returned home to tell about

13

a land of self-sown wheat and wild grapes. Thus begins the story of Norwegians in America.

The accounts of voyages to and settlements on the American continent as found in the sagas and other sources have been accepted, though not without controversy, as records of actual events. Nevertheless, one must proceed cautiously through the remote fogs of the North Atlantic in viking days, particularly in calling out place names and dates. Easier to accept has been the tradition that the viking sealords were a bold, overdaring breed of men, guiding with consummate skill their light boats, which rode the waves like peanut shells, across vast reaches of stormy, uncharted ocean. Perhaps our need for a heroic past has made them more daring and more skillful than they were. The odds against them may not have been as great as is commonly believed. Climatologists have advanced theories, for example, that between A. D. 500 and 1000 the weather in northern Europe was much warmer and drier than it is now, that the North Sea was generally calm and the North Atlantic considerably easier to sail across than it is today. An invasion of England from the Scandinavian peninsula in those days was not, perhaps, a major naval undertaking; and likewise, sailing to Iceland, farther to Greenland, and even to the North American continent were feats not beyond credence. At least the sagas, in matter-of-fact style, record such voyages, and since scholars now permit us to use the sagas for history as well as literature, we will go to them for the narrative of Leif Erikson and the Discovery of America.

The viking bands that landed on the North American continent in the eleventh century came from Greenland, not from Norway. In order to keep our bearings, we had better make clear the connection between Norway and Greenland and how it happened that Leif Erikson, who was born in Norway, lived out on the edge of nowhere among the icebergs and walruses. Except from the archeologists, we do not know much about the recorded history of Norway before 800. By that time, however, the vikings had already begun to menace the coasts of Great Britain and were heading their green and gold dragon boats toward the Netherlands and establishing beachheads in Normandy whose very name honors the conquering North men. They established themselves, too, on the Orkney, Shetland and Faroe islands, and between 860 and 870 began to visit Iceland. Kings were numerous and short-lived in those days and the only way a viking ruler could stay in power was to make war his business and keep fighting it out. They took turns conquering each other and with each new aggression a shift in the population occurred. When King Harald Fairhair, the Charlemagne of Norway, unified Norway and then made war on the western islands, several chieftains and their followers fled to Iceland.

Leif Erikson's father, Eric the Red, was one of those who left Norway and settled in Iceland. But he did not live in peace, turbulent viking that he was. It seems that he had unwisely loaned a friend the highseat pillars from his home, a mark of real friendship, for these were highly prized possessions. When Eric later came to claim them, the friend refused to give them up. Eric, consequently, made short shrift of his one-time friend. But the Icelanders had firm laws to take care of such unruly persons; Eric was banished from the land for three years. Having heard of lands to the west, he hoisted his sail and followed the path of the sun, finally coming to an uninhabited land. Sailing along the coast he saw a barren shore, innumerable small islands, rocky promontories; behind lay mountains of glistening ice and snow. But turning into the fjords that speared narrowly into the land, he found the inner parts edged by rich meadow grass, stunted birch and willow trees. Until it was safe for him to return to Iceland, he explored the desolate land, searching for a place where he could settle. When his time was up, he returned to his old home where, like a good real estate promoter, he peddled the charms of the distant "Greenland," as he called it, and lured a few adventurers and malcontents into going back with him. Twenty-five ships began the voyage; fourteen were said to have reached their icy paradise.

According to their custom of taking land, Eric most likely measured off a portion as large as he and his ship's crew could carry fire around in one day. He settled in Ericsfjord and from the red sandstone of the vicinity built his home Brattahlid. This was in about 985 or 986. Leif grew up there, pitting his strength against the roaring of the waves. Norwegian trading ships carried goods to Iceland and occasionally ventured beyond to Greenland to supply the settlers there with the products of a higher civilization. The crews of these ships told tales of Odyssean adventure, and Leif listened, growing more manful and determined with each ship's arrival. His silken beard was still short when he set out with his own boat and crew and sailed, not to Iceland first, but directly to Norway, thus making the first non-stop voyage across the Atlantic. Brave were he and his men to hazard the long and perilous journey with only their gods to bring them to a lucky end. King Olaf Trygvason of Norway, hearing of the singular voyage made by the bold youngster, invited him to spend the winter at his court. This Leif did and was Christianized. In the spring when the agreeable young viking went home, King Olaf sent with him back to Greenland one wearing a mitre, who was to bring salvation to the colonists. On the way Leif saved a shipwrecked crew and brought them also to Greenland. People, when they heard the story, named him Leif the Lucky, but his father, Eric, said that having restored life to the crew might be balanced against having brought the impostor, as he called the priest, to Greenland. The independent Eric refused the holy water, continuing to worship an old polar bear living in the neighborhood of Brattahlid.

One version of the discovery of Vinland is that it was on this return trip from Norway that Leif, driven off his course, accidentally came to the shores of the New World, and finding grapes and vines in abundance named the land Vinland. The other version, from another saga, discarded by some authorities as unreliable, is that Leif heard about the new land from a young trader, Bjarni Herjulfsson, who, sailing from Norway, had been carried by winds to the shore of strange lands. Leif was too much an investigator of the seas and lover of the roving life to let the rumor pass him by unheeded, and hearing that Bjarni intended to settle down quietly with his father in Greenland, Leif lost no time in making a deal with him for his vessel.

With thirty-five men crowded on the half deck of his small boat, he sailed in a southwesterly direction from Greenland, coming after many days to a land of flat rocks which he named Helluland. This probably was somewhere along the Labrador coast. Continuing south he again saw land, this time heavily forested, which he called Markland, probably Newfoundland or Nova Scotia. Still unsatisfied, he put out to sea again and sailed until he came to a region of grassy meadows, and there he stopped to explore. What he and his men found convinced them that a winter could be spent there. The streams swarmed with salmon; there was grass for cattle and timber for huts. Grapes and vines abounded; no frost came during the winter to wither the grass; day and night were more nearly of equal length than in Greenland and Iceland. Scholars believe that these observations, preserved for us in the sagas, identify this place either as the Cape Cod region, Narragansett

Bay, or the Long Island Sound area. The year is about 1003.

Whatever the time or the place, scholars are unanimous that Leif Erikson did reach the shores of the New World and called it Vinland, for references to Vinland have been found in manuscripts from the twelfth, thirteenth and fourteenth centuries. Also, it is certain that further and more extended expeditions to Vinland were made in the years following Leif Erikson's discovery. One interesting and, we are told, fairly reliable account tells of the first attempt of the Norsemen to colonize the New World. A wealthy Icelandic captain, Thorfinn Karlsefni, visited Eric the Red at Brattahlid one winter while the talk of and curiosity about Vinland was at its height. In the spring, after marrying Gudrid, the widow of another of Eric's sons who had been in Vinland, he organized an expedition. Three ships carried 160 people, livestock, and equipment for permanent settlement to the shores of the new land. The first winter was spent at a place they called Straumsjord, possibly the western extremity of Long Island, where Gudrid bore a son named Snorri. If we accept the sagas for more than colorful legends of the days of yore, then we have here the birth record of the first white child born on the North American continent.

Karlsefni and his party found the land hospitable—streams full of fish, timber in abundance. Permanent settlement appeared possible. But when spring came Indians (the sagas call them "Skraelings") issued from the forests in great numbers, and although they seemed willing to trade their bundles of furs for red cloth and milk food, they were suspicious of the invaders. Fear and mistrust finally led to open hostilities and bloodshed. After three years of increasing disturbances, Karlsefni and his people despaired of peace and returned home. The child Snorri was three winters old when they arrived in Greenland. Thus the Norse attempt to colonize America failed, but voyages to Vinland apparently did not cease.

A body of fascinating literature has accumulated on possible later expeditions. Viking relics, suggesting such visits, but whose authenticity has not yet been definitely proved or disproved, were unearthed along the Atlantic seaboard and as far inland as northern Minnesota. In 1898 a farmer near Kensington in northern Minnesota dug up a large stone slab inscribed with what appeared to be runic symbols. A young Norwegian-born American, Hjalmar Holand, began to study the stone and despite cries of "forgery" from many scholarly quarters, he doggedly persisted in his attempt to build history around the Kensington Stone.

Now, after half a century of painstaking research, he has published several books and many articles in defense of his theories about viking expeditions to America.

In the fourteenth century an expedition under the leadership of Paul Knutson was sent out by the King of Norway and Sweden to search for the Greenland colonists, who were rumored to have forsaken their Christian faith. Not finding them there, the Knutson party, so Holand thinks, proceeded naturally to Vinland, reaching Narragansett Bay in 1355. Again finding no traces of the colonists, Knutson set up headquarters and sent out a detachment to continue the search. According to Holand's theory, this smaller party sailed up the Atlantic coast into Hudson Bay, down to the Nelson River, into Lake Winnipeg, the Red River and finally reached northern Minnesota's lake region. There the Kensington Stone tells the rest of the story, the inscription according to runologists reading:

> [We are] 8 Goths [Swedes] and 22 Norwegians on
> an exploration journey from
> Vinland round about the West   We
> had camp by [a lake with] 2 skerries one
> day's journey north from this stone
> We were [out] and fished one day   After
> we came home [we] found 10 of our men red
> with blood and dead   AV[E] M[ARIA]
> save [us] from evil . . . year . . . 1362

Meanwhile the crew that had remained on Narragansett Bay had erected a building, the ruins of which are still standing in Newport, Rhode Island. Although mystery has surrounded this tower and the possibility of its being an ancient viking structure had been considered in the forepart of the nineteenth century, the most generally accepted tradition was that it had been built as a windmill in the late seventeenth century by Benedict Arnold, the first colonial governor of Rhode Island. In 1942 the distinguished archeologist, Philip Ainsworth Means, examined the whole question of the curious cylindrical, eight-columned tower in his book *Newport Tower* and concluded that it was not a windmill and had not been built by Governor Arnold. From that point Holand takes up the investigation and presents evidence that the building is a fourteenth century fortified church designed like those Paul Knutson had seen in Norway, Denmark, or even in the Holy Land. If this theory will hold up, then the Newport Tower is what remains of the oldest Christian church in the entire western hemisphere. Excavation of the ground around the structure is being carried on and if relics of viking seafarers should actually be found, a new page will have to be inserted in American history. Mr. Holand's fifty-year crusade for the acceptance of fourteenth century visits by the Norse will then not have been in vain. At the moment the controversy between believers and disbelievers still continues, with reputable scholars on both sides, but the increasing interest eminent Scandinavian archeologists take in the relics throws considerable weight in the direction of Holand's theories. When the Kensington Stone was placed in the Smithsonian Institution in Washington, D.C., in 1948, Dr. Matthew W. Stirling, chief of the government's Bureau of American Ethnology, called it "probably the most important archeological object yet found in North America."

For at least two or three centuries knowledge of Vinland stayed alive in northern Europe and on the inhabited islands of the North Atlantic. How far south it spread we do not know, although the tales of Vinland may have travelled with the viking ships that found their way into the warm waters of the Mediterranean, where, perhaps, they were heard by the crews of Venetian and Genoese galleys. Later on, when the expansionist spirit of the fifteenth and sixteenth centuries excited the imaginations of kings and explorers, voyagers of that day may have remembered these tales of a northern route to Cathay. By the fifteenth century the settlements in Greenland had disappeared, but Iceland still was peopled and in a legendary form the memory of the viking exploits may have lingered on in the group mind. We know, for example, that a Portuguese nobleman, Joano Vas Corte-Real, sailed in 1472 from Iceland to Newfoundland with Norwegian pilots, crew and equipment, perhaps seeking a northwest passage to India. Even Columbus, in February, 1477, made an expedition to Iceland, known then as Ultima Thule. Why he went and what information he gathered we cannot tell from the notes he left us. Yet, there gleams through these dimly lit spaces of history the imaginative suggestion of a thread that ties Leif Erikson to the great Genoese.

That voyages across the stormy waters of the Atlantic could be made in the small open skiff of the viking seafarers has been proved twice in modern times. When the World's Columbian Exposition was held in Chicago in 1893 to commemorate the discovery of America, some Norwegians built a ship patterned after a viking vessel found in 1880 in a burial mound at Sandefjord, Norway. Rigged with a square sail, the dragon-prowed *Viking* left Bergen on April 30 with a captain, two mates, and a crew of nine sailors. On May 27 the captain from the signal station at St. John's, Newfoundland, sighted the small vessel and, thinking it was a shipwrecked schooner with only part of the mast and sail left, he and his men steamed out to the rescue. When he learned that all was well and that the vessel had come from Norway under its own sail, his astonishment bordered on incredulity. The *Viking* continued its voyage, reaching New London, Connecticut, on June 14; from there it sailed to Newport, Rhode Island, then to New York, where it was taken up the Hudson River, through the Erie Canal, over the Great Lakes to Milwaukee and finally to Chicago. There the *Viking* became part of the Norwegian exhibit at the exposition. Enthusiastic Norwegian Americans in Chicago collected money, bought the vessel, and presented it to the Field Museum at the close of the exposition. Later it was moved to Lincoln Park, Chicago, where it was placed on permanent exhibition.

In 1926, a year after the centennial celebration of the beginnings of modern Norwegian migration to America, another Norwegian viking ship was built as nearly like the one used by Leif Erikson as it could be made. Only forty-two feet long and less than thirteen feet wide, the *Leif Erikson* was equipped with the usual red and white striped square sail, as well as a set of triangular sails, an ordinary rudder, a row of shields on each side of the boat, and the traditional dragon's head and tail, fore and aft. Perhaps food, clothing, and lifesaving gear were more adequately provided for on this modern viking ship; a few nautical instruments unknown to Leif the Lucky and his crew also gave the modern vikings a slight advantage; nevertheless, their equipment consisted of the bare essentials for such a voyage. The captain of this boat, Gerhard Folgerø, tried to duplicate the course taken by Leif. Heavy storms, drift ice, and dense fog almost brought disaster, but the crew finally reached the harbor at St. John's, Newfoundland, a month and two days after leaving Iceland. When the *Leif Erikson* arrived in Boston harbor on August 12, it had covered a distance of 6,700 miles, and had proved that, in spite of terrific hazards, the route taken by Leif in 1000 or so, could be travelled in the little open vessels of his day.

For some decades a few leaders of Norwegian American affairs have been vexed at the lack of attention given to the part played by the Norse vikings in the discovery of America. They have worked vigorously throughout the years, organizing in 1929 the Leif Erikson Memorial

Association of America to promote the establishment of a Leif Erikson Day. Long before Leif's accomplishment was officially recognized, Leif Erikson Day celebrations took place in cities heavily populated with Norwegian Americans. Such a one was held in Chicago in 1925 with parades, speeches by the mayor, a Congressman, an audience of thirty thousand, elaborate athletic contests, and an exhibition of folk dancing. A few years before that the Norwegian Americans in Chicago had been successful in getting the city to name one of its lovely new boulevards Leif Eriksen Drive; in Brooklyn a large open square was dedicated and named Leiv Eiriksson Square. Finally in 1935 President Roosevelt asked Congress to proclaim October 9 Leif Erikson Day throughout the land, that date being chosen because it was on October 9, 1825, that the *Restaurationen* brought the first party of modern-day Norwegians to this country.

Recognition of Leif Erikson Day has not been widespread throughout the nation; only a half dozen or more states in the Middle West and West have made it officially a day of celebration. Brooklyn, with its large Norwegian population, has enthusiastic festivities; Chicago, Minneapolis, and Seattle also observe the day with great pomp and ceremony. Even New Orleans, of Latin traditions, has for some years observed the day with commemorative luncheons, articles in the press, and speeches in the schools. Norwegian Americans are proud of the viking exploits and happy for the opportunity to celebrate them in speech and song. One cannot help wondering, though, how badly distorted by platform enthusiasm is the story of Leif and his luck, about which we know so little.

On May 24, 1630, ten years after Plymouth Rock had received from Holland the little band of dissatisfied English expatriates, a Dutch ship, *de Eendracht,* sailed into the sheltered bay of New Amsterdam and on the edge of the virgin forests of the Hudson Valley left a group of settlers. They had been firmly instructed to make good in the New World by the wealthy Amsterdam jeweler and patroon, Kiliaen Van Rensselaer. Prior to this event the West India Company, in an effort to colonize the land claimed for Holland in America, had established the system of patroons in which a grant of land was made to a person on the condition that he bring fifty adults to New Netherland and settle them on the Hudson River. The shrewd and successful Kiliaen Van

Rensselaer was responsible for the eight or nine Norwegians that were aboard *de Eendracht* that day at the threshold of summer.

Among them was a woman with her husband and three little daughters. She was Anneke Jans, "a small well-formed woman with delicate features, transparent complexion, and bright, beautiful dark eyes." She and her husband Roelof Jansen had emigrated to Holland from the Norwegian city of Marstrand; while in Holland they had met Kiliaen Van Rensselaer and now were bound for the colony of Rensselaerswyck, near the present city of Troy, where for $72 a year Jansen was to be a foreman on the patroon's farm. Two years after arriving, he was appointed to a judicial office, which gave him the right to wear a "black hat, with silver bands." As a farmer Jansen was not so successful; so neither he nor his patroon had any regrets when he left "de Laets Burg," Van Rensselaer's farm, to move with his family to New Amsterdam where he was given about sixty acres of land along the East River. It is this plot of ground, inherited by his wife, that has since become the wealthiest and most famous tract of land of its size in the entire United States. But more about Anneke before we reach that story.

Her good husband died shortly after acquiring the land in 1636, leaving Anneke with five children to support in a colony scarcely settled. However, a woman with "a well-balanced mind, a sunny disposition, winning manners," as she has been described, would not lack a suitor for long in a settlement where single men greatly outnumbered marriageable women. A Dutch Reformed pastor, Everardus Bogardus, claimed her attentions; two years after her first husband's death Anneke was settled in the parsonage, the first woman in the city of New York to marry a minister. As a pastor's wife Anneke was one of the ranking ladies of New Amsterdam and New Netherland. In 1647 Bogardus, while on a voyage to Holland, perished in a shipwreck. Left a widow again with several children and three married daughters, Anneke managed, in spite of some financial troubles, to buy a bit of property in Albany, where she built a house and lived the remainder of her life.

It was the farm on Manhattan Island that brought posthumous fame to the petite Norwegian lady and caused two centuries of legal headaches. In 1671, shortly after the English conquered New Netherland, Anneke's heirs conveyed the property to the governor of the province of New York. Confiscated by the Duke of York in 1674, it became the "Duke's Farm," the "King's Farm" when he ascended the throne, and the "Queen's Farm" during the days of Queen Anne. In 1705 the colonial authorities granted the land to Trinity Church. But since one of Anneke's sons, Cornelius, had not joined with the rest in the conveyance of 1671, his heirs soon advanced the claim that that sale was thereby invalidated, thus giving them a right to the property. Between 1750 and 1850 no less than sixteen or seventeen lawsuits were brought against Trinity Church by heirs who cast longing eyes on the riches coming from the plot of ground where merchant princes and money changers were establishing their counting houses. No court has ever sustained the claims of the disgruntled heirs, who have appeared with each new generation in spite of repeated warnings of the futility of suits against the Trinity Corporation. Societies such as the Anneke Jans Association and The Anneke Jans International Union have been formed in the hope that organized effort would succeed where individuals had failed. But to no avail.

Even during the twentieth century the case has appeared from time to time in the courts. In 1909 Mary Fonda, a direct descendant of Anneke, filed a suit against the wealthy Episcopal corporation for one per cent of its property. Another suit was filed in 1915. In 1922 a fantastic swindle revived interest in the case, setting droves of gullible persons on the trail of the Trinity gold. It seems that swindlers had sent out hundreds of letters and fake newspaper clippings with the information that the famous estate was to be distributed by orders of the Federal government, which had discovered a vault in New York City with millions in money, jewels, and other valuables belonging to the estate. The "clippings" also stated that the property to be assigned to the heirs included Trinity Church, nearly all of Wall Street, the Woolworth Building, the Carnegie Mansion, and the United States Treasury and Customs buildings. The government had intervened in the litigation, the "clippings" stated, in an effort to collect the enormous income tax that each heir would have to pay. Naturally the swindlers asked for contributions to help defray the legal expenses involved in the settlement. And literally hundreds of people fell for it, flooding the offices of the district attorney and police in New York City with inquiries. Little did the sane and sensible Anneke ever dream that the small "bouwerie" she and Roelof acquired out among the skulking Indians a mile north of the Fort would be a *cause célèbre* in the annals of American jurisprudence.

Anneke Jans was not the only Norwegian woman who held a prominent position in the colony at New Amsterdam. Her mother Tryn (Katherine) Jonas, also an immigrant from Marstrand, Norway, was a midwife by profession, the first in New Netherland. As the official midwife for the West India Company, she was paid from public funds and was held in high honor by the colonists for her service to the sick. This matriarch of the colony had many a distinguished child and grandchild. Her daughters married into prominent Dutch and German families—landowners, government officials, and professional men.

The Norwegians in the colony intermarried with the Dutch and Germans, who outnumbered them, more frequently than they married Norwegians or other Scandinavians. Many of the old Hudson River families—the Stuyvesants, Van Cortlands, Van Rensselaers, Knickerbockers, Schuylers, De Peysters, Jays, Gouverneurs, Bayards, De Lanceys, and Morrises—can trace their blood back to the Norwegian midwife, Tryn Jonas, and her distinguished offspring. The Vanderbilt dynasty is descended from the seventeenth century Jan Arentszen Van der Bilt, who signed his name with marks resembling a window sash with four panes, and whose first wife was Anneken Hendricks from Bergen, Norway. Her daughter married the German, Rem Remsen, who began the Remsen line in this country. The well-known Bergen family of Long Island and New Jersey is descended from the Norwegian ship carpenter, Hans Hansen Noorman as he was commonly called, who came to New Amsterdam in 1633 with Wouter Van Twiller, the governor of New Netherland. He married a Dutch girl of Walloon ancestry who bore him six children. Also from Bergen, Norway, came Herman Hendricksen, the progenitor of the Rosenkrans family in America, the most distinguished descendant, perhaps, being General William Stark Rosecrans, Brigadier General of the Regular Army in the Civil War, later United States Minister to Mexico, Congressman from California, and first Register of the Treasury under President Cleveland. Among the descendants of Arent Andriessen from Norway are the Putnams and the Bradts of New York.

How did it happen that Norwegians were among the Dutch settlers in the first place? There was, during the early part of the seventeenth century, a close commercial friendship between Norway and Holland; Norway's initiative on the seas had lagged with the loss of her political independence to Denmark, while Holland had risen for a short time to rule the seas. Thus, needing more sailors and ship carpenters than she had, she turned to her neighbor across the North Sea whose men had long been building ships and going down to sea. There were hundreds of Norwegian sailors on the Dutch ships throughout the seventeenth century, many of them bringing their families to Holland and settling there. So it is not at all strange that a few found their way to the Dutch colony along the Hudson River. How many there actually were during the period of Dutch rule it is difficult to say, in spite of the detailed records kept by the orderly Dutch, much better, incidentally, than by the English who followed them as rulers of the province in 1664. One noted historian of Scandinavian immigration to New Netherland, John O. Evjen, has reconstructed the biographies of fifty-seven Norwegians about whom there is no doubt of their emigration from Norway during the period 1630 to 1674, the date of the final conquest of the Dutch by the English. That there were more is quite possible. But counting these few heads is not meaningful unless one knows that the total population for New Netherland was never very great: 1,500 in 1647, 2,000 in 1653, and 10,000 in 1664. Although it is very likely that emigration from Norway to New York did not entirely cease after 1674, there was a marked decrease, mainly because Norway discovered through her connection with Holland that she had a future on the sea, and instead of sending her youth to help man foreign fleets she now employed them in building up her own.

However, the Norwegians were not the only representatives from the Scandinavian countries in the Dutch province; Danes were there in even larger numbers, Swedes fewer. We know that altogether some two hundred Scandinavians came as immigrants between 1630 and 1674, and from this group of northerners, small though it was, one can trace some rather distinct contributions to the life of the otherwise Dutch community.

Toward the establishment and maintenance of a firm economic basis for the colony, the Norwegians contributed the skills one acquires in a land where timber and waterfalls abound. The Hollanders, accustomed to flat land and windmills, gladly learned from them how to use the energetic streams of the Catskills for running their sawmills and grist-mills, two of the leading industries of the province. The Norwegians were particularly expert at sawing lumber. We see from the records, for example, that Laurens Andriessen operated two large sawmills, Laurens Laurensen another. The preservation of certain skills and trades in families and groups, generation after generation, turned many Norwegians to shipbuilding and sailmaking, several of them owning boats and freighting lumber and merchandise on the Hudson and Delaware rivers. Not only were they ship carpenters of note, but builders of sturdy houses. Thus it probably came about that the Scandinavians introduced a new form of architecture to America.

The first settlers apparently used bark-lined or log houses; when they began to replace these with permanent homes, the more wealthy took to the familiar Holland brick for their high and narrow-gabled houses; stone was used for the lower and smaller houses. The greater part of the houses in the colony, however, were built of wood in a design somewhat alien to Dutch ideas. It was the "clapboard" house, where the boards run horizontally, overlapping one another. This technique was not familiar to the Dutch; nor could the English, who used shingles when they began to build permanent homes, have given them the idea. The Norwegians, though, were accustomed to this type of construction. In Bergen, the Norwegian coast town from which many of the Norwegian immigrants had originally come, clapboard construction was exceedingly common during the sixteenth and seventeenth centuries. So it is not at all unlikely that America owes to the Scandinavians what is still the most common method of siding a house.

Farmers, fishermen, millers, sawyers, and tobacco planters these Norwegians were, fashioning their ways to the ways of the Dutch up to a certain point. On the more intangible side, the Norwegians helped sow a few seeds of democracy in a colony not founded on or ruled by democratic principles. Like most of the colonies in the New World, the Dutch were intolerant in religious matters. You may earn your bread as you see fit, the Dutch officials said in effect, but you must thank God for it in the way we think fit. But many of the Norwegians and other Scandinavians, reared in the Lutheran faith, were not willing to submit to the religious dictation of the Dutch Reformed Church. They therefore fought to secure Lutheran ministers and to establish their own churches, which they succeeded in doing, thus being one of the forces, albeit a small one, that made the Dutch respect the right of other religious groups, such as the Quakers, Mennonites, Catholics, and even the Jews.

In other ways, too, the Norwegians helped make the Dutch colony the timid anticipation it was of greater things to come. Although they were a small national minority, they did not suffer from political or other discrimination. They were elected to administrative offices; the demand for labor, as always in a frontier community, exceeded the supply, thereby giving everybody a measure of economic security; socially, they were close enough to the dominant group in language and behavior patterns to assimilate rapidly. Intermarriage with the Dutch was common, naturally enough, since the majority of the Norwegians had come single, although some families with children were among the immigrants. And among the immigrants' children, too, mixed marriages were frequent.

Because the Norwegians absorbed the new culture easily, as is evidenced by the Dutch endings they gave their names and by their adoption of the Dutch tongue, the group has remained unnoticed in colonial history until twentieth century historians, with their interest in ethnic groups, began to search the records of colonial trading companies, to consult ships' registers, family papers, wills, and legal instruments left by the early settlers of the American colonies. In the light of this new history we see many new people and hear the accents of many foreign tongues in the "Dutch" colony. Already in the grassy lanes of New Amsterdam in the 1650's several languages were spoken, almost as if history had been tuning up for the polyphony that now rises so richly from the pavements of New York. And the Norwegians, though they were not many, were there and in a small way contributed to the cosmopolitan air and the spirit of democracy that stirred in the colony.

A few other Norwegians may possibly have reached America in the seventeenth century, settling in New England, according to the Norwegian historian, Halvdan Koht, who has traced several Scandinavian names among New Englanders. One such family, the Gunnisons, seems to have come from Norway. Hugh Gunnison is believed to have been brought to Boston in 1631 by an English captain, and although family tradition has it that he was a Swede, Koht feels that his name points rather to Norway, probably to Bohulsen, a Norwegian province ceded to Sweden in 1658. Be that as it may, Hugh Gunnison served as an associate judge of the court of common pleas and in 1654 was made a deputy to the General Court of Massachusetts. Since then, the Gunnison family has spread over the entire country. One John Gunnison was a captain in the American Army in the middle part of the nineteenth century and has a fort and river in Colorado named after him.

There was also a trickle of Norwegians into the seventeenth century Swedish settlements on the Delaware that becomes quite noticeable toward the middle of the eighteenth. These early American Swedes maintained their culture and kept their allegiance to the Lutheran State Church of Sweden. The spires of their churches along the Delaware naturally attracted Lutherans from Norway who sought homes in the New World.

When the Moravian sect founded its colonies at Bethlehem, Pennsylvania, in about 1740 and at Bethabara, North Carolina, about a decade later, there were among them several Norwegians who carried on the trades of carpentering, shoemaking, and tanning. Others were teachers and spiritual leaders. Jost Jensen, a Norwegian, was an innkeeper in Bethlehem where between sixty and seventy Norwegian names have been identified on the gravestones in the old Moravian churchyard. In 1753 there arrived in Bethabara colony a Norwegian physician whose name was to rank among the leading medical men of colonial days. He was Hans Martin Kalberlahn from Trondhjem, Norway; in America he called himself John M. Calberlane, shedding as it were one of the outward marks of his immigrant status. Living but six years in the colony before being stricken by fever, Calberlane worked tirelessly to maintain decent health conditions in the settlement; the records afford glimpses of a man of marked talent and rare character.

In Philadelphia a Society of Scandinavians was founded as early as 1769. This society seems to have died shortly after the beginning of the nineteenth century, but in 1868 a few Philadelphians of Scandinavian birth founded the Scandinavian Society of Philadelphia, regarded by the members as a continuation of the original society.

Except for these groups, no other clusters are to be found in the eighteenth century. Names of individuals, however, and scraps of information about some of them have come down to us. Four or five Norwegian seamen are known to have enlisted as soldiers in the colonial army in New York. Torgus Torkelsen Gromstu, a seaman from Gjerpen, Norway, settled in New York about 1805. Thomas Johnson, the son of a pilot in Mandal, Norway, served under John Paul Jones during the American Revolution, taking part in the battle between the *Bonhomme Richard* and the *Serapis,* in which the latter was captured by John Paul Jones; Johnson later served on this ship, on the *Alliance,* and on the *Ariel.* We know, too, that another Norwegian, Lars Bruun, who had changed his name to Lewis Brown, also served under John Paul Jones.

Although Georgia, and the South in general, never was attractive to Norwegians, a Norwegian sea captain named Iverson settled there sometime near the close of the eighteenth century. The family remained, and an Iverson, one of the captain's grandsons, became United States Senator from Georgia in the years preceding the Civil War.

So far the Norwegians have not counted for much in the settlement of the eastern seaboard, but the few who were there farmed and traded, built a few ships and houses, sailed on American brigs and schooners, and fought for the independence of the new country. With peace came expansion. Lewis and Clark reported to the White House on the New West. Trails began to widen into roads; cartwheels grooved ruts where only footsteps had flattened the grass; mountain forests thinned to make room for caravans and cabins; canals sluiced inland creating new water lines and city-dots on maps. In the overcrowded capitals and port cities of Europe travellers and natives gossiped about Napoleon's campaigns and the unheard-of spaciousness and wealth of the New Republic. The hopeful and hopeless alike found their ways to the wharves of Liverpool, Bremen, Goteborg, and Havre to hear more about the charm of the New World and to watch gold-sailed vessels slide into the sinking sun.

2
Norway—The Land and the People

IN THE STUDY of America's national groups one must, first of all, turn one's attention to the past of the people who crossed the sea, for whatever habit patterns and mental traits a national group displays have been centuries in forming. There is a uniqueness about each immigrant group, a particular set of circumstances, a certain kind of cultural background that impels it to move, to think, and to live the way it does.

A thumbnail sketch of the "typical" Norwegian American of the mid-nineteenth century would look something like this: He has a fairly lean and long but sinewy body that moves with unhurried precision. His face is square or long, the cheekbones rather high and noticeable; his eyes a pale blue or light brown, going well with his light complexion—there is no guile in them; rather early in life fine wrinkles appear at the outer corners of his eyes, around his mouth, across his forehead. Puritanically he believes in hard work and little pleasure; he lives frugally, dresses simply, does not relax easily, rears his children with stern admonition, worthy precepts, and little demonstration of the love he feels for them. Intensely loyal to the Lutheran Church and the Republican Party, he is a great respecter of authority in all forms; yet he is somewhat contentious and doesn't allow himself to be led around by the nose. He runs his affairs in an orderly fashion and when he undertakes something sees it to a finish. His verbal facility is not great; he thinks neatly and slowly, but unimaginatively. His thought, innocent of all subtlety, plows as carefully to the point as he himself to the next corner of his 40-acre plot. Nor is he very flexible; when he has once adopted a pattern, he is not likely to deviate from it, be it in politics, religion, or the kind of tobacco he chews. In the face of trouble he is patient and uncomplaining. He solves his problems not through clever maneuvering, but by dogged and persistent attack. What he gets out of life he expects to get through his own efforts. He perceives clearly the details of his world and knows

30

how to handle them; but he doesn't often have the vision to do things on a grand scale, and therefore will not plunge into big enterprise where risks are great. His is a small-scale life, the peasant and artisan mind that gets its satisfaction from doing a job well, not demanding spectacular returns for its efforts. Modest in his ambitions for himself, he is also modest in his hopes for his children.

How did he come to be this sort of person? One is afraid to be misunderstood, after the Battle of Berlin, if one ascribes certain characteristics and traits to particular nationalities and racial groups. Descriptive phrases like "the hot-headed Irishman," "the silent Swede," "the vivacious Frenchman," "the warm-hearted Italian," or "the phlegmatic German," colorfully literary as they are, have at best some statistical truth. So we must be clear on what level we speak, lest through ignorance and intellectual laziness we give aid and comfort to the racemongers who want to sell us their vicious notion that whatever differences there are necessarily spring from the blood. Scientifically these assertions are unproved, to say the least. On the other hand, with the combined researches and analyses of historians, sociologists, political geographers, ethnologists, and psychologists, we have come to realize that whatever their cause there are some differences among the national groups, that history has built into them something that may, with reasonable precautions, be called their "national character."

Ignorant as we still are of the subtle alchemy of this process, it seems a shrewd guess that most basic, perhaps, among the many causal factors is the physical environment. A mountainous country nurses a different kind of people and favors a different kind of commonwealth than does, for example, a plains region. An insular people such as the British will develop traits that mark them apart from those who dwell in a landlocked country, such as the Swiss. And, of course, geography prescribes, or at least limits, the occupations of a people; nor is it unreasonable to expect that the different personality traits of those who engage primarily in seafaring, or in trade, or in agriculture and grazing are partly due to the differences of their callings. Even a people's attitude toward the supernatural may in some measure have been determined by its surroundings. Ultimately, the whole texture and flavor of a national culture must be seen against the background of soil, weather, waterways, and lay of the land, for the language of a people, its institutions, mores, and "national character" are in a very real sense a growth from the soil. Thus, when large fragments of several old nations come together, as it happened here, to form a new one, we should know something about the many lands that bred them.

Lying on the outskirts of the inhabited regions of the globe, Norway hangs like a small club from the hem of the North Pole area, extending 1,100 miles from the frosty tip of the handle to its bulging head. If this long, narrow strip of country were squashed together it would cover not quite all of Minnesota and Iowa or about half of Texas. If, without change of latitude, it were placed on the North American continent, it would stretch from the magnetic pole to central Labrador, a region of icy waste and hyperborean gloom. In reality it has a great variety of climates. Up north the winters are long, cold and dark; but the short summers are full of light, with the sun never setting. The western and southern coastal districts, favored by the Gulf Stream and warm southwestern winds, enjoy moderate winters and summers, not unlike those of our own Pacific Northwest. There orchards and flower gardens bloom without coaxing.

Most of Norway's area is mountainous and rocky, forbidding rather than inviting habitation. Three-quarters of the soil is barren; only about three per cent is actually under cultivation, most of that meadow. Grain is grown on less than one per cent. Most of these fields and meadows huddle in the deep and narrow valleys without which Norway would be almost desolate. There, in these little cracks in the mountains, the people and the culture of Norway have grown. Swift-running streams fall from sloping hillsides, fan in sprays over rocky ledges and hurry onward through the valleys, often widening into oblong lakes. The coast, abruptly dropping, is jagged and rocky, narrow fjords cutting into the land, short in the south, long and narrow in the west and north. Scattered along almost the entire length of the seaboard are small islands, called "skerries," vital to the fishermen and for coastal traffic.

Dense forests of fir, pine, and birch cover about one fifth of the country. From ancient times the main occupations of the people were agriculture, forestry, fishing, and cattle breeding. When we know that up until the industrialization of the country late in the nineteenth century, the overwhelming majority of the population (small though it was) * lived by farming and grazing, and that on an area of roughly about four thousand square miles, it helps to understand the small-scale life and personality of the Norwegian American farmer. Centuries of urg-

---

* In 1825 the population was a little over a million; by 1850 less than a million and a half; by 1900 something over two million.

ing each seed of grain to bring forth its kernels teaches a people to attend to the patient details of life.

Long before Norway became a kingdom, the Norse left their mark on the history of many European nations. Spreading fanwise from their land of brooding winter mists and mountain wilds, the vikings coursed the seas, sliding their long black ships with gaping-mouthed dragon prows into coves and up rivers of distant lands. Most of the knowledge of these pagan warriors comes from the Christian annalists who lived in the cities harried by the northmen. Small wonder, then, that the records dwell on the evil deeds of these conquerors—monasteries burned, villages devastated, women and children enslaved, all of which barbarous acts were committed with primitive exuberance. But some of these Norsemen conquered and stayed, as happened in northern France, in parts of England and Ireland, in the Faroe and Shetland Islands, in Iceland and Greenland, and, at the far end of the map, in Sicily. Wherever they stayed, they established their codes, mixed their language with that of the new tongue, and introduced many of their customs. More often than not, they left an imprint on the social and political fabric that is still discernible, faintly in some places, clearly in others. And strangely, to these Norse people their own law was important above all else. Their kings were powerful, but their law was supreme.

Before the end of the ninth century Norway was united into one kingdom and the ancient kings laid down the principle: "With laws shall we build our land, not with lawlessness lay it waste." But as the Middle Ages approached and the pennants of feudalism began to flutter from castle towers in other lands, her power declined. Her empire crumbled, her colonies were forgotten; king and court left the country; the nobility, never large since the land was not rich enough to support a "kept" class, all but disappeared. When in the fourteenth century the Black Plague reduced her population to a few thousand, Norway was no longer a match for the stronger states of Sweden and Denmark. Sometimes she was ruled by a Swedish king, sometimes by a Dane, until finally in the early part of the sixteenth century, losing what little independence she had feebly clung to, Norway became a province of Denmark. Until 1814 she was the Cinderella of the North; yet she had once known freedom and created a stern body of law. This the common people of Norway steadfastly remembered through three centuries of complete political and cultural subjection. And, preserving the spark to be kindled again into the bright flame of 1814, they kept fighting for their ancient rights against the foreign nobles who inched their way over the forested land.

Anchored in the law from the viking age down was the right to own and inherit land through the *odel* (allodial) system, by which the estate descended from father to eldest son. If the land fell into other hands, the heirs could buy it back. This institution the Norwegian farmers guarded as a sacred fire, and the Danish kings respected it. In spite of the infiltration of feudal nobles during the period of Danish rule, the Norwegian farmer remained free and personally independent, asking little or nothing from the favor of barons or kings. Well one might say of him what someone says to the hero in Undset's *Kristin Lavransdatter,* "Proud you are, Lavrans—you are like those udal farmers we have heard of in olden times, who would have naught to do with the titles the Kings would have given them, because their pride could not brook that folk should say that they owed thanks to any but themselves." Throughout Norway's history such self-reliance has determined her social make-up and molded the mentality of her people. Century after century a man, poor though he be in money, cattle, and goods, could pick up a handful of the soil he plowed and say, "This is my soil, my land, and it will be my son's after me." Thus is formed an attitude toward life that generations later, seasoned with frontier democracy and Yankee individualism, may well become self-reliance of a more Emersonian flavor.

Although Norway began to develop a merchant class during the sixteenth century, after the monopoly of the Hanseatic League had been broken, the farmers continued to be the backbone of the nation. When taxes became too high and too many of their privileges were taken from them by Danish officialdom, they rose in rebellion. But their cries against heaven were bootless and many of the rebel leaders were executed or imprisoned. Such acts of injustice only served to swell the indignation of the farmer against the official class, and the unhappy leaders became national symbols in the continuing fight for freedom.

During the Napoleonic wars Norway had virtually been isolated from Denmark by the British blockade. Thus forced to depend upon herself, she conducted her domestic affairs without guidance from the Danish throne. After Napoleon's defeat Denmark, having been allied with France, was forced to give up Norway. The Norwegians were not sorry to have their ties with Denmark severed, but when in 1814 the news reached Norway that she had been ceded to Sweden in the Treaty of Kiel, a storm of anger swept the country. Prince Christian Frederick, the Danish royal governor of Norway, who had already won the admiration of the people, understood that this was the time to act. He called for a constitutional assembly, which was presently elected in an atmosphere of universal enthusiasm. In April, 1814, the assembly convened at the Anker estate in Eidsvoll, some forty miles north of Oslo, where in the mansion that is now Norway's Independence Hall, the 112 delegates—merchants, farmers, civil and military officials, and a few noblemen—met daily to draft a constitution.

On May 17, 1814, the work of the assembly was completed with the acceptance of a constitution and the election of Prince Christian Frederick as king of Norway. Ever since, this date, *Syttende Mai,* has been celebrated in Norway as the Fourteenth of July in France and the Fourth of July in America. The rather democratic constitution declared Norway a free kingdom with, once again, a royal throne of her own. Thus, a tiny nation, weak in many ways, asserted her independence and established a political system much more liberal than was acceptable to the reaction that was then sweeping through the council chambers of Europe.

But Norway at this moment was stirred and emboldened by the rising spirit of nationalism. Few contemporary Americans realized what was happening in Norway, how similar to their own, in a quieter way, was Norway's fight for freedom. Nor did they realize that the little mountain country in northern Europe had established a government closer to the American than any other in Europe. The Norwegian leaders had watched the democratic experiment in the West with great interest, and with it and the spirit of the new nation they were wholly in sympathy. One American, however, did recognize the kinship between the two countries. John Quincy Adams, travelling through Sweden in the spring of 1814, commented in his diary that the desire for the acquisition of Norway was so strong in the hearts of the Swedish people that he felt there could be "no room left for any just or generous feeling in favor of America." Norway, on the other hand, he judged, was fighting for the same principles that America had fought for and was realizing. For the Norwegians America was the great symbol of freedom in the world. As the nineteenth century advanced and so many left for the New World, the lustre of that beacon became even brighter.

Although Norway had declared her independence, she had to fly the Swedish union flag on her ships, for she did not have the military strength to go to war with her more powerful neighbor, behind whom stood the yet more powerful England. But Norway's national assembly, the Storting, made it clear to the Swedish king that she would be governed by her own laws and her liberties safeguarded by her new constitution. Sweden was reasonable. Except for foreign affairs, Norway retained her independence, and the combined consular system did not bother her until later in the century her expanding shipping interests became impatient of all outside interference. Finally in 1905 the union with Sweden was peacefully dissolved. The Danish prince then elected to the throne, who took the ancient royal name of Haakon, is today still the constitutional ruler of the country. Indeed the monarchic form of government was chosen because of a long and ancient tradition that thought the king the guardian of his people's rights and liberties. During the recent war years King Haakon VII was in his quiet way as powerful a symbol and as steadying an influence as the royal house of Great Britain.

Belated as she was in her growth in almost every way, Norway's renewal of an independent political life in 1814 also brought new life on other fronts, the social, intellectual, and industrial. So, her nineteenth century was in spirit a blend of several different ages. Touches of the Renaissance and the Age of Reason intermingled with the dominant forces of romanticism and nationalism. The energies of the age were released in many directions, of which the emigration movement was only one. On the world's horizon appeared new faces and voices who spoke in Norwegian accents, and Europe listened curiously to this new tongue. Early in the century, there was the mathematician Niels Abel, who died at the age of twenty-seven with world-wide fame and who will rank forever as one of the greatest mathematical geniuses the world has seen. He was followed later by Sophus Lie who opened a whole new field in the same abstract discipline and thereby brought world renown to himself and his country. Sophus Bugge's research in all phases of Indo-Germanic philology, particularly his work on the origins of northern myths, the runic alphabet, and his interpretation of runic inscriptions turned even the eyes of the great generation of German linguists his way.

More important for the national life of Norway was the work of a self-educated peasant boy, Ivar Aasen, whose interest in philology led him to create a language that was distinctly Norwegian. Norway was, and in a measure still is, a country of many dialects, each with its own syntactical structure. This was a rural phenomenon, largely due to the relative isolation of the valleys. The official language, that is, the written language and that of schools, church, and educated people, was Dano-Norwegian, known as *riksmaal*. Of course, there were no grammars or dictionaries for the Norwegian dialects, no system of word forms, endings, conjugations, and gender. Aasen undertook the monumental task of writing a grammar and a dictionary of the people's language. Sifting the dialects for the forms most commonly used and closest to the Old Norse, he systematized them into a new language known as *landsmaal*. The movement to spread this tongue, purely linguistic at the start, was opposed by those who still looked to Denmark as Norway's cultural mentor; gradually, however, it joined and merged with other forces, economic, political, and religious, all of which together produced the most significant social phenomenon of nineteenth century Norway—the cleavage between the rural population or *bønder* as the farmers were called, on the one hand, and officialdom, government and church, on the other.

The age also brought forth a group of historical writers who helped to fan the spirit of nationalism; foremost among them were Rudolf Keyser, P. A. Munch, and J. E. Sars. Two writers of international stature, Bjørnson and Ibsen, interpreted Norway, her history and her people, through plays, novels, and poetry, early in their careers in the vein of romanticism, later as the leaders of the realistic movement in literature. Grieg, whose ancestors came to Norway from the Scottish Highlands bearing the name Greig, gave to the world romantic melodies from the northern mountains. Compared to countries like Germany and France, Norway's gifts to the world have been small, but for a nation whose population reached the two million mark only by the end of the nineteenth century, it was a show of some magnitude.

The century also brought to Norway a university for which she had long been working, a national theater in which works of native authors were presented by native actors. But these advances did not come without struggle. Not all the people of Norway were confident that the country could stand on its own feet intellectually and culturally. Many intellectuals, a large portion of the burgher class, and the official class still took their cues from Copenhagen. Three centuries of thinking Danish could not be changed overnight. But, on the other side, a small but vigorous group of intellectuals had long been alarmed at the thick crust of Danish culture that had overlaid and stifled Norway's own life. Language and literature, the schools and the church—everything was molded into the Danish form. Yet these men knew that Norway

had once had a life of her own, that a forgotten but glorious past had
only to be remembered. So they set out to reconquer this heritage by
studying in the spirit of romanticism the history of their people, thus
reviving the traditions of an ancient and independent Norway. And,
seeking to uncover the real Norway, they found the farmer, untouched
by Danish influence in his remote valley, speaking the Norse language
of olden times, reciting the sagas of Snorri, the tales of the trolls and
the mountain creatures. Stimulated by this romantic vision, writers, historians, and linguists went into the hidden valleys of Norway to record,
and by recording, preserve what they saw and heard. Thus drawn into
the center of the social and cultural scene, the farmer, the new hope of
Norway, was at last also to have his political chance. But it takes time for
the inarticulate to find speech after centuries of silence.

Finally, in the 1830's the *bønder* found a leader to give voice to their
ideals and their aspirations. He was the radical young intellectual,
Henrik Wergeland, who had returned to Norway from Continental
travel deeply steeped in Rousseauistic and egalitarian ideas. His writings
and speeches urged the people to break away from all foreign influence,
particularly Danish and German. Norway, he declared, had a rich past,
and if she would only rely on herself, she could build a national culture,
independent and peculiarly her own. Wergeland's nationalism was
openly opposed by the brilliant young poet, Johan Welhaven, who felt
that Norway's strength lay in developing a world outlook, absorbing as
much as she could culturally from the cosmopolitan atmosphere of
the Continent. These two young poets personified the intellectual clash
that kept the Norwegian atmosphere electrically charged during so
much of the century, but it was Wergeland's ideas that won out in the
end; Wergeland himself, who died early, did not live to see this con-
summation. But there was more to him than his nationalism. His fierce
love of Norway, her people, and their rights contributed in no small
degree to the spread of democratic ideas among the *bønder* and encouraged them in their demands for social and political reform.

Although a bright new sun seemed to be rising over the Norwegian
mountains, social and economic repairs were made slowly in the new
democracy where the national assembly met but every third year. To
the tax-burdened landowner of the first half of the century, whose worn-
out soil bore more debts than crops, progress was indiscernible. To the
cotter whose service to his landlord left him scarcely enough time to
plow and seed the few leased acres of his own, the new age did not

seem to bring greater economic opportunity or more social equality than he had enjoyed in the past. Over the span of the century, however, the lot of the farming class did change for the better, though to thousands of individual land dwellers the chance to win a way out of poverty during their lifetime seemed slim. When the emigration movement began to spread over the mountains and through the valleys, these tillers of a meagre soil were swept into the current like dry leaves from the banks of a flooding stream. And yet, curiously enough, no class in Norway was so close to the traditions, history, and inmost life of the nation as were these farmers, none so deeply attached to the fjells, the fjords, and the mountains of their land.

Viewed from the vantage point of the present, the nineteenth century Norwegian farmer was something of a split personality. The political and cultural climate in which he lived can best be described as "national romanticism." The literati who had "discovered" him made him the possessor of Norway's finest virtues, his life one of idyllic beauty. With so much attention, he became self-conscious, proud of his role as the carrier of ancient traditions of democracy and freedom. The very thought energized him into action to win his place in the councils of the mighty, where once again, after centuries of silence, he could at least speak his mind and voice his demands. But the struggle against conservatism, inside and outside of officialdom, was slow and often disappointing. In this mood the farmer fell easy prey to the emigration fever.

Emigration became for him another way of asserting himself, another form of challenging the official class. So, while the forces of national romanticism restrained him and tied him more securely to his native soil, other forces prompted him to rebel or at least to go out and conquer new worlds. In the end America gave him greater security and, in most instances, a better social position than he had had before. But it also became his fate to carry with him to the end of his days a heart heavy with longing for the sight of his home fjord glittering in the sun, for the early spring call of the cuckoo, and the endless roar of the mountain torrent hard by the cottage where he was born.

During the forepart of the nineteenth century the bulk of the Norwegian population was engaged in agriculture, in spite of the fact that less than a quarter of the land was tillable. There were a few well-to-do landowners, particularly in the eastern districts, but for the most part those who tilled the soil were eking out a bare existence, some not even that. There was a distinct stratification within the farming class, the largest and most powerful group being the independent landholders, the *bønder,* who during the century rose to become for a time the most influential political and social element in the country. Most of their farms were ancestral estates, in the family since the fifteenth and sixteenth centuries. But in spite of the prestige this brought them, they were often but one cut above poverty.

Next in the social and economic scale came the *husmaend,* or cotters, who were given a few acres and a hut in return for services to the land-owner. Almost never was a *husmand* able to rise to the step above and become a *bonde.* (An exception to this social rule is found in Bjørnson's romantic novel *A Happy Boy* where Öyvind, the *husmand's* son, after years of sorrow and hard work, finally marries the daughter of the *gaard.*) Few were his possessions in life; yet thousands of them sold what little they had and managed with the help of others to finance the journey to America. Not infrequently this help came from a kind-hearted *bonde* for whom the *husmand* had faithfully toiled. Besides these two groups, the agricultural population included close to two hundred thousand renters, laborers, and servants, who could expect no change for the better either in their lives or that of their children except through emigration to the land of liberty. These were the people, then, natured and nurtured by a reluctant and secretive earth, who furnished the courage, strength, and patience to clear and plow the untouched tracts of the Mississippi River basin one hundred years ago.

3

"And Out You Sweep to Sea"

The yards are trimmed and the sails set,
And out you sweep to sea.—*From an emigrant ballad*

EXCEPT FOR IRELAND, Norway gave to America a larger proportion of her people than any other nation during the Atlantic migration of the nineteenth and early twentieth centuries. In that period over a million were to move from some pocket-sized valley hemmed in by craggy mountains to the land of lush meadows and sun-bleached prairies. They were part of the century that gave birth to a new face, for America became a country that "changed the bone in the cheek of many races," as Carl Wittke phrased it.

The first group of emigrants, fifty-two in number, left Norway in 1825. For the next decade emigration ceased. Then, from 1836 on it became a yearly phenomenon, increasing from a few hundred to something over a thousand each year in the 'forties. In 1849 a sudden increase to four thousand took place, and until after the Civil War the number zigzagged between one thousand and almost nine thousand annually. A jump from four thousand in 1865 to fifteen thousand the next year gave warning that a period of mass emigration was at hand. This marked the beginning of the first of two great waves of emigration from Norway, the one from 1866 to 1873 when 110,896 people left, the other from 1879 to 1893 when 256,068 left. In this second period the high point was reached in 1882 when almost twenty-nine thousand Norwegians left their native land for America. Through the remainder of the 'nineties emigration dropped to five and six thousand annually, then after the turn of the century rose to high points of from twenty to twenty-five thousand a year from 1902 to 1907. Once again emigration levelled off, dropped during the first World War, increased slightly in the few years before the quota system was established by the United States.

The present quota for Norway is 2,377. In 1947, 2,316 persons were admitted from Norway, slightly less than two thousand being quota immigrants.

The story of why Norwegians came to America is in outline similar to that of other northern Europeans. They were both pushed and pulled, but the pull was stronger than the push. The relationship between European emigration and American business cycles has been well established. Norwegian emigration follows the pattern of relatively few arriving during periods of depression, many during years of prosperity and expansion. Likewise, the number of immigrants returning to Norway rises whenever American business slumps. On the other hand, Norwegians were not, as many other European peoples, uprooted by wars and political disorder.

They left mainly because their life ration of land, bread, and meat was, compared with America's generous measure, too scant to satisfy them. But a variety of influences, coming from all directions, acted upon the potential emigrant. In most instances he himself was not aware of the larger forces. Sometimes these stimuli fused in him so that no single motive stood out; sometimes one particular thing, a letter from America or a crop failure might have set him in motion; but, psychologically, years of economic and social oppression had been preparing him for the break. It is hard to describe the tangle of motives and emotions that attend the momentous decision to turn one's back upon family, friends, and country, and to face a strange continent, a new life, and an unknown language.

We have already noted that the prevailing spirit of nineteenth century Norway was one of change, of transition from a three-century dormancy to a fairly abrupt consciousness of identity and independence. Swords were turned into plowshares, young men stayed home and reared families instead of going off to war. This, and the introduction of a better sanitary system, vaccination, and new foodstuffs, such as the potato, led to a population increase, not paralleled by a proportionate growth in economic opportunity. Naturally, the population surplus resulted in unrest that expressed itself in a movement from farm to city as well as in emigration. Both were parts of the same thing, the break up of an old agrarian system. Though many additional factors enter the picture, the population surplus throughout the century was, no doubt, one of the major causes for the push to America. Had the Norwegian government been on its toes during the early part of the century, a considerable portion of the surplus labor could have been absorbed through land reclamation and redistribution, a vigorous exploitation of water power and other natural resources, and the creation of new industries. But the emigration movement took the government by surprise, and not until the exodus from the country became alarmingly large and steady did the government bethink itself of counter measures.

Taxes on land were so high that in many cases farmers had to sell part of their land to lighten their fiscal burdens. This break up of the land into thousands of farms of less than ten acres each meant that, even though more people acquired property, not enough to support a family was produced on each homestead. After a succession of crop failures, as happened late in the 'thirties, it looked as if a huge broom had swept through some of the valleys, wiping them clean of people. To America or to the growing cities of Norway they went, hoping to escape famine and privation. Those who stayed, borrowing money to tide themselves over until better days, found the exactions connected with the loans so burdensome that they soon preferred to sell their property and follow the others. In 1843 in order to get a loan of $50 a person had to pay over $8 in official fees. In addition to the high taxes on his land the farmer had to pay tithe to public officials and the clergy. Then, too, it was his duty in those days before railways to provide horses for travellers, often a burden that was hardly worth the few shillings it brought in. To sum it all up, the cloud of debt, hard times, and official oppression hung heavily over the Norwegian farmer during the first half of the nineteenth century.

The relationship between the agricultural, or productive class, and the official class, consisting of the clergy, governmental and military groups, must also be understood if we are to keep our fingers on all the strings that became wound together in the skein of causes that were to leave their effects on the prairies of the Mississippi Valley. Until the beginning of the eleventh century there had been no priesthood or kept secular classes in Norway, but with the coming of the church and the new semi-feudalistic state the clergy, military, and state officials multiplied over the land and dominated the country "in a teamwork of misrule, extortion, and waste, apparently somewhat beyond what prevailed elsewhere in Europe," wrote Thorstein Veblen.

When the Reformation swept north from Germany, the substitution of Lutheran ecclesiasticism for Roman Catholicism made little difference as far as this exploitation of the rural class was concerned. The Lutheran

Church during the sixteenth, seventeenth, and eighteenth centuries in
the Scandinavian countries ran pretty much on the same plan of charg-
ing all that the traffic would bear. It bore down so heavily and set its
stamp so indelibly on the people that it took until the year of Our Lord
nineteen hundred and forty-six before one body of the Lutheran Church
in America was willing to give up its national character and drop "Norwegian" from its official name. The church and all that was connected
with it, its doctrines, its representatives, its liturgy and hymns, its vest-
ments even, were something to be looked up to with awe. The Norwegian people were devoutly, if not abjectly, Lutheran. Religion usually is
deep-seated and compulsive with people who must struggle with the soil
and the sea to get their five loaves and three fishes. Otherworldliness
appeals to them; the vision of a gentler life softens and colors the gray
bleakness of existence as they know it.

In 1736 an ordinance was passed introducing the rite of confirmation
in Norway with a rigid public examination in Luther's Catechism,
Pontoppidan's explanation of it, and the Bible. The officials found out,
however, that this was putting the cart before the horse; not enough
people had learned to read to pass the examination successfully. So in
1739 a compulsory education law was passed, and this, though never
completely enforced, did much to improve the literacy of the people.
Confirmation came to play a decisive role in the social life, which was
later carried over onto the American scene. Lined up in front of a
curious, expectant, and sympathetic congregation of relatives and friends,
the young people in their new clothes, the very best the family could
afford, trembled through the two-hour ordeal of reciting long, mem-
orized answers to questions on the faith and doctrine of the Lutheran
Church. The person who "stood first"—the one who had the best memory and the most facile tongue—was held in high esteem by the whole
community. From his group he was thought to be the one most likely to
succeed in the world. Also, confirmation marked the division between
childhood and adulthood. From that day forward a young person was
allowed to make his own decisions. Many a young man chose this day
to tell his parents he was going to America.

That alone was difficult to do; but, worse, he had to inform the pastor,
who had just confirmed him, who in many sermons had denounced
emigration. In his pulpit high above the humble congregation, the
pastor in sombre black gown and fluted white ruff kept his parishioners
in spiritual submission. Unconsciously they invested him with some-

thing of a halo, and to go contrary to the word of this representative of the church was a thing only the more daring had the temerity to do. But from him the emigrant had to obtain a certificate of good character, a sort of honorable dismissal from the country, and in this last heart-to-heart talk the pastor used all his skill and authority to dissuade his restless parishioner. How many potential emigrants the pastors have kept at home will never be known, but some of the more yielding must certainly have been intimidated by the authoritative voice of the clergyman.

The clergy tried hard to stem the tide of emigration, publicizing widely any complaints about the new land that came to their ears. They sensed, though, that the rising determination of *bønder* and *husmaend* was stronger than anything they could say or do. To stop the movement was like trying to gather the wind in their fists; yet they made every effort. In 1837 the bishop of Bergen, Jacob Neumann, published a pastoral letter entitled, "A Word of Admonition to the Peasants in the Diocese of Bergen Who Desire to Emigrate." Hundreds of copies of the pamphlet were distributed, but, although he appealed to the people on religious, patriotic, and economic grounds, playing on their unconscious fears and guilt feelings, the bishop's words had but a momentary effect on this movement that was already falling into a pattern. One emigrant, when he read the bishop's text, "So shalt thou dwell in the land, and verily thou shalt be fed," said the bishop had forgotten that the Bible also enjoined people to "multiply and replenish the earth," and since the land in Norway was already overpopulated they had to go to new, unsettled parts of the world to carry out the biblical command.

The church, whether it realized it or not, was also feeling the effects of the deep-seated discontent that the *bønder* were voicing politically. The rights they had secured in the Constitution of 1814 were theirs but in theory; practically speaking, their condition had changed very little for the better. They were in a rebellious mood, which in the religious field reacted against the formalism and narrow orthodoxy that then dominated the church. Since the eighteenth century the dry winds of rationalism had been blowing north from the University of Copenhagen, where the Norwegian clergy were educated before the establishment of their own university in 1811. Opposition came from a singular man of peasant stock, Hans Nielsen Hauge. If the effects of the Haugean movement had been confined to Norway alone, we would merely mention him as a pivotal figure in early nineteenth century Norway; but the loyalties and resentments that crystallized around him were carried across the ocean with the early emigrants. On the American prairies they gathered even greater strength, decisively influenced the development of Norwegian American institutions, and thrived long after the original differences between the *bønder* and the clergy had been forgotten in America and settled in Norway.

Hauge came from the lower class and was but slightly educated. Shocked in youth by a narrow escape from drowning, he felt keenly that he was spiritually unprepared for death. So he began to study the Word of God with great zeal, and looking at the world with new eyes, as it were, he saw that most people were going through the rituals of the church without ever being touched by the finger of God. They cared not about the state of their souls, knew next to nothing of the horror of sin nor of the beauty of God's grace and forgiveness. The rationalistic-minded Norwegian pastors, he saw, were concerned only with the paltry affairs of this world. They organized reading circles; they improved the schools; used their parsonage farms as experimental stations for new ideas in agriculture, and delivered lectures from the pulpit on such secular matters as the vaccination of cattle. Hauge felt that by thus busying themselves these clergymen neglected their real work, the saving of souls for the Kingdom of Heaven. This, then, became his duty.

Travelling from farm to farm, from community to community, Hauge called people together in the farmyards by day, around the hearth at night, pleading with them to open their hearts to God. He railed against the spiritually lazy clergy who were offering such frugal, dry fare to a people hungering for spiritual food. His fervent conviction made him eloquent, made those who heard him quiver in anguish for their sins, tremble in hope of mercy. By the hundreds they became his followers, many leaving their work to go about and preach like the disciples of old. Like the warm winds of sudden spring, a religious revival swept through the valleys of Norway into the homes of the farmers and fishermen, as Methodism had appealed and was to appeal to the poor and humble of the English-speaking world. Again, part of Hauge's attraction was that he combined practical reform with religious fervor. He established paper, stamping, bone, and flour mills; a tannery, a foundry for church bells and small cannon. He engaged in trade in Bergen and along the sea coast, and in many different ways introduced the people to new ideas, new methods of doing things, new habits of work.

When the church and government officials began to feel the challenge all this was to their system of law, order, and obedience, they remembered a sixty-year-old law that forbade travelling around and holding meetings, as well as a later ordinance that prohibited trade along the coast without royal privilege. Hauge was arrested for violation of these statutes. Except for a brief period when he was released to help manufacture salt during the English blockade, Hauge was kept in a dark, unwholesome prison from 1804 to 1814. Naturally and deservedly, this action backfired. Hauge became a martyr, and what had started out as a simple religious awakening assumed the proportions of a social revolution as it drew political, economic, and cultural issues into its field. The *bønder,* sharply differentiated from the official class by language, customs, and economic outlook, were more often than not sympathetic to Hauge. Many of the leading *bønder* in the national assembly were stanch Haugeans, and the majority of the early emigrants had been infected with his dislike of the state church.

Once the excitement of 1814 had died down, the traditional political leaders were reluctant to give up the power they had in principle agreed to share with the rising classes. Measures providing for more popular control of local affairs were gradually put through the Storting, but the larger demands of the *bønder* were often ignored or defeated, and with every defeat their antagonism toward the official class mounted. Universal military conscription, for example, was still merely a hope, the rural districts continuing to furnish the manpower for the army. Finally in the middle 'forties a law was passed that, though it paid its respects to the principle of universal military service, in practice still left the burden on the poorer classes, since it permitted those who had enough money to escape service by the hiring of substitutes. It is no wonder, then, that this and other such irritations caused many to look to America. "In earlier times," commented a Norwegian newspaper writer of the 1860's "many a young *bonde* maimed himself to escape military service; in these more civilized times he emigrates."

On the other hand, it must be pointed out that two attitudes toward emigration existed even among the *bønder,* the landholding class of farmers. Those who were close to the lower levels of the economic scale favored emigration as a practical measure. Their sons, particularly the younger ones who would not inherit the land, left first and often through letters persuaded the parents to follow. The *bønder* who had become influential politically, and they were among the economically better-off, joined with the urban middle class, church and state in opposing emigration. To these people America was a place for ne'er-do-wells, malcontents, and the tenantless. When Andreas Ueland, son of the Storting's most prominent *bonde,* Ole Gabriel Ueland, decided to emigrate after his father's death in 1870, the magistrate in Stavanger, who inspected the young man's papers, remarked sadly, "What would his father have said if he was living and saw one of his sons go to America?" This attitude notwithstanding, many a *bonde* joined the swelling stream of emigrants from the two lower rural strata, the *husmaend* and the landless.

While the government did little, constructively, to prevent emigration, letters kept arriving from the first groups of emigrants describing the land of wonder, the richness of the soil, the limitless expanse of prairie. These "America letters," as they came to be called, were indeed most effective in drawing the people across the Atlantic. Later came visitors from America, old friends and neighbors who had been poor and now were as well dressed as any Norwegian official. Nay, they even spoke to the pastor as if they were his equal. With each report America became more fabulous, a sort of fairytale land where every poor Askelad could win the hand of a princess and half a kingdom; a sugarplum land where, in the words of an emigrant ballad,

. . . raisins and almonds grow in huge clusters on the trees, and they cost you never a penny.

Barley-sugar there is as big as biscuits; and the chocolates are like loaves of bread; it hails and snows sugar-cracknels and rains lemonade.

Incredible as it seems, there were people, particularly in the remoter mountain districts, who had never heard of America until a letter from the new land came into the community or one of its inhabitants brought news back from a visit to another valley. One day in 1836 two brothers from Numedal left their farm home to journey to the port city of Stavanger. According to the standards of their day and their class they had been decently educated; but when they were in the city they heard people talking about a country, the name of which was new to their ears— America. Friends showed them letters written by Norwegians who had already sailed across the ocean to the new land, while others told them that a certain Knud Slogvig, who had gone to America many years earlier from Stavanger, had returned to visit his native city. He had given such a glowing account of life there that 150 people in Stavanger and Hardanger had decided to leave Norway and return with him. That very summer they had sailed away in two brigs.

This news came as a thunderbolt from the skies to the two young men, and on their way back home they could talk of nothing else. A year later they, too, had decided to emigrate to the country that had better laws than any other in the world, or so they heard. These two Nattestad brothers were later responsible for swelling the streams that found their way to the sea about 1840, Ole by keeping a journal of his trip to America and his experiences there, Ansten by returning to Norway with letters from nearly all the earlier Norwegian emigrants and with two manuscripts, his brother's journal and Ole Rynning's book, *True Account of America,* both of which were published, the latter in 1838, the former a year later.

Ole Rynning, the author of the book, rises out of the anonymity of the crowded ships that were taking Norwegians to America in the 'thirties by his class, education, as well as by his unusual concern for the welfare of the downtrodden and dispossessed. His father, Jens Rynning, was a curate of the church and agreed with his ecclesiastical colleagues that emigration was a fearful disease that ought to be stopped or at least checked. His son Ole thought otherwise. Though he had been given a good education, he somehow escaped the prejudices of his class. Instead of becoming a minister as his father had hoped, he decided to go to America and to help as many others as possible to emigrate to a country where freedom of speech and belief and freedom from want and fear were more of a reality than in any other country in the world.

Together with several other emigrants, Rynning left Norway in 1837 with Illinois as his destination. And mindful of the thousands back home who were dreaming about America, he shared with them his sane and sensible observations, giving them a sober account in writing of what conditions were like in the New World. In thirteen question-and-answer chapters he briefly told the history of America; described the soil, crops, livestock, and natural resources; discussed religion, education, and language; advised some to come, others to stay in Norway; provided information about costs and kind of transportation, the proper season for leaving Norway; and, very important to the emigrant, he stilled his fears about the journey across the ocean, the danger of which had been magnified by rumor all out of proportion to reality. He assured them that they would not die of seasickness, as many opponents of emigration had maintained. Knowing that his book would stir many half-decided people into action, he concluded, "For those who wish to leave next spring, there is a good opportunity to go with Ansten Knudsen Nattestad from Rolloug parish in Numedal, who is now on a trip back to Norway."

In the district of Numedal and other parts of southern Norway the news and contents of the book passed by the way the crow flies from farm to farm. Nattestad himself left us a picture of what happened:

> I remained in Numedal throughout the winter and until the following spring. The report of my return spread like wild-fire through the land, and an incredible number of people came to hear the news of America. Many travelled as far as twenty Norwegian miles [140 English miles] to talk with me. It was impossible to answer all the letters which came to me containing questions in regard to conditions on the other side of the ocean. In the spring of 1839 about one hundred persons from Numedal stood ready to go with me across the sea. Amongst these were many farmers and heads of families, all, except the children, able-bodied and in their best years. In addition to these were some from Telemarken and from Numedal who were unable to go with me as our ship was full.

In Rynning's home town in Norway the book created a furore; the author became a local hero. An eyewitness later described the reaction:

> For a time I believed that half the population of Snaasen had lost their senses. Nothing else was spoken of but the land that flows with milk and honey. Our minister, Ole Rynning's father, tried to stop the fever. Even from the pulpit he urged people to be discreet and described the hardships of the voyage and the cruelty of the American savage in the most forbidding colors. This was only pouring oil upon the fire.

As more and more people found their way to America new ties were established between many a farm home in the land of nisse and huldre folk and some dugout or log cabin by the side of an Indian-named stream. Letters postmarked Illinois or Wisconsin Territory arrived in increasing numbers in southern and western Norway, spreading like the web of a giant spider from the large centers into the valleys and up the mountainsides.

Reports varied according to the experiences and personality of the writers; some were full of praise: "Norway can no more be compared with America than a desolate waste with a garden in full blossom." "Every man here has a large number of pigs and also chickens. There are some who have as many as a thousand chickens." "Here a young but poor man can soon become a well-to-do farmer if he works hard and uses good sense. He can look forward to becoming rich without usury, a difficult task in Norway," wrote Johannes Nordboe in 1837 from La Salle County, Illinois. And in the same letter he excited his readers with fabulous figures; "Other Norwegians who secured land made a profit from their labor of $200, others $300 to $400, and so on. Some made $1,500 to $1,600 depending on how poor they had been, and one . . . had only three dollars when he came . . . in 1825. When he sells his improved farm, he will have $2,000."

Over a decade later one of the leaders of the Norwegian migration into Texas wrote to a friend in Norway:

. . . all of the Norwegians who came to this country in 1847 from the mountain communities in western Norway have, without exception, become well-to-do people. Most of them possessed very little surplus capital when they arrived; some were without a penny and a few were even in debt for their passage across the ocean. Now, all of them have bought land and have paid for it; they have built good houses; they have sufficient cattle, oxen and horses for the management of their farms; and they get annual crops so large that there is a surplus to be sold to the newcomers. A few of these men, who had large families and debts of more than one hundred dollars each, can now be estimated at being worth more than one thousand dollars per family. They have succeeded even under unfavorable circumstances; and all of them are actually independent farmers, free from any fears of either taxes, mortgages, or foreclosures. . . . These are the facts, which the statistical data can verify whenever that is desired.

Little wonder that such words fell like a quenching rain over the parched lives of the struggling farmers in Norway. For those who were choking in the staleness of Norway's social and political air, the letters of Hans Barlien, whose outspoken advocacy of the ideas of the French Revolution had put him in such bad odor with the official class that he had to seek refuge in America, sounded like a call from a magic new world. "At last I can breathe freely," he wrote in one of his letters. "No one is here persecuted on account of his religious belief; anyone is permitted to worship God in his own way, as his conscience dictates. Pickpockets, lawyers, unscrupulous creditors, a corrupt government, and

vagabonds have lost all power to harm the people. . . . By wise legislation the American citizens are safe against oppression." In another
letter he wrote: "Intelligence and manliness are honored, but stupidity
and cowardice are despised. . . . Let the government of Norway and
some of its officials slander the American government as much as they
please, their government will never match this."

But not all the letters were so full of cheerful and naive enthusiasm.
One immigrant wrote from Wisconsin Territory in 1839: "But though
we believe that no one who is determined to come should be frightened
away by fear of sickness and though we are convinced that every industrious and able-bodied man can live better here than in Norway,
we do not seek to persuade anyone to come, but rather to advise against
it in the cases of those who are earning a good livelihood there."

In a letter from Wisconsin, dated July 4, 1857, an immigrant wrote:

Dear Friend and Cousin:

I have received your most welcome letter which in part pleases
me and in part causes me much pain. You will perhaps wonder why
I say it pains me, but the reason is that I see that you, with your little
ones, intend to come over here. If you can stay at home and in some
way make your living, you must retain your farm and never think
of coming to America.

In the first place, the journey across the ocean is so difficult that
one can hardly endure it, and if you should live through it and land,
where, then, would you go? Certainly everything would be strange,
even the language. A farm for a small family like yours, costs at
least $800, for land has raised in price during late years. If you should
buy farm implements much more money would be needed and yet
your stock would be comparatively small. . . .

The winter here is shorter than that in Norway, but it is usually
much colder, and when summer comes, that in turn, is much
warmer. Our minister told me that the heat this week has been
between 88 and 94 degrees, so you see it is very hard to endure the
labor that is necessary under such conditions. Many people not
adjusted to the climate break down.

If you still do not give up the idea of coming to America, kindly
write me as soon as possible in order that I might be of as much help
to you as possible. But yet, I must, as I have already said, urge as a
friend and relative, that you never think any more about this journey. I will tell you straightforwardly that I hardly think that you

will have enough money left, after you arrive here, with which to buy land, and if you should go as far as Iowa before buying land where it is said that land may be had—then all that you may have would not suffice to pay the journey's expense, since travel by railroad and stage coach has in late years become much more expensive. I might also say that various kinds of diseases often attack newcomers. Among these, the fever is the worst. I, too was in bed for sixteen weeks at one time because of this sickness, and although I have often been troubled with it since this time, others have suffered much more. . . . I hope that the information I have given you will help you in deciding to think no more of coming to America.

Some were completely disillusioned and returned to Norway, eager to corroborate anything that the clergy and the officials might say. Only those who were completely bereft of their senses, they said, would consider leaving Norway to live in America, where only sickness, misery, and godlessness prevailed, where the immigrant was cheated on every hand and beset by difficulties he never had anticipated. Such doleful accounts retarded emigration here and there where the letters and returned emigrants were listened to, but looked at as a whole America remained the land of dreams, a magic, faraway land, whose glamor could not be darkened by the shadows of such occasional disappointment.

Out of the collective experience of almost half a nation uprooting themselves has grown a remarkable body of folk literature, the emigrant ballads and songs. They tell the story of the longing for a richer life, the grandiose visions of America, the feelings of guilt for having broken away from the motherland, the bravado and courage of the travellers, the sharp grief of those who stayed. But not only do they express, undisguised, the emotions of a people in transition, they also reflect, for our benefit, the attitudes and social conditions of the times. Again and again the economic motive is sounded:

Farewell, Norway, and God bless thee. Stern and severe wert thou always, but as a mother I honor thee, even though thou skimped my bread.

From another:

Norway is a poor and wretched land, and now I am going to America.

Here I have to slave and suffer want: In America every one can make a living.

Frequently the emigrant's resentment of his social and political inferiority is expressed:

For the land is fertile there, and wages are high, and I can easily earn what here I may never hope for, there where Fortune smiles on the humble, and all are equal before the law.

Those who disapproved of emigration also expressed themselves in song:

My brothers, hear a word of counsel: remain at home here in the friendly North! From a sorrowful heart I beg you to stay here at home; do not sail over yonder. Little do you know what it is you are doing, nor the bitter disillusioning that may be yours.

And in the same vein:

Where in this wide world do you imagine that you will find greater happiness than here at home? Think of your father's silver hair, your mother's voice, your brother and sister; think too of friends and kin. . . .

Think you that you will find in those new lands to which you go the same music in the streams? the same sun? the same summer? . . . Soon will you forget the speech and customs of your father; and however life may deal with you, you will live an exile always. . . . Nay, stay rather at home in the land of your people. Your cottage, indeed, may be humble and your fortune poor; but when all is over, friendly hands will deck your grave with flowers.

The poetic qualities of the ballads are not always of the highest. More often they read like prose tracts, but one that rises above the rest, both for its literary qualities and its historical importance is the rollicking, satirical "Oleana," popular on both sides of the Atlantic for two generations. The background for this song was violinist Ole Bull's grandiose scheme to found a colony in Pennsylvania. In 1852 he bought, in good faith, 120,000 acres of land there, planned the town of Oleana, mills, a cannon foundry, a polytechnical school, and invited the underprivileged of Norway to come to his New Norway, "consecrated to liberty, baptized with independence, and protected by the Union's mighty flag." Excitement ran high when news of the project reached the people of

Norway. Ole Bull was praised as a great benefactor of the poor and oppressed. Over a hundred went to the new colony where they found conditions anything but Utopian. Tales of disillusionment filtered back to Norway, and when in 1853 Ole Bull discovered that he had fallen into the hands of frauds and did not legally own the land, the enterprise crumbled, the colony disintegrated. The ballad "Oleana" was written by a Norwegian newspaper editor, Ditmar Meidell, in 1853, as a satirical thrust at the exaggerated claims made for Ole Bull's American colony.

> I'm off to Oleana, I'm turning from my doorway,
> No chains for me, I'll say good-bye to slavery in Norway.
> Ole—Ole—Ole—oh! Oleana!
> Ole—Ole—Ole—oh! Oleana!

They give you land for nothing in jolly Oleana,
And grain comes leaping from the ground in floods of golden manna.

The grain it does the threshing, it pours into the sack, Sir,
And so you take a quiet nap a-stretching on your back, Sir.

The crops they are gigantic, potatoes are immense, Sir,
You make a quart of whisky from each one without expense, Sir.

And ale as strong and sweet as the best you've ever tasted,
It's running in the foamy creek, where most of it is wasted.

The salmon they are playing, and leaping in the brook, Sir,
They hop into your kettle, put the cover on, and cook, Sir.

And little roasted piggies, with manners quite demure, Sir,
They ask you, "Will you have some ham?" And then you say, "Why sure, Sir."

The cows are most obliging, their milk they put in pails, Sir,
They make your cheese and butter with a skill that never fails, Sir.

The bull he is the master, his calves he likes to boss, Sir,
He beats them when they loaf about, he's never at a loss, Sir.

The calves are helpful, themselves they skin and kill, Sir,
They turn into a tasty roast before you drink your fill, Sir.

The hens lay eggs colossal, so big and round and fine, Sir,
The roosters act like eight-day clocks, they always tell the time, Sir.

And cakes come raining down, Sir, with chocolate frosting coated,
They're nice and rich and sweet, good Lord, you eat them till you're bloated.

And all night long the sun shines, it always keeps a-glowing,
It gives you eyes just like a cat's, to see where you are going.

The moon is also beaming, it's always full, I vow, Sir,
A bottle for a telescope, I'm looking at it now, Sir.

Two dollars for carousing they give each day, and more, Sir,
For if you're good and lazy, they will even give you four, Sir.

Support your wife and kids? Why, the county pays for that, Sir,
You'd slap officials down and out if they should leave you flat, Sir.

And if you've any bastards, you're freed of their support, Sir,
As you can guess since I am spinning verses for your sport, Sir.

You walk about in velvet, with silver buttons bright, Sir,
You puff away at meerschaum pipes, your women pack them right, Sir.

The dear old ladies struggle, and sweat for us and labor,
And if they're cross, they spank themselves, they do it as a favor.

And so we play the fiddle, and all of us are glad, Sir,
We dance a merry polka, boys, and that is not so bad, Sir.

I'm off to Oleana, to lead a life of pleasure,
A beggar here, a count out there, with riches in full measure.

> I'm coming, Oleana, I've left my native doorway,
> I've made my choice, I've said good-bye to slavery in Norway.
> Ole—Ole—Ole—oh! Oleana!
> Ole—Ole—Ole—oh! Oleana!

Nonetheless, packing continued on farm after farm. Spinning wheels whirred busily before they were stowed away at the bottom of a box, not to be used again until the housewife was sitting before a hickory fire in a Wisconsin cabin. Piles of dry, crinkly *flatbrød* were baked and packed into round wooden tubs, cheeses were cured and many pounds of fish were dried and salted; and when all the food for the journey was ready and the clothes were packed, the auction was held. Many tears were shed as cows and horses were led away, as carved chairs, tables, and beds were carried off in a stranger's cart. But when it was over and all goodbyes were said, they journeyed to the port and gravely and bravely swept out to sea, these thousands of hopeful Norwegian farmers.

For a century they left the ports of Norway in ships that were frequently unseaworthy, nearly always unsanitary and poorly equipped. In large, dark and unwholesome quarters scores of emigrants were crowded into open bunks, were ill with contagious diseases that quickly spread through the ship, died, gave birth to children. Meals were inadequate and irregular, cooked when there was room in the small galley that was provided. Most of them lived on the *flatbrød,* the dried meat, cheese, and sour milk they had brought with them in casks. Diaries and letters that have survived describing these voyages reveal in simple unadorned style the hardships and discomforts of the majority of the emigrants, but they also record that in good weather there was hilarious fun on deck. They played rough games, like Barber of Seville, they sang and danced to the accompaniment of a fiddle or an accordion, celebrated birthdays, the Seventeenth of May and the Fourth of July, or a wedding, the culmination of a shipboard romance.

At the end of the six, nine, or even twelve weeks' voyage the passengers and crew caught fresh cod off the Newfoundland Banks, not unfrequently a lifesaver for those whose supplies had been exhausted by an overlong voyage. When the ship cast anchor in the St. Lawrence River, for most of the emigrant ships landed at Quebec during the middle decades of the century, men and women in rowboats quickly swarmed around the vessel offering bread, buns, cakes, milk, butter to the emigrants. This feast on fresh foods, after the weary weeks of eating dry bread and salt meat, became one of the most pleasant episodes in the emigrant's memories of the long journey to his new home.

4

From Stavanger to "Ellenaais"

A FIFTY-FOUR FOOT single-masted boat, the *Restaurationen,* lay in the afternoon sunshine of Stavanger harbor on July 4, 1825. Chances are a passerby on the waterfront would have failed to notice this undistinguished-looking craft. Indeed, even the forty-five people boarding her and the seven-man crew, intent on riggings, sails, and the distribution of barrels and boxes, were completely unaware of their historic roles. For the *Restaurationen* was to be Norway's *Mayflower,* less than a quarter as large as the famous Pilgrim ship, yet sturdy enough to cut a new path from the Old World to the New.

Standing on the foredeck, Captain Lars Helland checked with a careful eye the progress of the loading, noting that the last of the rod iron to be sold in America had been stored in the hold of the ship. Then his glance rested a moment on the lad Jacob Slogvig, nimbly climbing the rigging, and he decided the boy would hold his own on this long voyage, his first, with the more experienced crew. As the captain's eyes slid down the ropes to the deck, he saw Fru Larsen, heavy with child, struggling with a box whose rope had come loose. Captain Helland hurried forward to help her. For the next hour or so he was busy assigning space to his passengers.

After a while an air of settling-down came over the groups of quiet-voiced men, women, and children, tired ones resting in their fathers' arms. One by one they found places at the side of the boat where they could look at the town and pick out a rooftop and chimney or a clump of trees that marked homes they had known. When twilight crept over the stilling harbor all the passengers were aboard. The sloop was ready. Sometime during the night, or perhaps it was in a dawn wind, the canvas unfurled and the tiny vessel headed toward sea.

This party of half a hundred Norwegians is known as the Stavanger Quakers. The leader of the band, Lars Larsen, was the only one among them officially a member of the Society of Friends, but most of them were in sympathy with its principles. To be a dissenter in Lutheran Norway then took courage. Enough evidence has come to light to show beyond doubt that church and government officials had virtually driven these Norwegian Quakers into emigration.

During the Napoleonic wars a few Norwegians, among them ship carpenter, Lars Larsen, had been captured and held on an English prison ship, where Quakers had visited them and converted them to their faith. Returning to Norway at the conclusion of the peace in 1814, they became the nucleus of a group of Quakers. In 1818 Stephen Grellet, the noted Quaker missionary who had spent several years in America, and William Allen, of a famous English Quaker family, visited Norway. They secured for the Friends in Stavanger a meeting house large enough to seat 250 people. At the missionaries' first morning service fifty listeners were present; but news of the visiting Quakers spread so rapidly that by meeting time in the afternoon "there was too great a crowd to be accommodated."

This sort of thing irritated the Norwegian officials. They used whatever old laws they could find to make the Quakers feel the authority of church and state. Official action of the state church was attendant upon each birth, death, and marriage. Thus, fines for not having their children baptized and for burying their dead in unconsecrated ground could be imposed upon the Quakers. At one time twenty young persons were committed to a house of correction for having neglected to learn the Lutheran Catechism, thereby disqualifying themselves for confirmation by a Lutheran pastor. In spite of all this, and, though they were strictly forbidden to proselytize, the simple faith of the Friends made some progress among those who had long been dissatisfied with the rationalism of the state church. The circumstances that favored them were, of course, the same that had produced the Haugean movement. So one is not surprised to find Haugeans as well as Quakers and Quaker sympathizers in the little group that left Stavanger in the summer of 1825. Whatever the press of economic constraint, there is no doubt, then, that the religious motive played an important role in the emigration of this first boatload of Norwegians. And, indeed, one finds it referred to again and again in the old documents that record their venture.

Probably we will never know exactly how and when the idea of emigrating to America came to the Stavanger Quakers. Living in a

seaport, however, they had undoubtedly heard of America from Norwegian sailors; newspapers sometimes carried items about the country
and its opportunities; Stephen Grellet may have told them about his
years with the Friends in America; Lars Larsen, who spent a year in
England after his release from the prison ship, most certainly must have
heard about America from his English associates. Then into their
midst came a man who brought their "America" thoughts to a head,
a man who was to become a link between Norway and the New World
for them and others after them.

His name was Cleng Peerson, a *bonde*'s son, quixotic, restless, adventurous. Somewhat of a failure in the old country, he was yet to become one of the great leaders of the huge migration of his people, a
strange figure, half Daniel Boone and half, in his own way, a new
Moses. Some people said that his marriage to an elderly, well-to-do
widow with a shrewish temper drove him to America. Be that as it
may, he seems to have travelled a good deal in England and on the
Continent during his youth. At home he got into trouble by inducing
the people in one of the parishes where he lived to abstain from com-
munion. Also he seemed to have had some genuine sympathy for the
Quakers, though later in his life, according to his friends, he became a
freethinker, believing little or nothing of the Bible.

Small wonder, then, that Peerson was more than willing to go to
America when in 1821 the Stavanger Quakers had raised enough money
to send him there to investigate conditions for them. But in America
misfortune overtook him. His money was lost; his travelling companion, Knut Eide, took sick and died. Penniless and alone, Cleng
Peerson had to work at whatever jobs he could find if he was to carry
out his duties as agent for the Stavanger Friends. But in doing so he
learned a good deal about America, travelling on foot, meeting the
people, and exploring what a contemporary account calls "the vast
regions of the west," probably western New York, since Peerson mentions friends he had there. For three years he thus lived and worked in
America, then in 1824 made a flying visit back to Norway to make his
report to the Quakers. Staying just long enough to advise them about
buying a ship and iron, both of which could be sold when they reached
America, he hurried back to arrange with a Quaker agent for the pur-
chase of land in Orleans County, New York. The ship—a little under
forty tons—was bought for less than fourteen hundred dollars.

After leaving the English Channel, Captain Helland, for some unknown reason, set his course too far south and by the end of July found himself at the Madeira Islands. A somewhat amusing and un-Quakerlike story is reported of their arrival there. Just before reaching Funchal harbor they sighted a floating cask, and, hauling it aboard, found it filled with good Madeira wine. The inevitable happened, with the result that "the ship came drifting into the harbor like a plague-ship, without command, and without raising its flag."

For almost a week the deck-weary passengers remained in the pleasant island city where they were shown many courtesies. On board again, the days seemed endlessly stormy as week after week crept slowly over the sea. On September 2 the monotony was broken by a little flurry of excitement among the women. Then, "It's a girl" went quickly through the ship. Lars and Martha Larsen's first child was born and they named her Margaret Allen after his Quaker friend in England.

On October 9, fourteen weeks after she had left Stavanger, the *Restaurationen* entered New York harbor. That her arrival was somewhat out of the ordinary is evident from a New York newspaper account under the caption "A Novel Sight," which read in part: "The appearance of such a party of strangers, coming from so distant a country and in a vessel of a size apparently ill calculated for a voyage across the Atlantic could not but excite an unusual degree of interest. An enterprise like this argues a good deal of boldness in the master of the vessel as well as an adventurous spirit in the passengers. . . . Those who came from the farms are dressed in coarse cloths of domestic manufacture, of a fashion different from the American, but those who inhabit the town wear calicos, ginghams and gay shawls, imported, we presume, from England. The vessel is built on the model common to fishing boats on that coast, with a single mast and topsail, sloop-rigged."

Perhaps some of the immigrants felt that now that they were on American soil all their troubles were over. They would simply sell their boat, go inland and buy land. But unfortunately they had violated an American shipping law by carrying many more passengers than the tonnage of their boat permitted. The sloop was confiscated and the leaders of the party received the shattering news that they were liable for a fine of over $3,000. Quaker friends in New York had to intercede in their behalf to make customs officers put the best possible construction on this unintentional breach of law. Nevertheless, the case had to go through the courts and was not settled until the middle of November when President John Quincy Adams and Secretary of State Henry

Clay put their signatures on a proclamation pardoning the master, Lars O. Helland, and the owners for having violated a law "through ignorance, the said Master and owners being Foreigners, and entirely unacquainted with the language and Laws of the United States." And so even the head of the United States government knew that a little band of Norwegians had come to find homes in the "great American asylum." Glad to be released from the awkward situation they had blundered into, the owners now sold the troublesome little boat for $400.

Meanwhile, most of the party, which had been met in New York by Cleng Peerson and the agent with whom he had negotiated for land, had proceeded inland to Orleans County, some thirty-five miles north-west of the city of Rochester. There on the shores of Lake Ontario in Kendall Township the immigrants bought 40-acre tracts of heavily forested land at $5 an acre, on the installment plan. Had they known what a hard winter was before them, the pilgrims from Norway might not have boarded the little sloop so willingly in July. Cold weather and illness overtook them before they had even finished getting a few inadequate huts ready. They had no money, no provisions. But Cleng Peerson did not forget them now that he had piloted them thither. He called on his American friends in the neighborhood and asked them to find employment for the newcomers. Without his steady encouragement and help the colony might easily have disintegrated in that first distressing year. Nor were the next four or five years easy. Gradually, however, the colonists cleared enough land to support themselves, and once the heartbreak of those first grim years was behind them they admitted they were better off in America than they had been in Norway.

Lars and Martha Larsen meanwhile had settled in Rochester, since Lars felt that he would have more success by following his trade as a carpenter than by trying to farm. And he was successful, even becoming fairly well-to-do as a canal boat builder. His comfortable home, cheerful with a flock of youngsters, was for years a haven for newly arrived Norwegian immigrants. The good-hearted Larsens not only housed, fed and clothed them, but went about the city looking for employment for the newcomers. Eventually this burden became too heavy even for the generous Larsens; at least we have a letter of Martha's asking a friend in Norway to dissuade people from coming to America unless they had money enough to take care of themselves. The Larsens remained faithful to their Quaker religion, travelling to Philadelphia and New York for meetings which to Martha were, according to one of her letters, "as a kingdom on the earth."

For twenty years Lars enjoyed the freedom of his adopted land; then one autumn day in 1845 he lost his life in a canal boat accident. But he had lived to see many of his people follow him to the great new continent. A few had settled in the little colony in Orleans County. But western New York was no longer the "Far West." The Erie Canal had brought many settlers into the region; land prices had risen to a level beyond the reach of new arrivals. So, when they heard that, farther west, plans were afoot to build more canals they rumbled on over the bumpy trails in open wagons and Conestogas, or on canal and river boats if they had money to pay the fare. And if they were bold and curious and had nothing to lose they went by foot, as did Cleng Peerson.

He couldn't sit idly by and watch people in the markets buying flour, rifles, hammers and nails, listen to them talk about the West without catching the fever himself. So one morning in 1833, when the sky was bright overhead and the retreating frost had left a spongy earth for the sun to play on, Peerson and a friend named Narvig started out, knapsacks over their shoulders. They went through the forests of New York, stopping at settlers' cabins to gather news and directions, into Ohio, following streams and rivers, resting at little settlements, but soon pushing on again into Michigan. Here Narvig stayed; Peerson went on alone across Indiana toward Chicago, his destination.

Chicago, when at last he reached it, was disappointing, far smaller than its reputation. Here was a midget town of wooden boxes, straggling like a few old, brown teeth on the flat gums of the river's mouth opening to the Lake. Land around the village was low and marshy, but to the south, he heard, lay open prairie. In the busy village there was talk about a canal that was going to be built between the Illinois River and Lake Michigan, the sort of talk that made land prices skyrocket. Peerson's mind was as full of ideas and plans as ever, but first he wanted to see what things looked like farther north. Following the shore of the Lake he came to a place called Milwaukee, where he met a French fur trader, Solomon Juneau. It was wonderful country, but no place for farmers, Juneau told him. Too much timber to clear away. So he walked back to Chicago, continued southwest from the village, trudging on and on through the wind-bent grass of the prairie, examining the soil, looking for the right spot for his people.

There is a story, probably apocryphal, about how Peerson chose the location for a settlement. After plodding for some hours through hot sunshine, he reached the crest of a hill and threw himself down in a shady spot. Below him rolled the luscious meadows of a green valley through which wound the Fox River, glistening between clumps of pale willow trees. Maybe he dozed, maybe he lay there idly dreaming. But he thought of Moses leading the children of Israel into the Promised Land. He envisioned his people living in this beautiful valley, saw comfortable homes, spacious barns, herds of well-fed cattle, fields of grain ripe unto harvest. Inspired by this bucolic musing, the indefatigable scout walked back to New York as fast as foot would take him, reported to the Kendall settlers and promised to lead those who desired to follow him to the valley of his vision.

The next summer, 1834, half a dozen families left for the "place which is called *Ellenaais,*" as one of the Kendall settlers wrote to a friend in Norway, adding, "We and another Norwegian family have also sold our farms and intend to journey, this May, to that state, where land can be bought at a better price." Thus, the year 1834 marked the beginning of a new and vastly important chapter in our history, a chapter whose story is acted on the undulating land of the upper Mississippi. For the first travellers to "Ellenaais" were but the vanguard of the mighty procession that scattered Norwegians all over the great Northwest.

Others from the New York settlement followed their friends and, family after family, the first Norwegian colony in America was depleted. But for some years it was a halfway house for many newcomers who stopped there for a few weeks, months, or even a year to replenish their pocketbooks and their courage before making the inland journey to the region of $1.25-acres. Before long, however, the friends and relatives of the prospective emigrants were largely settled in the West, and the newcomers made their way to the newer settlements directly. The center of Norwegian life in America had moved to the banks of the Fox River in La Salle County, Illinois.

When Cleng Peerson led the first settlers to Illinois, he, too, bought land, but only to turn it over to relatives who soon arrived. His part was not to till the soil; his call was to aid and comfort his countrymen and be their leader. When children spied him coming across the fields they shouted his name and ran to meet him, while the housewife called her husband from his work. Peerson was their newspaper, bringing messages and gossip from friends in distant cabins. He told them how their American neighbors did things, how they thought and felt. When he entered a cabin, it was said, he would pick up the housewife's knitting, and while he talked would add several inches to the socks or mittens she was making. With never more than a few pennies in his pocket at any time, he made his way from settlement to settlement, doing a little carpentry for the pioneers when they needed it, accepting the shelter and food his people gladly offered.

Knud Slogvig, one of the settlers in the New York colony who had gone west with Cleng Peerson in 1834, returned to Norway in 1835 to marry and bring back his bride. This visit stirred the people in his and surrounding districts in southwestern Norway into such a pitch of excitement about America that two brigs were made ready and quickly filled, leaving behind many more to wait for the next sailing. Thus it came about that the autumn of 1836 brought a sudden and large influx of new settlers into the Fox River region. By the time ice slivers began to edge the creeks, dozens of new shanties were going up. Aside from the sloopers, only scattered individuals had left Norway for America between 1825 and 1836. This 1836 group, almost two hundred emigrants bound for the Fox River settlement, was the first large contingent to go directly to the West. From this time on there was no break in the annual hegira from the fjords to the prairies.

During the same winter more news of America reached Norway, particularly in the district of Hardanger, north of Stavanger, through the letters of Gjert Hovland, who had left Norway in 1831, farmed in New York, and then joined the trek to Illinois in 1835. Copies of his enthusiastic letters were widely circulated through the district. A lay preacher travelling into other districts carried one of them with him. After the people had read it, there was no peace in their hearts until they, too, had sold their possessions to pay for their fare. So, in the spring of 1837, two more ships left Norway with 177 passengers aboard, all eager to join their friends in that wonderful place called "Ellenaais."

Coming, as they did from wooded hillsides and sheltered valleys, the settlers found the open prairie cold and bleak as winter crept over the land. Their log shanties shielded them but poorly from the driving November sleet. Fires built in stone-circled holes in their dirt floors gave forth scant heat. In the morning they awoke to find little drifts of snow on their bedcovers. When someone in the family fell ill with a cough and fever, there was faint hope of escape for the others. Three, four, or even more slept in the same bed. Eating utensils were frequently so scarce that sick and well alike ate from the same bowl and shared spoons. Water was used sparingly. Food stood uncovered on an open shelf, often above a sick bed. Refuse and excrement fouled the air from a swill pail in the corner. Attended by a neighbor lady, a woman bore an infant one day in her dark, inconvenient little cabin and on the second was up and about her chores. But somehow they plugged through the winter, knowing that spring and summer work would bring them a few more comforts with which to face the next cold season.

At the first sign of spring a party of men from the settlement hitched their oxen to wagons and pulled through the mud to the "Chicago mire," as the settlers called that hustling city northeast of the settlement, where they bought seeds and a few simple implements. To the housewives' delight some wagons even returned with iron stoves. But summer brought tribulations of its own. Swarms of flies invaded the cabins; yet the sizzling heat that soured the food also yielded a wider patch of ripened wheat and a few more rows of potatoes and corn. So, after two or three seasons had passed, the firstcomers were established in solid log cabins with floors underfoot, lofts overhead, and windows with panes of glass. The original huts were occupied by the new arrivals that kept coming. Altogether the colony on the Fox River was changing from a camp in the wilderness to a stable farming community.

As the land was taken up the Norwegian immigrants spread into adjacent townships and from there into neighboring counties. Some, who came to Chicago intending to proceed to the Fox River, stayed in that ugly little town, where two Norwegians, Halstein Torrison with his family and Johan Larson, a sailor, had settled as early as 1836. Others hearing that conditions at Fox River were not good, thought they could do better by starting fresh colonies elsewhere. Such a group of about fifty, led by Ole Rynning, whose "America book" was to cause such a stir in the old country, went to Iroquois County, some seventy miles south of Chicago.

There along Beaver Creek the low lands, cloaked in heavy grass, looked promising when the immigrants arrived late in the summer, but the heavy rains of the following spring wrought great distress on the new colony. Worse than that, the summer brought an epidemic of malarial fever, killing many, among them Ole Rynning. Panic-stricken the survivors sought shelter with the Fox River people, abandoning their cabins for the winter wind to whistle through. The Beaver Creek settlement was one of the more tragic episodes in the story of the first Norwegians in the Middle West. Indeed, reports of this disaster in Norway cooled the emigration fever in quite a few communities.

Another offspring from the mother colony, led by the untiring Cleng Peerson, struck southwest toward Missouri. But this northeastern Missouri colony, off the course of general frontier movement and uncomfortably far from trading centers, did not last. Besides, Missouri permitted slavery, something abhorrent to the Norwegian mind. The only successful Norwegian settlement in the South was the Texas colony, founded in the middle 'forties. Although never large, it was well known through the writings of its dynamic leader, J. R. Reiersen, a liberal Norwegian editor who chose the northeastern Texas site for what he hoped would be a large colonization project for his oppressed countrymen, and through the letters of the Wærensjolds, Wilhelm and Elise, a former Norwegian schoolteacher.

Their vibrant reports, published in a Norwegian labor newspaper and in a magazine Reiersen had started before leaving Norway, brought Texas to the attention of many people both in Norway and in America, but because of the immigrants' dislike of slavery the region attracted relatively few. Cleng Peerson and a handful of Fox River settlers joined the colony, and it was here that the great pathfinder, who had "travelled back and forth across the Atlantic, and trudged from frontier to frontier" in search of land where his people could find happiness and prosperity, lived until his death in 1865. This colony and two or three later ones continued to attract occasional immigrants through the years. Even today there are about five thousand first and second generation Norwegians in Texas.

The story of these first settlements, their leaders, and their growth has been so well recorded by the professional historians of Norwegian American life that a detailed account here would be ill considered. Only a broad pattern needs to be outlined. Generally, the Norwegians followed the northwesterly movement; the period of the 'forties saw their center shift from northern Illinois to southern Wisconsin. The Fox River colony gradually lost its parental role, becoming just another kin to settlements of greater importance. In spite of this it continued to grow, increasing from about four hundred souls in 1840 to over a thousand by 1850. Others had been started in northern Illinois, so that the total Norwegian population in 1850 was close to two thousand five hundred among a total of eighty-one thousand for the state of Illinois. By 1860 there were almost six thousand, by 1870 over thirteen thousand Norwegians in "Ellenaais."

The Norwegian-stock population in northern Illinois is still fairly high. In June, 1934, the centennial of the founding of the Fox River colony was celebrated in La Salle County. Ambassador Morgenstierne, Arne Kildal, a Norwegian prominent in national affairs, and several well-known Norwegian Americans from the Middle West took part in the festivities. On the spot where Cleng Peerson was supposed to have passed his first night after completing his long search for a dwelling place for his people a monument was erected in memory of this early scout and the other pioneers, who with their descendants, many of whom still live in the region, contributed so largely to the development of that section of Illinois.

5

Wisconsin

THE NATTESTAD BROTHERS, Ole and Ansten, came to the Fox River colony in 1837. Ansten, in his exuberant enthusiasm for the new land, returned to Norway the next spring just to urge people to join him and his brother, who, in the meantime, explored the land to the north of the Illinois settlements. In Wisconsin Territory he came to a region where, as he later reported, "the soil [was] especially fruitful and the melancholy uniformity of the prairie . . . relieved . . . by intervening bits of woods." He built a shack there, the first Norwegian settler in that state. Eight Americans had already taken land in the township, some distance from his lonely winter abode. By the end of summer he had a cabin ready for the new immigrants Ansten was to bring along, and with their arrival, in the fall of 1839, the well-known settlement at Jefferson Prairie in Rock County was started. Meanwhile another party of Norwegians had arrived in Milwaukee, choosing land in Waukesha County near Lake Muskego, while a third party was inspecting land farther west near Lake Koshkonong. Thus began the settlement of Wisconsin.

These colonies, particularly Koshkonong, were centers for the incoming tide of Norwegian immigrants that flowed into the West during the 'forties and early 'fifties. But, like the Fox River settlement, they themselves continued to grow, for many of the new arrivals found the settled, prosperous conditions of these older colonies more inviting than the prospect of subduing the newer frontier, cheap though the land there might be. Generally it may be said that the Muskego area in lower Waukesha and upper Racine counties, Rock Prairie in Rock County, and the Koshkonong region in Dane County were the first nodal points in the dense net of Norwegian settlement that the 'forties and early 'fifties wove over southern and western Wisconsin and which has held firm to the present time. In these early days Muskego and

Koshkonong were names almost as familiar to the people of Numedal and Telemark valleys in Norway as they were to the Norwegian immigrants of the Middle West.

By the time of the Civil War there were thirty thousand Norwegians scattered throughout the southern half of the state, the majority of them concentrated in Dane, Vernon (then known as Bad Ax), Columbia, and La Crosse counties. After the war they pushed north into the lumbering and fishing regions; in one county, Eau Claire, the Norwegians came to outnumber the hitherto predominant French and Irish. Today every county in Wisconsin has Norwegian communities, but the areas of concentration follow the pattern of the 'forties and 'fifties: Rock, Walworth, and Racine counties in the southeast; Dane, Jefferson, Columbia, Lafayette, and Iowa counties in the south central; Vernon, Crawford, La Crosse, Jackson, Trempeleau, Eau Claire, Dunn, and Pierce counties in the west. In 1920 the foreign-born population of Dane County was almost half Norwegian, that of Vernon County two-thirds. Until 1870 Wisconsin ranked first in number of Norwegians in the United States, then fell to second, and by 1940 to fourth place with a Norwegian population (first and second generation) of 105,611, which represented about nine per cent of the foreign stock in the state.

They had been farmers in Norway. Here, too, they tilled the soil. A few had enough money to buy land immediately, but most of them hired themselves out a year or two—the firstcomers to Yankee settlers, the later ones to their already prospering countrymen. After such a period of working for wages, the pioneer bought a team of horses and a few implements. This advanced him to the level of a "shareman," a sort of tenant farmer who received half of the crop which he grew on another man's land. From Pierce County two brothers, Anders and Ole Jensen Stortroen, wrote to their parents in Norway, in 1861, "we wanted to wait until after harvest and threshing so we would know how much we raised on the farm we worked this past year. . . . We got 200 bushels of wheat and 104 bushels of oats for our share. . . . Wheat is 62¢ a bushel now, and oats are 25¢. We made about a dollar a day for the time we worked with it." The next year Anders wrote: "Last winter we worked a little on our own land, and in between times I made shoes and Ole did some tailoring. Last spring we worked out almost all the time. We did mostly carpenter work." Thus they accumulated money to pay for their own land. This was the common pattern in Wisconsin.

Until about 1875 wheat was the principal crop raised on Wisconsin farms, but when year after year the stems grew shorter and the yields smaller, the farmers began to follow the advice of the state's agricultural scientists who urged them to change from the plow to the cow. Norwegian and other immigrant farmers adopted the new line of agriculture more quickly than the Yankee farmers, largely because they had been accustomed to handling livestock, making butter and cheese in their native lands. Most of the Norwegian immigrant women had spent their girlhood summers on the *sæter* (mountain meadows) in Norway, caring for the herd and making the winter's supply of butter and cheese. The tradition that milking the cows was woman's work carried over to America. The son of a pioneer settler in Bush Creek Valley, Vernon County, reported in his memoirs that his father had never milked a cow in his half century of farming. The Yankee farmers led the way in improving the herds, but gradually the Norwegians, too, came to see the value of scientific breeding. In many communities they banded together to build creameries for the processing and distribution of their milk. Insufficient experience sometimes brought failure to these cooperative attempts, but, on the whole, prosperous creameries outnumbered the failures.

Tobacco raising has been an established industry in certain southern sections of the state ever since the first crop was planted by American settlers in the early 'forties. Norwegian immigrants soon entered the field, first as laborers, then as sharemen, eventually as independent growers and merchants. Since 1875 the principal producers of tobacco in Wisconsin have been Americans of Norwegian descent. As a matter of fact, the two main tobacco regions coincide with the two most densely populated Norwegian areas, Dane and Vernon counties.

Andrew Jenson, who came from Norway in 1869 and settled in Edgerton, Dane County, became the leading independent leaf tobacco merchant in the state, served as presidential elector in 1892, and was a candidate for state treasurer on the Democratic ticket in 1906. His nephew, Christian A. Hoen, is the publisher and editor of Edgerton's weekly newspaper, *The Wisconsin Tobacco Reporter*. From its pages one sees that Dane is still the high-ranking tobacco growing county in the state. Stoughton and Edgerton, mainly Norwegian in make-up, are the county's chief market centers. Vernon County closely follows Dane in tobacco yield, the towns of Viroqua and Westby, hardly less Norwegian than Stoughton and Edgerton, its marketing points. These two counties produce about sixty per cent of the state's yearly crop and for each community it is a million-dollar business annually.

Some of the growers have formed co-operatives, one of which, the Northern Wisconsin Co-operative Tobacco Pool, celebrated its twenty-fifth anniversary in October, 1947. It is apparent from the names of its officers that the membership is heavily Norwegian American: George Nygaard, president, M. T. Jenson, vice-president, L. A. Peterson, secretary, A. J. Peterson, manager. Among the directors are Peter Stromstad, Clarence Aamodt, Ole Quale, and others with unmistakably Norwegian names.

However, not all the Norwegian settlers who started farming continued in that occupation. Frequently those who had learned the blacksmith trade or had been carriage makers in Norway established small shops on their farms where they made agricultural implements and wagons for their neighbors. Some of these shops grew into sizeable manufacturing concerns. T. G. Mandt, for instance, produced the "Stoughton wagon," used by thousands of farmers in the Northwest during the last three decades of the nineteenth century. From his boyhood days in the 'nineties my own father remembers the Stoughton wagon on his father's South Dakota farm.

Targe G. Mandt came with his parents from Telemarken to Dane County in 1848. In the blacksmith shop his father set up on their farm Targe built and sold his first wagon. Too young to serve in the army during the Civil War, he worked in a Missouri factory that supplied wagons to the Union forces. Before he was nineteen he was foreman of the shop. When the war was over, he went back to Wisconsin with $40 and started his own factory in Stoughton. After a decade his trade extended into Minnesota, Iowa, and the Dakotas. During the 'eighties his plant covered seven acres and employed over two hundred men. Year after year he improved his wagon; this burly, brusque Norwegian had one dominating interest in life—to create the perfect farm wagon.

A few of the early settlers worked in the lead mines in the southern counties. A diary kept by one Charles M. Tuttle during a cross-country journey in 1859 from Rock County to California records: ". . . we came to the village of Wiota [Lafayette County] settled principally by Norwegians who are principally miners working in the lead mines. We went to see some of them at the mines it is rather hard looking business. Some of them told us they had been to work about a week and had obtained about a *dollars* worth of ore." But they stayed in the mines only long enough to get cash for the down payment on a piece of farm land.

As settlement spread north, the Norwegians went into the pineries. It was common for teen-age lads like Nils P. Haugen, who later served in the Wisconsin legislature and in Congress, was tax commissioner for Wisconsin and nationally recognized as a tax expert, to spend a few youthful winters in the lumber camps and ride the logs down river in the spring "drive." Some of those who stayed in the lumbering business eventually bought sawmills from Yankee owners. But, generally speaking, the Norwegians were hewers of wood rather than owners of mills.

The communities that grew up on the shores of Lake Superior attracted Norwegian sailors and fishermen as well as lumbermill workers, and even today such fishing areas as the Apostle Islands are largely populated by descendants of those pioneer Norwegian fishermen.

Many small towns and communities in the southern and eastern parts of the state are still very Norwegian in character. These valley and village inhabitants had managed to preserve the language and folkways of their forefathers unto the third and the fourth generations. A Norwegian sociologist, Dr. Peter A. Munch, has in the last two years made a study of Vernon County, believed to have kept the customs of ancestral Norway more purely than any other Norwegian American region. Within this cultural island interesting smaller divisions appear. The northern part of the county is inhabited principally by descendants of immigrants from western Norway, the southern part by eastern Norwegians. Between them sits a conglomerate population whose forebears came from many different sections of Norway.

The political and cultural cleavage between western and eastern Norway that arose early in the nineteenth century was prominent in the heritage of the early immigrants and likewise with the later, since in Norway it has lingered on in one form or another even into the twentieth century. These attitudes, transferred to and perpetuated in America, are still very clearly discernible in this one county. Descendants of western Norwegians are slightly suspicious of and reserved toward their fellow Americans from eastern Norway. A large percentage of the population is still bilingual, and within the Norwegian tongue dialectal differences remain apparent. And, as in Norway, the speaker of one dialect holds all others in mild contempt.

The Lutheran Church is, undoubtedly, the strongest single force that kept this culture so insular and deeply rooted in the past. Out of the eleven thousand church members in Vernon County in 1936, over seven thousand were members of the Lutheran Church, most of them belonging to the body that until 1946 called itself the Norwegian Lutheran Church of America. The majority of the young people who go away to college from rural communities like these are sent to St. Olaf College, the largest Norwegian Lutheran educational institution in the country. Some, of course—an increasing number—attend the University of Wisconsin at Madison, but in the minds of a great many stanch Norwegian Lutherans, the taint of sin still clings to the secular halls of state universities, and even though they might live but an hour's drive from the university campus they send their children to the wholesome, properly Lutheran atmosphere of one of their church colleges.

In these areas, too, folk games and dances have survived; the famous Halling dance is still known and performed by agile young men. Native costumes—bright red caps, beaded or embroidered bodices, full dark skirts, white blouses and aprons, probably bordered with the lovely Hardanger lace, and the exquisite filigree brooches known as *sølje*—have been preserved in many families and are brought out for *Syttende Mai* celebrations and singing festivals. On display in homes one sees the old spinning wheels, the immigrant chests, perhaps a *salmodiken,* a one-stringed instrument the pioneers used to accompany hymn singing. One original and a few copies of Norwegian calendar sticks have been preserved by some descendants of the pioneers. A calendar stick is a notched wooden rule with symbolic markings used from the sixteenth to the nineteenth century in Norway to measure the seasons and mark the holidays of the year. When American interior decorators discovered the charm of folk art, many old hand-carved articles were brought out of dusty corners in attics and used again in these homes. Some of the people have even gone into the handicraft business. Per Lysne, a Norwegian in Stoughton, established a shop in the basement of his home, and with the aid of several elderly men, many of whom had learned their craft in the old country, he makes Norwegian chairs from hollowed logs; large round platters, trays, and boxes decorated with *rosemaling,* a highly intricate rose pattern used by the Norwegian folk artists in past centuries. I have heard Norwegian American housewives, when showing a friend a painted wooden platter or a carved chair, say, "It's a Per Lysne," with as much pride as a New Englander would say, "It's Chippendale."

A unique spot in the Middle West is Little Norway, a museum in a valley some thirty miles from Wisconsin's capital city. The hillsides are dark with spruce and pine trees, a stream twists through the "Valley of Elves" or Nissedahle, as this estate is called. Many years ago, Isak Dahle, a munificent Chicago businessman, began to build this museum spot for his countrymen to preserve on as large a scale as possible the memory and atmosphere of the old country as well as of the pioneer days. He bought a 160-acre plot where one Austin Haugen had settled in the 'fifties. Some of the log buildings Haugen had built were faithfully restored, even to the sod roofs. Inside one sees handmade furniture and tools of pioneer days, as well as priceless Norwegian antiques. Perhaps the most singular of the several structures in the valley is the Norway building, constructed in Trondheim, and taken to the Paris Exposition in 1889, then to the Columbian Exposition in 1893. An example of old Norse church architecture, this building houses valuable seventeenth and eighteenth century antiques. High up on a piny hillside overlooking the valley is the mountain hut of the *sæter jente* (milkmaid who takes the herd to the mountain meadows for the summer) which houses a library of rare Norse literature. Before his death in 1937 the creator of Nissedahle stipulated that the entire estate should eventually be given either to an educational institution or to an historical association.

Quite apart from the well-known Norwegian American areas in southern and eastern Wisconsin are settlements that have had little or no contact with the older strongholds, that have a pattern of life in many ways different from that of the "typical" Wisconsin Norwegian groups. Such is the settlement on Door County peninsula in the northeastern part of the state.

The first Norwegians to come there were a group of Moravians who founded the village of Ephraim in 1853. Their story before coming to Ephraim has for its central character Nils Otto Tank, one of those glamorous figures one finds occasionally on the periphery of the main story of immigrant life. He has been blessed and mildly cursed, called by some a well-meaning idealist and philanthropist, by others a paternalistic lord of the manor who snorted with rage when his policies were questioned. His father, a wealthy, ambitious, and powerful aristocrat in Norway, educated his son for political leadership and hoped, in the upheaval following the Napoleonic wars, for nothing less than the kingship for him. But Nils Otto spoiled his father's shimmering plans. While travelling in Germany he was converted to the Moravian faith by a clergyman whose daughter he married, and with her went to Dutch Guiana as a missionary. While there, he discovered gold fields that brought great wealth to the Dutch government and from which he, too, realized part of his large fortune. His great concern, however, was with the welfare of the natives, and after the death of his wife, he sailed for Holland to plead with the king for more enlightened colonial government.

In Holland he met and married Caroline Van der Meulen, whose mother had been the first lady-in-waiting at the court, and whose grandfather, Baron General van Boetzelaer, had once won a victory over Napoleon and was one of Holland's heroes. In 1849 Tank and his aristocratic Dutch wife came to the American frontier to work among the Norwegian Moravians in Wisconsin, arriving with priceless Dutch heirlooms, a million and a half dollars in gold, it is said, and plans for the founding of a communistic colony. Tank bought several thousand acres of land in the Green Bay region, gave ten acres to each Moravian family, and provided them with buildings, tools, and livestock. A Moravian minister from Norway, A. M. Iverson, was put in charge of the religious and educational work, establishing an academy in 1851, the first high school founded by Norwegians in America.

The colony, which Tank called Ephraim, did not prosper. Iverson disapproved of Tank's lordly treatment of the "tenants." When Tank refused to give these settlers deeds to their land, on grounds that it would defeat the purpose of the communistic enterprise, Iverson offered to lead the dissatisfied to a new frontier. Thus, in 1853 Iverson led most of the colonists to the northern part of the peninsula and established another Ephraim overlooking the waters of Green Bay. The original Ephraim disintegrated; the new Ephraim flourished as other Norwegian Moravians joined the first settlers and successfully engaged in lumbering, fishing, and shipping. It is, of course, the Ephraim of today.

After the Civil War, settlement of the peninsula progressed rapidly, Scandinavians and Germans particularly being drawn to this region of bays, fish, and towering pine trees. The religious and economic forces that have molded the lives of these peninsula Norwegians were different from those that shaped life in the southern and eastern Wisconsin settlements. Although the majority among the Protestant church members in the area belong to one of the several branches of the Lutheran Church, many of these peninsula Norwegians are still Baptists or Moravians.

When I came to know some of these Norwegians, their acquaintance gave me a new experience. I myself had spent my childhood in Norwegian or American communities of South Dakota, Wisconsin, and Minnesota, and no matter where we lived the Norwegian Lutheran church traditions were with us. We grew up hearing names like Preus, Ylvisaker, and Kildahl mentioned as great ecclesiastical luminaries of the tribe; college graduates in our world were either "St. Olaf" or "Luther"; the *Lutheran Herald, Lutheraneren,* and *Decorah-posten* belonged, we thought, to all Norwegians. Later, of course, I learned many new and different things, among them even that not all Norwegian Americans were Lutherans. Yet, I believe I had a mild shock and a quick adjustment to make when I first heard these Door County Norwegians, in a familiar brogue, mention names and events that spoke of a lifetime of allegiance utterly alien to those in which I had been bred.

A detailed account of the lives of these people may seem out of proportion to the role they have played in the larger story of Americans from Norway, but, on the other hand, many aspects of their experiences are representative of the life led by Norwegians who settled individually or in small groups in the fishing and lumbering areas of northern America.

The present-day traveller ascends the peninsula by car, or by bus, as we did the summer we chose it for a vacation spot. At Manitowoc, situated at the base of the peninsula, we left the train and crowded into a bus that sped north along the shore of Lake Michigan to Door County. Signs on the buildings—Olson's Machine Works, Hauge's Food Market—showed that we were following the trail of Norwegians, who, we knew vaguely at the time, had settled there in the nineteenth century. Mile after mile we saw cherry pickers harvesting the peninsula's main crop, in orchards that glistened with ripe fruit. Between the orchards were small fields of corn, white-blossoming timothy, and purple clover, separated by old stone fences. The names on the mail boxes, we noticed, were running increasingly to Chas. Johnson, O. Pederson, H. Seaquist, and Knut Halvorsen. Fashionable resort hotels often indicated Scandinavian ownership. Little villages quickly came and went—Egg Harbor, Fish Creek, and Ephraim, one of the most popular and beautiful villages on the peninsula. As we curved over a brow the town nestled in the crotch of two cedar-covered hills, looking for all the world like a Norwegian fishing hamlet, or, as my husband observed, like a lakeside village in the Austrian Alps. Two white church steeples rose out of the green hillside. Sails made white triangles on the blue water of the harbor. Gray fish nets hung drying on their square forms. Our destination, Little Sister Resort, lay a few miles beyond Ephraim. Soon we turned into its pillared gateway, drove down a gravelled road past a stony pasture, a big white barn, and braked to a stop in a grassy farmyard.

A little towheaded youngster and a fat puppy were playing tug-of-war with a gunny sack. Norwegian or Swede, I wondered. A voice from a screened porch called, "Bruce, come in here and keep out of Daddy's way—he's busy now." "Daddy" seemed to be the blue-eyed, tan-faced young man who was calling off the names of the guests he expected, and greeting them with more than a hint of Norwegian accent and dignity in his speech and manner. We learned that he was Mr. Anderson, the manager. I was curious for more information about this place, which, except for a 1947 Buick in the yard, had an undeniable Old World quality. After a few conversations with guests who had been coming to the resort for years, and who had watched at least one generation of Andersons grow up and another get started—the little towhead with the puppy—I knew that here was a story of Norwegians in America I had to hear about.

Then, one afternoon I met Grant Anderson, pitting cherries on a shady porch. Three score years and ten, spent in vigorous out-door life, had been gracious to this sturdy man. For thirty years he and his wife had managed their farm and resort; now two sons and their wives were carrying on. So, Grant Anderson had time to tell me about his family, show me documents relating to the history of their piece of land, and take me to visit his Norwegian friends whose memories easily reached back to the 'eighties and 'nineties of the last century. The history of the Andersons, I found, follows the pattern of most of the Norwegian peninsula families.

In August, 1865, Endre Endreson and his twenty-one-year-old son, Gunnar, who wanted to escape compulsory military service in Norway, left their home in Trondheim. Gunnar's sister had preceded them to America and was settled in Ephraim, Wisconsin, to which place they therefore naturally went.

Opportunities for a living, particularly in lumbering, were good, for exploitation of the forests by companies that had bought large tracts of timber land from the government at a low price had started. Gunnar's first job was cutting trees and stripping the bark for a company engaged in extracting tannin. The peeled logs, useless to this company, were stacked in enormous piles and burned.

Five years after arriving in America, Gunnar, now spelling his name Gunder Anderson, bought 108 acres of wild timber land along the shores of Little Sister Bay. Having no cash to pay for the property, he contracted, instead, to furnish 550 bushels of potatoes over a period of three years. Grant showed me his father's contract, on the margin of which was inserted a clause reading: "all the Small and Rotten Potatoes to be picked out, & if the Potatoes should fail then the deficiency is to be paid in Cash, at the rate of Seventy Five Cents pr Bushell, at the time of the last payment." At that rate, Gunder Anderson paid $412.50 for a piece of land that today is valued at thousands of dollars. His signature on the contract was an X.

Each day Gunder walked the three miles from his sister's home to work on his land, clear space for a cabin, and build a pier where schooners could stop to haul his logs to Green Bay, Sturgeon Bay, and Chicago. Another Anderson family settled not far from Gunder's land— Swedes who had come to Chicago first, then, after the Big Fire, to Door County. In that family Gunder met his future wife, Emma, whose father had been active in establishing the Baptist Church in Sweden. Gunder and Emma reared ten children in their primitive home on the shores of Green Bay, taught them the Baptist creed and, by example, how to use resources at hand. Emma wove cloth for their clothes; they lived on fish, venison, bear meat, and a few grains and potatoes from the land Gunder was gradually clearing of trees and stumps. In the autumn the children gathered beechnuts and butternuts from the woods. Water was carried from the bay, and often when Emma dipped her pails she also drew enough fish for the next meal.

Other Norwegians began to settle near by. Around the curve of their bay John Thorson set up a blacksmith shop. Close to him was Jake Lindem, who later moved across Green Bay to Marinette and established a sash and door factory. Jake Lindem's daughter Edith later married F. Melius Christiansen, a young musician from Norway, who was to achieve national fame as the founder and director of the St. Olaf Choir at St. Olaf College, Northfield, Minnesota; this group led the way in the a cappella choir movement in America and set the standard for similar choral groups all over the nation.

Jake Lindem kept his property on Little Sister Bay, and ever since the early 1900's the Christiansens have spent the summer months in their lovely stone house close to the water's edge in the shadow of mighty pines. Proud of "his peninsula," the aging music master took us on long rides over its winding roads, telling us leisurely stories of old settlers and their families.

Gunder and Emma Anderson's children married into families of other Norwegian and Swedish settlers. Some are still living on the peninsula, Grant on the home farm, and a sister, Martha Erickson, less than a mile away in a trim, flower-bordered white house atop a wind-swept hill, which offers a bird's-eye view of coves and bluish green fingers of forested land that pointed into the wide waters of Green Bay. Sitting in her kitchen, while she ironed pillow cases and sheets with meticulous care, I listened to more stories of bygone years in Door County.

From 1900 until after the first World War Grant Anderson was engaged in commercial fishing. He and his brother paid for their first net in two years by furnishing a company in Menominee, Wisconsin, with eight hundred packages of salted fish, two hundred each spring and fall at the rate of one dollar a package. Their fishing rig then consisted of a thirty-foot sailboat—later replaced by a gasoline motorboat and a couple of skiffs—and many hundred feet of nets. Twice a year they lowered the nets, using the "pond net" method of fishing then common in the Bay. During the fishing seasons, from May to the middle of June and from September until ice forced them to lift their nets, they kept as many as ten men busy at the dressing bench in the fish house, salting the herring and packing it in hundred-pound wooden kegs called "packages." Between seasons they cleaned and mended their nets, and in winter went into the woods and cut trees for the sixty-five-foot stakes that had to be driven into the floor of the bay for the nets. The demand for salted fish kept Anderson in the business for twenty years. But after the peak of $6.35 a package during the first World War, prices dropped, salted fish was replaced by fresh fish on America's dinner tables, and Anderson sold his business. In 1911 he had taken over the management of the farm from his aging father, and gradually changed from grain farming to dairying.

During the latter part of the nineteenth century travellers, escaping the summer heat of Chicago and other cities, began to dock at piers in the villages along Green Bay and Lake Michigan. Soon they were buying land and building summer cottages. At first, the farmers and villagers were a little ruffled by the invasion of strangers, but they soon realized their quiet countryside and beaches had a destiny that could not be ignored. Old houses were converted into tourist hotels; farmers built cottages on their property down by the water's edge. During the booming 'twenties wagon ruts became roads to accommodate the Reos and Hupmobiles that had begun to take America sightseeing. With the coming of the auto, the future of the peninsula as a vacation land was secure.

By the time the first World War was over the Anderson family had already started their resort business, lodging and feeding a few guests at the farm house and building cabins for those who were asking for accommodations. Each year Grant, with his horse and buggy, met more guests at the piers in Sister Bay or Ephraim. Once they had tasted Mrs. Anderson's juicy roasts, spicy pickles, and luscious cherry pies served with instructions to "eat as much as you want of everything," once lived in the unsophisticated comfort of a small cabin under the pines, they joined the ranks of the "repeaters." The place, even with modern equipment and conveniences, is still unpretentious; it still has an atmosphere of family living; it still has a tinge of Norway—more than a tinge, perhaps, for the white-haired, blue-eyed great-grandchild of the first Anderson to own that land could have come straight from a Norwegian mountain *gaard*.

When the flaming sumac begins to shed its slender leaves, the Andersons and their neighbors board up the cottages and settle down to peninsula affairs again. They visit friends the next bay over, take up activities in their Baptist, Moravian, or Lutheran churches, spend quiet winter evenings studying new catalogues from the nurseries where they buy their cherry trees. For many of them cherries have become a big business. Orchards stretch the length of the peninsula, some owned by individual farmers, others by large companies. The peninsula supports its people well. If the grain crops fails, they count on the cherries; if frost or blight kills the cherries, they tide over on their dairy products. And summer always brings the tourist. The peninsula dwellers scarcely felt the depression in the 'thirties, for their varied pursuits always provided them with some cash, their dollars went far; there were no unemployed.

One day Grant Anderson took me to visit Herman Hogenson, over seventy and a life-long resident of Ephraim. His father, Fordel Hogenson, who came from a family of Lofoten fishermen in northern Norway, arrived in America in 1870 at the age of twenty-one and went to Ephraim where an uncle, Nels Fordelson, operated a hotel. Fordel Hogenson married a Norwegian girl whose parents had come to Ephraim in 1853 or 1854, just after the settlement had been started by Iverson's group of Norwegian Moravians. He combined farming with hotel business;

later he built himself a sixty-nine-foot three-masted schooner, the *Eben-ezer,* which he used for coastwise trading, mostly on Green Bay, occasionally on Lake Michigan. It was on this and subsequent schooners his father built and operated that Herman Hogenson came by his profession as a Great Lakes sailor. For the most part he served as a wheelsman on the sidewheelers and propeller boats owned by the Goodrich Line, operating between Chicago and Ephraim, or by the Hart Line, with headquarters in Green Bay. When sails were in their heyday in the 'eighties and early 'nineties many Ephraimites owned and operated schooners. Some of the schooners and their owners were:

Arrow—Peter Goodlet	*Gen. Hancock*—H. N. Anderson
Ebenezer—Fordel Hogenson	*Jeannie*—Sam Nelson
Active—Fordel Hogenson	*Lark*—Ole Abrahamson
Guide—John Hogenson	*Elizabeth*—Jas. Johnson
Rose Bud—Soren Hanson	*H. J. Wright*—Jas. Johnson
J. S. Stack—Ole Abrahamson	*F. H. Williams*—Anton Hanson
	Katie Laurie—H. N. Anderson

It is interesting to note that the names given to these boats by their Scandinavian owners were Anglo-Saxon rather than Scandinavian.

Another old-time Ephraim resident is Hjalmar Holand, cherry grower and private scholar. His books on Vinland and viking explorers are reviewed by *Time,* but his Door County neighbors know him best for his cherries and his *Old Peninsula Days,* a gracefully written history of their island-surrounded neck of land.

6

Crossing the Mississippi: Iowa

Two FIGURES ON skis appeared through the trees at the brow of a slope. Below them lay the Mississippi River, in the distance the snowy hill-sides of Iowa Territory. Farther west on the Turkey River, they knew, was their destination, Fort Atkinson. Ole Valle and Ole Tollefson Kittils-land had left their jobs in the lead mines at Dodgeville, Wisconsin, in the winter of 1843, when they heard that work was available at the new government fort built in Iowa Territory for the protection of the Winne-bagoes. Both of them, a few years later, bought land in the northeastern part of the state and began farming. Their letters to friends at the Koshkonong and Rock Prairie settlements in Wisconsin resulted in a migration from these places to Iowa in 1849 and 1850. In the next decades hundreds of Norwegian families from Wisconsin, Illinois, and Norway came to clear the Iowa woodland and plow the prairie where the "grass growth was so luxuriant that if it could have stood at its full height it would have served to conceal a horse and wagon," as a Wisconsin Nor-wegian American newspaper reported in 1852. Many of the early Nor-wegian immigrants, however, preferred wooded areas and were glad to let the German, Bohemian, and other settlers claim the prairie to which, in their letters and newspapers, they frequently referred as a desert.

Before the main tide into northern Iowa began, a small Norwegian colony, the first in the state, had been founded in southeastern Lee County, near Keokuk. This Sugar Creek settlement, as it was known, though it faded into obscurity rather soon, has some historical interest.

Its founder, Hans Barlien, once a member of the Norwegian Storting, was filled with the spirit of the French Revolution. As was to be expected in the Norway of the 'thirties, his radical opinions led to persecution and when even his friends grew too timid to support him actively, the embittered agitator turned his back on Norway. In 1837 he arrived in America, visiting the settlements in the West where he hoped to found a colony "with a government in harmony with nature, and in a manner to preclude the thriving of injustice." Joyfully he exclaims in his letters from America that at last he can breathe freely. A few families came to the southeastern Iowa site that Barlien and his Norwegian companion, William Tesman, selected in 1839. Sometime in 1840, it is thought, Cleng Peerson brought there a small group from the dying settlement in northeastern Missouri. Thirty or forty families were living in this Iowa colony in 1843, according to the report of the Norwegian journalist, J. R. Reiersen, who visited the settlement before he himself founded the Texas colony.

However, soon after Barlien's death in 1842, the Sugar Creek settlement began to disintegrate. Many of the colonists were converted to Mormonism by the Saints across the river at Nauvoo, Illinois. Records show, for example, that a widow, Martha Larson, and her children were baptized into the Church of Jesus Christ of the Latter Day Saints on January 23, 1843, in Lee County, Iowa, joining, with others from the community, in the Mormon trek to the new Zion in 1846. Yet others in the settlement were Quakers who moved away to places where they could be closer to their fellow Friends. In the course of time, these Norwegian Quakers came to be quite a substantial group in Marshall County, Iowa, organizing the Stavanger Meeting, the only Quaker meeting in America conducted in the Norwegian language. In the 'nineties they even opened a boarding school that existed for about two decades.

But it is time to return to the main story. The immigrants of the late 'forties and 'fifties concentrated in the northeast, in Winneshiek County, and, in the central part of the state, in and around Story County. Yet, compared with the neighbor states in the Middle West, the Iowa Norwegians were always small in numbers. In 1870 Wisconsin had some sixty thousand people of Norwegian stock, while Iowa had only about twenty-five thousand; in 1900, when Minnesota had about 258,000, Iowa had 71,000. But the Iowa group has been culturally more important than many of the larger centers, mainly because from the college it founded and from one of its newspapers many significant influences have flowed into the expanding stream of Norwegian American life. In 1862 Luther College was started in Decorah; a dozen years later the first issue of the weekly *Decorah-posten* appeared. Decorah was, and still is, the "Norwegian capital" of Iowa. Professors, writers, church leaders—many of them educated in Norway's university—came there to teach in the college and work on the staff of the newspaper. Though on the edge of the western frontier and primitive in its setting, the school had some of the atmosphere of a European gymnasium and attracted many budding intellectuals from among the sons of the settlers.

Since 1877 there has been a Norwegian-American Historical Museum in Decorah. Replicas of Norwegian landscapes and buildings have been constructed, and a large collection of pioneer relics is on display. Here one can see the clothes the immigrant wore, the chests he brought, the *kubberulle* (large wooden wagon) he built to carry his family and possessions over the hills and plains to their new home, the exterior and completely furnished interior of the log houses he lived in, the primitive tools he used on his farm. Unfortunately this splendid collection is crowded into a run-down, creaky building where many of the valuable objects are lost to sight in dark, dusty corners. However, a project has recently been inaugurated to establish a $250,000 foundation for the proper care and housing of this unique collection of Norwegian Americana. Supporting the project are such leaders of Norwegian descent as Leif Erickson, chief justice of the Montana Supreme Court, Henry O. Talle, representative in Congress from Iowa, Ernest O. Melby, dean of the college of education at New York University, C. A. Elvehjem of the University of Wisconsin, Henning Larsen, dean of the college of liberal arts at the University of Illinois, Enoch Norem of the Mason City (Iowa) *Globe Gazette,* Orlando Ingvolstad, secretary of Norwegian Relief, Inc.

These institutions, attracting as they did the educated immigrant, have given the Decorah community a flavor of middle class Norway. Ties to the old country continued unbroken in many families; memories of the homeland remained a little sharper in these minds; the Norwegian language lingered a little longer on these tongues; the secrets of skilled fingers descended more easily. Norwegian Christmas customs, for instance, still survive in many forms, for the most part now not as something consciously alien, but simply as part of the established order of things, like "having the tree" on the twenty-fourth instead of the twenty-fifth of December. The hours of Christmas Eve are the breathless, shining hours for the family, starting with the traditional dinner of *lutefisk,* meat balls, and *lefse,* ending with a special fluffy cream pudding and Norwegian pastries, and maybe, in a few families, a glass of wine for old and young. When they gather around the lighted tree after dinner, father reads, "Now it came to pass in those days, there went out a decree from Caesar Augustus," from the gospel of Luke; then they sing their favorite Lutheran Christmas hymns, and the gifts are distributed. There is no Santa Claus, no " 'Twas the night before Christmas" in the homes of these Americans whose grandfathers came from Norway, except, perhaps, in occasional third-generation families where intermarriage with Anglo-Saxons may have introduced other traditions.

On Christmas Day festivities are divided between home and church. Following the church service in the morning, friends and relatives gather for big dinners with more special dishes, such as the hot, spicy fruit soup. In the evening they go back to church for the children's program. Whoever has spent his childhood in a Norwegian American community vividly remembers the dim church, the enormous tree inside the altar rail, blazing—before the days of electric tree lights—with a thousand flames, men hovering in the shadows ready to snuff out danger with wet pads tied to the ends of long poles; the "pieces" he spoke, the gauze angel costumes she wore, and the primary class singing, "Thy little ones, dear Lord, are we, And come Thy lowly bed to see." And when it was all over, we stepped from the hot, tallow-smelling church into the frosty night, clutching the evening's reward, a small paper bag of peanuts and hard "Christmas" candy.

Sometime during the Christmas season the young people, even today, mask themselves and go *julebukk,* visiting from house to house where they are served goodies and make their hosts guess their identity. Of course, these traditions are fast disappearing and survive now mainly in the rural neighborhoods, particularly around such old centers as Decorah.

Only of late a countercurrent to this "assimilation" makes itself felt. Like all other immigrant groups, the Norwegians were first ashamed of their old country paraphernalia and discarded them as soon as they could afford to buy Grand Rapids tables, rockers, beds, and Sears Roebuck curtains and crockery. Grandfather's sturdy homemade chairs were put in a storeroom with grandmother's wooden cooking bowls. Now these things are hauled down again as interesting antiques and, also, as the material witnesses of a past sufficiently remote that one may well be proud of it without jeopardizing one's secure Americanism.

Like Per Lysne in Stoughton, Wisconsin, Mrs. Sigurd Reque, wife of a Luther College professor and also curator of the Norwegian-American Historical Museum, has developed her hobby of producing replicas of the Norwegian decorated woodenware into a small business. In other places, too, the old Norwegian crafts are finding their markets. In Council Bluffs, Iowa, Chris Loseth, now in his eighties, has found that American housewives are eager to own the salad bowls and other woodenware he shapes out of blocks of black walnut. Chris and Karen, his wife, came to Council Bluffs from Norway over fifty years ago. For many years he earned his living as a brick mason and a shoemaker. When he became too old to do heavy work he took up woodcarving, a craft he had learned as a boy in Aalesund, Norway. Tourists from all over the country stop to watch the aproned old man in his stocking cap sit at the window of his little shop, chips flying from the block of wood in his lap.

Story City has also been a center of Old World culture. One of its most remarkable families are the Tjernagels, farmers and musicians. Ole Andreas Tjernagel came to America in 1859, settled in Iowa and reared a large family. There was music in their pioneer home, an organ and an accordion which Ole played. When his sons earned a little money they bought instruments, and with four neighbor boys organized a band that played at Fourth of July celebrations, political rallies, and the State Fair. As the Tjernagel children grew up, they settled on farms close to each other and continued their musical association. Their Follinglo Orchestra, named after their mother's home in Valders, Norway, was unique. For many years the farmers and villagers around Story City listened to the Tjernagels, a dozen more or less, play Bach, Beethoven, Brahms, and Grieg. One of the brothers carved lyre-back chairs for the group, music stands with old Norse designs, and a massive music cabinet, each drawer inlaid with a composer's name. Another brother, Nehemias, who celebrated his eightieth birthday in 1948 on the old homestead, now one of Iowa's most modern farms, went abroad twice to travel and study music. He has published books in English and Norwegian; his compositions, including band selections, anthems, and hymns, have been played and sung both in this country and in Oslo at the royal palace.

Though they could not essentially change it, such exceptional families as the Tjernagels at least break the midwestern rural pattern of stolidity, drabness, and cultural barrenness, which Hamlin Garland, Ole Rölvaag, and other writers have portrayed so well. That Iowa's Americans from Norway have largely been farmers is not strange in a state whose biggest industry is agriculture. In the 'seventies a few of them went into business on a small scale; later they trickled into the professions. But, generally speaking, they have stayed on the land, served their communities by holding local, county, and state offices on the side, while they tended their fields of corn and their pastures full of hogs.

7

A Considerable Norwegian Settlement: Minnesota

GOVERNOR RAMSEY LOOKED up from the letter he was reading to glance out the window in the room that was his office by day, in the evening the Ramsey drawing room. When this first governor of the new Territory of Minnesota arrived in the spring of 1849, St. Paul was a village of fur traders' huts perched atop a bluff over the Mississippi River. Now only a year later, there were a few hundred houses and stores, a newspaper, and over a thousand people, with more arriving every week. To the west were the rich lands he hoped to buy from the Sioux Indians and open for such settlers as this Norwegian minister from Wisconsin was writing him about. His eyes returned to the carefully written page. "Those Norwegians, in whose behalf I now principally write, are generally poor, but sober, hardy and industrious farmers and mechanics; but I have received letters from Norway & Denmark, informing me, that several men with considerable capital, wish to get over here, if I can lead them to places where they can invest their capital profitably, in improving water powers erecting mills and other machineries, and building towns, etc: and I should therefore be much gratified, if your Excell: would please to let me know how far those objects might be gained in your section of country. . . . If Your Excellency's Answer is so, as to encourage emigration up there, I am determined to go there myself, and will in all probability have a considerable norwegian settlement on the banks of one of the lakes or water courses next fall." A considerable settlement it was destined to be, indeed.

The writer was Danish-born C. L. Clausen, who had come to the United States in 1843 with a Norwegian party, and until his death in 1892 remained identified with Norwegian American life. We will encounter his name later on, for he was, in truth, one of the important figures of the pioneer period. When he wrote to Governor Ramsey in January, 1850, he was the Lutheran pastor for the large Luther Valley settlement of Norwegians in Rock County, Wisconsin; so, naturally, newcomers often appealed to him for advice about land. Since what was left in the southern counties of Wisconsin was by that time in the high-priced hands of professional land grabbers, Clausen felt he couldn't sit back and let the innocent be exploited by these "interested speculators" as he politely described them in his letter. No record of Governor Ramsey's reply has been found, but when warm weather opened the Mississippi River for traffic, Clausen went to St. Paul, investigated land in the vicinity, finally deciding on the Rush River Valley in eastern Wisconsin as a likely settlement spot. But, he had set eye on Minnesota land and imparted information about it to the people in Luther Valley.

Apparently Governor Ramsey did not forget the Norwegian clergyman, for some months later, in October, 1850, his house guest, Fredrika Bremer, the distinguished Swedish writer who was travelling in America, wrote from St. Paul: "I have been told that the Norwegian pastor in Luther's Dale, Mr. Clausen, is intending to remove hither with a number of Norwegians in order to establish a settlement. Good. There are already a considerable number both of Norwegians and Danes."

About one of the Norwegians, a cook in the governor's household, Miss Bremer commented frankly, "she is not above twenty, and is not remarkably clever as a cook, and yet she receives eleven dollars per month wages. This is excellent country for young servants." The cook, Ingeborg Langeteig, had come with her brother from Hallingdal, Norway, to Rock County, Wisconsin, in 1849. It is altogether possible that they heard about Minnesota from Clausen shortly after his return, for by early autumn they were in St. Paul. She left the governor's kitchen after a year, married an Irishman, and later, after his death, became the wife of a Norwegian, who lived to be a patriarch among his people in Minneapolis.

Meanwhile Governor Ramsey had other Norwegian immigrants in his employ. His coachman for five years was C. Amundson, who later became a merchant in Winona. Twenty years after he had driven the governor's coach, Amundson was speaking on the floor of the Minnesota legislature as a representative.

The first permanent Norwegian settlements in Minnesota were in the southeastern part of the state, the arrival of immigrants in Goodhue County in 1851 marking the beginning. Every year thereafter new families crossed the Mississippi River, usually at La Crosse, Wisconsin, one of the main points of departure for the southern Minnesota frontier, particularly after the railroad was extended that far in 1858. Merchants in the river town did a thriving business supplying the immigrants with wagons, oxen, implements, and food. Ferries were clogged through the summer months with the bulky paraphernalia of the westward moving settlers. For many years Fillmore, Houston, and Goodhue counties attracted most of the Norwegians. By 1860 twelve thousand Norwegians had settled in the state, over half of them in these three counties. The shock of the Sioux War in 1862 momentarily halted the advance, but when the frontier had calmed again the Norwegians thronged into the valleys of southeastern Minnesota. In 1870 the three counties had almost half of the fifty thousand people of Norwegian stock in the state.

A typical journey to the Minnesota frontier in the early 'fifties is Steener Knutson's, whose children later took the name Steenerson and whose son described it in his memoirs. Knutson left Telemarken, Norway, in 1850 with his wife and children. In Milwaukee they were met by a friend who took them in a hayrack to Dane County, Wisconsin. A year later Steener Knutson travelled into Minnesota Territory, and, in spite of the general opinion that Minnesota was too far north for good crops, he took a claim in Houston County. In the spring of 1852 his family joined a caravan of fourteen wagons bound for the new frontier. And there, like so many of the immigrants who built the inland empire, Knutson not only cleared his land but helped organize the community. He was chairman of the settlement's first town meeting in 1858; and when a Norwegian Lutheran church was established, he became a member of the board.

By the time the Civil War was over, land prices in these settled areas were already too high for the moneyless newcomers. To the west was cheap government land, recently and reluctantly given up by the Sioux. The Minnesota River Valley—rolling prairie land spotted with timber and broken by willow-edged creeks—formed a natural westward passage for those who streamed into the state.

The experience of a member of Steener Knutson's family, this time his son Knute Steenerson, again typifies a pattern, the westward thrust of the late 'sixties and 'seventies. In the spring of 1869 Knute headed west in a prairie schooner, following the old Indian travel route along the Minnesota River Valley. Beyond Redwood Falls there were no white settlers. When he reached Lac qui Parle County on the western edge of the state, Steenerson staked out a claim on the rich soil where the Lac qui Parle and the Minnesota rivers join. There he built his shanty. Except for a few Indians who camped near by, he was alone. But the next season brought settlers and from his hundred acres of timber he sold logs for their cabins. After a few years a flourishing Norwegian settlement extended fifty miles along the Minnesota River Valley, with Montevideo as its center.

Among the hundreds who came to this region Steenerson had opened were my maternal grandparents, Sven and Elsa Anderson. Elsa Lundefaret married a young Swede who came to work in her home parish in Telemarken. About 1872 they emigrated to America and went directly to Fillmore County, Minnesota, worked for the older settlers until they had enough money to buy a yoke of oxen and a wagon and then started west, following the wheel trails along the Minnesota River bottom. When they reached Lac qui Parle County, where stretches of meadow lay between gentle hills, they stopped. Around them they saw the wooden shacks of other Norwegian immigrants.

Grasshoppers ravaged the patches of grain the settlers sowed the first few years, and when, summer after summer, noondays became dusky night and wheat stalks were left naked, the defeated turned their backs to the prairie, now truly a desert. Several had gone into debt buying machinery and implements; rusting seeders and mowers in the open fields mutely told a tale of despair. Knute Steenerson was employed by the machine companies to haul the abandoned machines into the little town of Montevideo and auction them off. They covered over an acre of ground when the sale was held, and the only bidders were the companies' agents, who bought them back for a song.

I don't know how, but my grandparents struggled through those bitter times. Every two or three years gentle, brown-haired Elsa had a new baby until there were three sons to help Sven with the land and five daughters to help Elsa with the house, chickens and cows. The children had country school educations, three of the girls a few years of Lutheran academy training. They all learned the English language, the younger more easily than the older children, but Norwegian was spoken exclusively in the home because of Elsa and Sven. Six of the children married, all of them into Norwegian immigrant farm families like their own; most of them stayed on the soil and all of them handed the language of the old country on to their children. By the time I came to know my frail, weary-looking grandmother, English from a small-town grammar school in South Dakota had replaced the Norwegian of my early childhood. I remember well how she tried to talk to me with the few words she knew and how I tried to make her say "sugar" instead of "sooger," which was closer to the *sukker* of her native tongue.

When the railroad came to the Minnesota River Valley, towns began to sprout along the tracks. The founding of Sacred Heart, in western Renville County, is typical of how thousands of villages came into being. Sacred Heart township had been organized in the late 'sixties by a German and several Norwegian settlers. For a decade the post office shifted from farm cabin to farm cabin, changing names with each shift until finally, while on the Eric Gunderson farm, it was called Sacred Heart. In 1878 the Chicago, Milwaukee, and St. Paul railroad extended its line through the county and located a station in the township. The post office and its name moved to this spot on the prairie where the train stopped, a town without people, without buildings. But a year later, when the railroad company began to erect a depot, two Norwegian settlers moved to the new site. Ole Torbenson, who had started a store on a farm four years earlier, now built a shack across the tracks from the rising depot and moved his merchandise there. Hans Field, who probably had been Hans Fjelde before he came to America, a widower with three daughters, put up a shanty next to Torbenson's store to shelter his forge and anvil which he, too, had brought into town from a near-by farm. He also built a house for his family and a slightly larger wooden structure, which he called a hotel, to provide quarters for the men working on the depot.

Like the house that Jack built, one thing led to another. A saloon appeared; two elevators, two hardware stores, a general store were doing business within a year's time. Board sidewalks were laid and hitching posts appeared along the short dirt street. A few of the newcomers were German and Irish, many were Scandinavians, and most of these Norwegians. Conversations and business transactions were carried on in a mixture of these languages. The spirit of America arrived the day a sign appeared in one of the store windows which read: "English spoken har." The Norwegian *her* (here) is pronounced somewhat like "hair"; so the "har" in this notice is obviously a compromise between English and Norwegian. Such was the village of Sacred Heart.

The same spring the railroad came to Sacred Heart township a young Norwegian, Hans Vorkin, also came there, leading a pair of steers with which to start his farming. He wrote to his twin brother, Ole, back in Dovre, Gudbrandsdalen, urging him to come and farm with him. Two years later, in 1880, Ole and his bride, Anne, arrived, and the three of them worked a farm the two boys had rented. In 1882 Anne's sister, Kari, came to live with them. The brothers bought the farm. Hans and Kari were married. When children were born, the families separated, but still lived on neighboring farms. Even after Ole and his family had moved into town they were still close enough to celebrate their holidays together.

In 1947 the Vorkin twins were ninety years old. While their children are running the farms, they live in Sacred Heart, sit at the kitchen table close to the stove and the coffeepot, and in between gossip of present and pioneer days these life-long partners try to beat each other at card games. By themselves they are but two humble drops in the nation's sea. Yet, when I come to think of the span their memories cover, I am awed by the grandeur of the American dream and by the fullness with which it has come true. For, generous as this span was, how often can it be said in the history of mankind that a nation of such pioneers grew as fast as we did to what is now, for better or worse, the greatest power on earth.

The prairie and pleasantly wooded sections of Minnesota filled up, but still the Norwegians came into the state. By 1900 a third of the some eight hundred thousand immigrants and their children in the United States lived in Minnesota, where they constituted close to a fifth of the foreign-stock population. With indomitable courage they pushed north into the region of pine forests and red earth. Here they homesteaded, cleared patches of ground, planted potatoes between the stumps, wheedled a few grains out of the cool, stony soil. Many gave up the battle and moved west.

Some, like Bjørgulv Bjørnaraa, stayed in the North where the air was light as dry wine. The son of a well-to-do merchant in Norway, Bjørnaraa was educated to be a teacher, but failing to get a position, came to America in 1903. For eight years he taught school in a Norwegian farm community in southern Minnesota, published poetry, essays, and newspaper articles; travelled constantly throughout the region lecturing on Norwegian culture to the immigrants and their children, who were forgetting the language and traditions of their forefathers. In 1911 he moved his family to the newly opened north woods country, taught school for two more years, then took up a homestead of four hundred and fifty acres. For almost three decades he poured his immense energy into the stubborn land. As a friend wrote about this poet-farmer, "He walks around'on his niggardly farm, dreaming and thinking and yearning for something which I suppose he shall never have." * Like his friend, the novelist O. E. Rölvaag, he saw and felt the spiritual tragedy of the immigrant, drifting between two cultures, losing the core of the old, attaching himself to only the surface of the new. Glowing with purpose, he joined organizations that tried to keep alive the old country culture among the Norwegian Americans. In their interests he continued to travel, lecture, and write. But neither he nor others who felt as he did could stem the steady progress of acculturation among their people, and as he grew older a mist of bitterness hung over this stalwart Norwegian on his stony farm in northern Minnesota.

Since 1870 Minnesota has had more Norwegians than any other state in the Union, and in spite of their wide scattering over the nation in the last few decades, the North Star state still has within its borders about a quarter of the close to a million of the first and second generations. Of these about sixty per cent live on farms or in towns of less than 2,500. Though the Swedes outnumber them in the state as a whole, there are considerably more Norwegians than Swedes engaged in farming. Of the seventy-one thousand Norwegian-born in the state in 1930, fifty-five per cent were classified as rural, while only forty-four per cent of the ninety thousand Swedish-born Minnesotans were rural. At the same time there were 196,000 natives of Norwegian parentage and only 180,000 of Swedish parentage, indicating less mobility on the part of the children of Norwegian immigrants. This agrees with the fact that in this second generation group over sixty per cent of the Norwegians were rural, while forty-seven per cent of the Swedes were so classified.

The twin cities of Minneapolis and St. Paul, particularly the former, attracted the majority of those who went to the cities. The character of the two cities is, nevertheless, quite different. In Minneapolis in 1930 the Swedes (26.6%), Norwegians (18.7%), and Germans (13.4%) were the dominant non-native groups; in St. Paul the distribution was: Germans (24.3%), Swedes (16.4%), Irish (8.5%), Norwegians (8%).

Pioneer settlers in St. Paul, the older of the two cities, were German and Irish Catholics, as well as a group of German and Czech Jews, who were established economically and socially before the Swedes and Norwegians came in any great numbers. The flavor of the city has remained Catholic and Democratic because of the later arrival of Polish and Austrian Catholics, even though the Swedes rose to second place and

* In a letter from Jarle Leirfallom to Louis Adamic, September 5, 1939.

the Norwegians to fourth among the foreign stock. Minneapolis, on the other hand, was first settled by Yankee families who gained control of the major industries—milling, lumbering, manufacturing—and still occupy the highest rung of the social ladder. The next wave brought middle class Scandinavians into the professions, trades, and politics. Later came Russians and Poles, many of them Jewish.

The predominant tone of Minneapolis is Protestant—mainly Lutheran—Republican, and, it has been frequently observed, anti-Semitic, a trait absent from the social pattern of St. Paul. Some observers believe the cause of this difference to lie in the social structure of the two cities. Jews were among the pioneers in St. Paul, some of them rising to economic, social, and civic leadership in the city, thus establishing a tradition of assimilation and participation in community affairs. In Minneapolis anti-Semitism became, for the social elite of closely interrelated Yankee families, a device for maintaining their socio-economic monopoly. This attitude has more or less sifted down to the middle class groups and even to the working class. The Scandinavian Lutherans, almost totally unfamiliar with Jews from their old country backgrounds, did not bring any tradition of anti-Semitism with them. However, in their tendency not to participate in civic affairs as a group, they have left a vacuum and thus, at least passively, contributed to the persistence of a pattern that only recently began to yield to the conscious efforts of an Americanism more generously conceived.

Every major industry in the state has used the labor of Norwegian immigrants and of their children, not to any great extent on the managerial level, but as foremen and laborers. The great milling and lumbering companies are in the hands of the Pillsburys, Washburns, Crosbys, De Laittres, Boveys, Morrisons, and Walkers, pioneer Minnesota families, many of old New England stock. Giant eastern concerns—mainly Rockefeller and Oliver—control the vast mining interests in the state. The Finnish, Polish, Yugoslav, and Scandinavian immigrants and their children supply the labor and mechanical skill in the pits. But there are exceptions, of course. Recently Dreng Bjørnaraa, the son of Bjørgulv Bjørnaraa, was appointed to the important post of public relations representative in the St. Paul office of the Oliver Mining Company. On the whole, though, educated Scandinavians strove rather for political and educational leadership in this state they have done so much to build. In 1892 Knute Nelson was elected governor, the first Norwegian American to serve at the head of an American commonwealth. In 1921 Jacob

Preus became the second governor of Norwegian descent, and since that time five chief executives of the state have been of part or full Norwegian stock. But the mass base has remained in agriculture, naturally, since agriculture is still the main source of Minnesota's wealth.

Many institutions in the state reflect the Norwegian concentration. The Evangelical Lutheran Church, which embraces more Norwegians than any other single organization, has its headquarters in Minneapolis. So does Sons of Norway, a fraternal order and the largest secular organization. No state university in the country has so many students of Norwegian stock as the University of Minnesota, which, likewise, has many department heads and deans of Norwegian descent. Scores of Norwegian Americans have held high administrative positions in the state teachers colleges. St. Olaf College, the largest of the schools founded and maintained by the Norwegian Lutherans, is an hour's drive from Minneapolis in the little town of Northfield. The Norwegian-American Historical Association is incorporated in the state of Minnesota, its archives located at St. Olaf College.

It was altogether fitting that Minneapolis was chosen as the scene for the elaborate centennial commemoration in 1925. The official historian of the occasion wrote that if he were asked to give in one word the Norwegian contribution to America, he would say, "Minnesota." Indeed, though the Swedes have come to outnumber them, there is still, a century after Fredrika Bremer's visit, "a considerable Norwegian settlement" in Minnesota.

8

The Red River Valley and the Dakotas

THE CIVIL WAR did not stop the flow of emigrants from Norway. On the contrary, 1861 and 1862 brought a sharp increase over preceding years. Perhaps it should be said here that the United States immigration figures, which, by the way, did not separate Norwegians and Swedes until 1869, give only a few hundred arrivals for each of these years. Closer to the truth, undoubtedly, are the official Norwegian reports, which reveal that from four to eight thousand left Norway for America annually, except for 1863 when the number dropped to about a thousand.* One reason for the wide discrepancy is that during this period the majority of the emigrants landed at Quebec and, without being counted, passed over the laxly regulated border into the States. Statements of American consuls in Scandinavia also bear out the greater accuracy of the Norwegian figures. In the fall of 1862 Carl J. Kraby, consul in Porsgrunn, Norway, wrote to Secretary Seward that with "proper encouragement" emigration from Norway "may literally become an 'Exodus.' Four thousand emigrants for the United States left the several ports of Norway from May to August inclusive, ten thousand the spring and summer of 1861."

The early 'sixties were gray years for the rural population of Norway. Crops had failed in 1860; agricultural conditions were generally unprofitable; no relief from high taxes was in sight. Then, in 1862, came the momentous news of the passage of the Homestead Act. America was calling for labor. The Federal and state governments, railroads, steamship lines, and land companies were working feverishly at home and abroad through a network of agents to bring people into the factories and onto the land of a nation at war. Norway's dispirited farmers answered the call, streaming to the offices of government officials and shipping lines to secure emigration permits and tickets.

* Reports of the Sioux massacres in 1862 undoubtedly cooled the ardor of some prospective emigrants.

The efforts of American consuls in northern European cities shed an interesting light on the immigration policy of Lincoln's administration. The consular system was expanded; consuls were directed to distribute copies of the Homestead Act, to stop rumors that emigrants were tricked by scoundrels at the ports and taken South to be sold into slavery, and to allay fears that young men would be drafted into military service the moment they stepped on American soil. On the other hand, Norwegian youths, hoping to get free passage across the Atlantic, volunteered to serve in the Union Army.

Consul B. F. Tefft in Stockholm faced this perplexing problem. In a report of January 9, 1863, he stated: "My office is overrun with applicants, from Sweden and Norway, who wish to go to the United States and enter the Army. . . . Had I the means of sending such applicants to America, I believe I could send a thousand per month for a year or two to come. I have had, sometimes from ten to twenty Swedish and Norwegian soldiers, with their uniforms upon them, together seeking a way to get to America for the above purpose. . . . What shall I do in relation to these numerous, increasing, and altogether troublesome applications?" The Department of State discouraged this form of emigration, advising the consuls to aid only civilian applicants.

In the early 'fifties a few states in the new West began to encourage immigrants to settle within their borders, but it was not until the 'sixties that they all made a serious bid for a share in the human wealth that was pouring in. Most of them established immigration commissions. Pamphlets, extolling the virtues of soil and climate, stressing the political, religious, and economic freedom of the state, were printed in German, Norwegian, Swedish, and Dutch and distributed on boats, in hotels, and in taverns at the port cities in this country and in northern Europe. Agents were sent abroad to persuade people to emigrate and assist them in getting passage. Other agents were stationed at ports of debarkation to escort immigrants safely past the intriguing propositions of wily runners who haunted the piers. As late as 1871 Wisconsin was offering several thousand acres of desirable land in a few central counties at prices ranging from fifty cents to $2.25 an acre. Minnesota, trying to counteract the prevalent notion that the state was a wasteland of ice and snow the year around, pointed out that common grains and garden vegetables could be raised with great success. During the grasshopper raids of the 'seventies the state government, as well as the railroad companies, provided some relief to stricken settlers and officially minimized the devastation wrought by the 'hoppers. The territorial governments of Dakota and Montana also issued alluring invitations that helped dispel the myth of the Great American Desert beyond the Mississippi.

Railroad and land companies clamored for immigrants like hawkers at a county fair. On the whole, these companies were more extravagant in their claims, more generous in their promises, frequently less scrupulous in keeping them, and, generally speaking, more successful in actually settling immigrants. The Northern Pacific, the St. Paul and Pacific (later called the St. Paul, Minneapolis and Manitoba when James J. Hill took it over) and the Great Northern were the main lines that brought immigrants into northwestern Minnesota and the Dakotas. By providing huge reception houses where wives and children could live while the men hunted for land, free transportation for those who bought railroad property, and favorable terms of payment such as the rebate system, the railroads eased the transition for many an immigrant family in the 'seventies and 'eighties. Yet, in spite of these improvements over the ox carts of earlier times, the immigrants, crowded for days on the hard benches of railroad cars inadequately equipped for human needs, found the journey to the frontier arduous and nerve-wracking.

And while all the noisy advertising of transportation and land companies went on, a quiet stream of "America letters" flowed back to the parishes of Norway, many of them with money for parents, sisters, and brothers to make the journey. In the total picture, they were more important than any other single factor in drawing families out of their cottages in Norway to live in the sod shanties of the American West. The opening of the Dakota Territory for settlement marks the beginning of the biggest wave of migration, the peak year being 1882, when almost thirty thousand Norwegians entered the country.

A Norwegian journalist, Paul Hjelm Hansen, followed the movement with particular interest. Having turned to writing after the Norwegian government halted his career as a state official because of his activities in the Thrane labor movement,* he advocated emigration, and, in 1867, himself left Norway for America where he joined the staff of *Faedrelandet og Emigranten,* a newspaper published in La Crosse, Wisconsin. In 1869 the Board of Immigration of Minnesota, hoping to direct settlers to the western part of the state, asked him to explore these areas.

---

* Marcus Thrane (1817–1890) the founder of the organized labor movement in Norway.

For several weeks during that summer Hjelm Hansen travelled through the Red River region around Fort Abercrombie; often he slept at night under the stars. His enthusiastic reports of the fertile valley where there was "not as much as a stone or a stump to obstruct the plow" were printed in two Norwegian American newspapers as well as in Norway. Paul Hjelm Hansen's praise of the Red River Valley, which he prophesied would become, within a decade, one of America's most productive and beautiful regions, undoubtedly helped direct the movement of Norwegian Americans into western Minnesota, South and North Dakota.

The story of how people settle in a region is inextricably bound up with its rivers. As the Norwegians moved westward their choice of homes was determined to a large extent by the waters of the Missouri, the Big Sioux, the James, and particularly the Red River, pouring wide and straight through the plains between Minnesota and Dakota. A network of smaller rivers with tree, plant, and animal names—Willow, Elm, Maple, Wild Rice, and Mouse, Goose, Turtle, Snake—formed paths to the larger channels. Settlements grew along these water veins. Caravans of canvas schooners crept northward from Iowa and westward from Minnesota and when they reached prairies where the grass brushed the bellies of their oxen, they halted.

An eyewitness, who lived on the old Pembina trail near Crookston, Minnesota, described the caravans that passed daily in the summer of 1882: "We watched the schooners come up from the south zigzagging up the tortuous trail like ships beating up against the wind. Slowly they drew nearer—sometimes one, sometimes five or six in a fleet. . . . Sometimes they stopped to inquire about the road or to chat a few minutes. They told us . . . they came from Fillmore or Goodhue County in Minnesota, or Wisconsin, or Iowa. Most of them were on their way to Larimore, Devil's Lake, Church's Ferry, or some other point far distant from a railroad in Dakota. . . . The number of schooners that passed our shanty in the summer of 1882 seemed endless. From ten to fifty would pass day in and day out. The year 1882 marked the beginning of a big migration to Dakota."

Year after year they streamed over the land. On the Northern Pacific, on Jim Hill's "Manitoba" and his Great Northern they chugged into the Red River Valley and beyond as the railroads flattened the grass across the plains. The Norwegians settled thickly on fat-soiled river bottoms and spacious prairie under the large and potent sun. They grew heavy-headed wheat, raised elevators and built towns that were called Norway Center, Oslo, Veblen, Voss, Brandt, Hetland, Bygland, Kragnes, Rustad, Halstad, Hitterdal, Dahlen, Fossum, Flom.

As was customary the pioneers came to the frontier both from the older settlements and straight from Norway. The Rölvaag family runs true to this pattern, although when Ole Edvart Rölvaag himself came to America in 1896 at the age of twenty directly to the South Dakota farm of an uncle, the frontier there was almost two decades in the past. Jennie Berdahl Rölvaag's family, on the other hand, came to America in 1856. Her grandfather settled on the Iowa frontier, then four years later moved to Houston County, Minnesota, and six years later to Fillmore County. In the early 'seventies they caught the Dakota fever and again pushed west, taking claims near Sioux Falls. There the trek of this branch of the Berdahls ended, and there Jennie grew up and met the young immigrant from Norway who later used the stories of these pioneer Dakotans in what has become a classic in American literature, *Giants in the Earth*.

My father's father, Christian Nelson Boe, a fisherman and farmer from north of Bergen, came to America in the 'seventies, married Kari Kvam who had come from the district of Valders, and, after spending a few years near Spirit Lake in northern Iowa, moved west with the rest. They homesteaded in a region of small hills and numerous sloughs bordered by cattails—what is now northeastern South Dakota. There my father was born.

In 1880 there were already over twenty thousand people of Norwegian stock settled in Dakota Territory, most of them concentrated in the eastern counties. One of the attractions of the Red River Valley, especially for single men, were the bonanza farms that flourished between the panics of 1873 and 1893. After Jay Cooke's failure, eastern shareholders exchanged worthless bonds of railroad stock for immense blocks of land given to the railroad by the government. Managers were hired and thousands of acres sowed with wheat. These plantations of the North, twenty and thirty thousand acres in size, employed as many as three hundred men each, used three hundred horses, one hundred plows, fifty seeders, seventy-five binders, ten separators, and ten threshing engines to plant and harvest a crop of wheat. Several crews of two dozen men cleared fifty acres of land a day. Tons of butter, cheese, and meat were shipped into the region for these farms that had no livestock and poultry. The bonanza farms, in spite of their mass production, did not bring great wealth to their eastern owners, but they established the Red River Valley as the "No. 1 hard wheat" region of the world, and that brought people.

Hundreds of laborers—immigrant homesteaders, small farmers, lumberjacks from Wisconsin and Minnesota, and college boys—came to the bonanza farms for harvest and threshing. Many Norwegian settlers worked on the farms to get enough cash for "improvements" on their claims required by the Homestead Act. Knut Hamsun, the novelist to be, who visited America twice during his salad days, drifted into the valley early in the summer of 1887 and joined a crew on one of these farms, dreaming through the shadeless days atop a machine that crawled over the furrowed earth. On Sundays he wrote letters for the clumsy-handed workers not accustomed to tools as small as pens or pencils. To his poet friend, Kristofer Janson, in Minneapolis, he wrote about his loneliness, about the oceanlike prairie where wagons in the distance seemed to swim, the houses to float, the staring, white hot sun and, when it set, the crimson foam, no words could describe, around it. By autumn Hamsun was gone again.

When the 1890 census was taken, the Norwegians were the most numerous of the foreign-born in Dakota, North Dakota having almost fifty thousand and South Dakota over thirty-five thousand. Resolutely they had toiled across the plains in the wake of Jim Hill's railroads into the country of wind and broken buffalo bones. Quickly they tidied up the prairie, for the bones were bought by companies for as high as fifteen dollars a ton and sent east to be ground into fertilizer. Beside each cabin could then be seen a pile of bleached bones rising higher than the house, wagon loads of them.

Jim Hill needed settlers to make his railroad pay, so he beckoned them west by laying out towns along the tracks—a red depot, a barren park, a Main Street—drearily uniform across the state. He donated money for their schoolhouses and churches, gave them pure-bred bull calves. The settlers were grateful until they realized this was sugar-coated exploitation; then their newspapers reflected uneasiness and growing suspicion of the railroad builder, and the saying spread among the farmers of the Red River Valley, "After the grasshoppers we had Jim Hill." For there was the army of grain dealers, graders, shippers, merchants, who worked hand in glove with the magnate. One had to move one's grain in his cars, store it in his elevators where his henchmen graded it as second-class wheat, ship it on his lake steamers. When in

1887 Hill acquired control of the Norwegian-language newspaper, *Nordvesten* (Minneapolis), such a storm of protest arose in the Norwegian American press that he was forced to sell it back to a Norwegian two years later. Certainly Jim Hill's empire was one of the causes behind the rise of agrarian radicalism in the Dakotas, particularly North Dakota.

During the late 'eighties and 'nineties, as the price of wheat dropped, the Dakota farmers rebelliously left the Republican Party and joined the Farmers' Alliance, which became part of the Populist Party. For a time they had some political power. Two Norwegian newspapers, *Nordmanden* (Grand Forks, North Dakota), edited by a well-known writer, H. A. Foss, and the later *Nye Nordmanden* (Moorhead, Minnesota) under the same editorship, reflected the Populist sympathies of the Norwegian farmers of the Red River Valley during this period. The first governor of South Dakota with a Norwegian background, Andrew E. Lee, was a Populist, serving from 1896 to 1900. But when this party failed to bring the reforms the farmers hoped for, and when rising wheat prices in the late 'nineties brought a measure of prosperity again, most of the Dakota farmers returned to the Republican fold. Since 1921 there have been several Dakota governors of Norwegian birth or descent, all of them Republicans. The present governor of North Dakota, Fred Aandahl, as well as his predecessor, John Moses, have Norwegian backgrounds.

By the turn of the century there were over fifty thousand people of Norwegian stock in South Dakota, about seventy-five thousand in North Dakota. Close to a third of the population in the latter state was of first and second generation Norwegian stock, the largest of any of the foreign-born groups in the state. Some counties, like Traill, Griggs, and Steele, were almost entirely, several others at least half, Norwegian. At the time of the 1940 census the first and second generations numbered about ninety-seven thousand in North Dakota, approximately forty-two thousand in South Dakota. Compared with the number of Norwegians in other states they ranked fifth and eighth respectively. Fargo and Grand Forks, North Dakota, and Sioux Falls, South Dakota, have long been centers of Norwegian cultural life in the Red River region.

The pattern of one man's life could be multiplied a thousand-fold. At the age of twenty-seven in 1887, John O. Engesather left Sogn, Norway, arrived in Nelson County, North Dakota, where two thousand people had already settled, one thousand of them Norwegians. He had fourteen dollars in cash, owed sixty dollars, filed on a piece of land, produced a couple of crops, married a girl from Norway, reared five children, worked hard, made money, retired in 1920 at the age of sixty. He helped establish a Lutheran church in the community, served in many of its offices, sang in the choir for several years. He came to live in the village of Petersburg, and for many years was school treasurer and town treasurer; he was one of the organizers of the local Farmers State Bank, its cashier and finally its president. He was active in the Sons of Norway, helped organize the Norrøna Male Chorus in his town, was a member of the Norwegian American chorus that toured Norway in 1914, for two years was president of the Red River Valley Norwegian Singers Association. In 1947 he died on his eighty-seventh birthday.

9

Montana

WHEN THE FIRST Norwegians came into Montana, newspapers in the territory still ran columns of "News From America" and printed items about residents who went to "America" on business trips. As economic and political links were established with the rest of the country, "America" became "the States." Norwegian miners and lumbermen began to enter the territory in the 1860's and continued to arrive all through the 'seventies and 'eighties. When the Great Northern tracks crossed the Dakota line into Montana in June, 1887, lengthening at the rate of almost four miles a day, many Norwegian laborers worked in the gangs. After the line had been completed between Great Falls and Helena and construction temporarily halted, most of the Norwegians stayed in Montana, some of them taking up homesteads in the Great Falls region, some going into the silver mines to the south, others into the coal mines at Sand Coulee. About this time, a group of expert smeltermen from Haugesund, Norway, came to Great Falls to work in the smelters. Most of them, too, later took up land and became prosperous farmers and stockmen, as did the majority of the Norwegians who first came as miners, lumberjacks, or railroad workers.

One young man caught the vision of Montana's future earlier than most of his countrymen. He was Anton M. Holter, one of the state's leading pioneers and certainly the most notable of the Norwegians who settled there. Holter arrived in America in 1854, worked in Illinois and Iowa for a few years, joined the gold rush to Pikes Peak in 1860, but after three years of hard work and meager results left with a Norwegian friend for Montana's pistol-shooting frontier near Virginia City. With some of their gold dust they bought a second-hand sawmill, built most of their own machinery, and started operating one of the first mills in the territory. Later Holter and his brother started another mill in Helena, paying ten per cent interest a month on the loan they needed to start the enterprise. So great was the demand for sluices and timber for the mines that Holter made money in spite of such usury. When his mill was destroyed by fire, he rebuilt, put up new mills and bought others. Lumbermen were playing a freeze-out game, but Holter was astute enough to remain on the winning side. As his lumber interests increased he also branched out into the tool, implement and machinery business. In 1872 he heard about a German machine for concentrating ores, and, obtaining the manufacturing rights for Montana, Wyoming, Idaho, and Washington, he introduced it in the Montana mining industry. Although his business affairs involved him in railroads, banking, manufacturing, and commercial enterprises, it is as a lumber baron that he is remembered, for until he sold most of his interests in 1898 to Marcus Daly, one of Montana's copper kings, the lumber industry in the state centered around A. M. Holter. And from it all he made a fortune.

Compared to the copper barons who "controlled" Montana, Holter's political influence was negligible; nevertheless, his power and his interest in the welfare of the state reached far. In 1878–1879 he was a member of the Council (upper chamber) of the territorial legislature, and from 1889 to 1891 served in the House of Representatives of the state legislature. He was active in the first movements to develop hydroelectric power on the Missouri River, and when a dam was built in 1912 on the Missouri about forty miles from his home town, Helena, it was named Holter Dam. This pioneer Montanan lived to be ninety years old. After his death in 1921 two of his sons carried on the Holter business in the state, while a third became an attorney in New York City.

The Scandinavians, it is said, have contributed more to the development of lumbering in Montana than any other national group. The Gyppo contract system, commonly used in Montana's lumber camps, was introduced largely to satisfy their demands after the 1917 general strike of lumbermen in the Inland Empire. Under this system a camp foreman contracts for the various logging operations with different crews, such as a sawing crew—usually two men—and a skidding crew, at a price per thousand feet of lumber. Every member of the crew, after agreeing on the terms, signs the contract. Until the job is completed the camp foreman retains twenty-five per cent of the contract wage. The lumberjacks like the system because it gives them independence, they don't work under the supervision of a foreman at a fixed daily wage; the lumber companies have found that it has decreased labor trouble and increased production. When the contract is completed, the Gyppo, a term thought to be derived from Gypsy, heads for another camp and another contract, always his own boss. In the middle 'twenties about seventy-five per cent of the Gyppo contractors were Scandinavians. So were the majority of the employees of the Anaconda Copper Mining Company, also the largest lumber business in Montana.

A considerable number of Norwegians settled on the grazing uplands of the Crazy Mountains, the Big Belt and Little Belt Mountains, and the Flathead Mountains. Late in the 'sixties Martin Grande came to Montana, located on the Musselshell River in Meagher County and during the years acquired vast tracts of grazing land, thousands of sheep and cattle. Many newcomers found their way to his ranch and got their start in the West working for this generous, energetic man from the broad valleys of Trøndelag, Norway. Ruling over his domain like a king, as he rose in power and prestige, Grande was held in such high esteem by his countrymen that—so the story goes—when they were asked who the president of the United States was, they answered, *"Det måte vel vaere han Martin Grande"* (It must surely be Martin Grande).

But the glamorous figures are not the rule. The main body of Norwegians are small farmers and businessmen, miners, lumber, mill, and railroad workers. In 1900 there were almost six thousand Norwegians of first and second generation in the state whose total population numbered less than 250,000. A decade later there were between thirteen and fourteen thousand, comprising seven per cent of the foreign-stock population. The Irish, German, English, and Canadian immigrants and their children outnumbered them. By 1920 the Norwegians had risen to second place in the percentage (10.2%) of foreign-born, topped only by the Canadians. Although the number of Norwegian-born residents dropped from 9,962 to 8,991 between 1920 and 1930, they ranked first in percentage (12.3%) by 1930. Of the thirty thousand first and second generation Norwegian Americans in the state half were then farmers, the largest group of foreign stock engaged in farming. The Germans and Russians ranked second and third among those who tilled the soil.

Montana's copper deposits and forests have yielded great riches, but the general population in the state has benefited only moderately from this tremendous wealth that flowed into the vaults of eastern banks. For longer than Montanans care to remember, mining interests have controlled their political life. Farmers, stricken by drought and dust storms during the decade from 1910 to 1920, were paying thirty-two per cent of the taxes in the early 'twenties, while the mines contributed less than nine per cent. One of the more independent of Montana's governors, Joseph Dixon, called in a tax expert from Wisconsin—a Norwegian, Nils Haugen—to advise the state tax commission. Although some adjustments were made and Governor Dixon managed to put through a few further reforms, the 'twenties proved so unprofitable to Montana farmers that many of them moved away. Norwegians were among the outgoing population, as is indicated by the drop in their numbers between 1920 and 1930. Yet, as we saw, they rose to first place in percentage of foreign-born. Undoubtedly, this proves again that, come what may, Norwegians cling a little harder to their land.

The peregrinations of the western Norwegians are illustrated in the life of Ole Tangen, born in Trondheim, Norway, in 1880, who came to the United States shortly after the turn of the century, took a homestead in the northwest corner of North Dakota, and farmed there until the first World War. Then he moved to Wolf Point, Montana, a railroad center, where he was employed as a boilermaker for a few years. When the state of Washington began to boom in the early 'twenties, he went to the newly platted town of Longview where he worked on the early construction of the city. Later he was employed by the Pacific Paperboard Company, remaining in Longview until his death in 1948. I can remember the circulars my father, then a small merchant in Wisconsin, received in the early 'twenties from Longview, Washington, which was then being built on the Columbia River. He wrote to the chamber of commerce inquiring about business possibilities and subscribed to a Longview daily to watch developments for a few months. But in the end his "western fever" subsided and we remained in the Middle West.

About half of the twenty-five thousand first and second generation Norwegians in Montana in 1940 lived on farms and in rural communities; the rest concentrated mainly in Great Falls, Butte, Anaconda, Missoula, Billings, and Helena. In some of these towns there are Sons of Norway halls where *lutefisk* dinners are served in the winter, where the Norwegian townspeople gather to play whist, dance, and sing Norwegian songs. About half of the Norwegian Americans in the state belong to the Lutheran Church.

Unlike the Norwegian stock in the middlewestern states, who have been predominantly Republican in their political sympathies, many of those who came to Montana became Democrats. One of the Democratic governors, John E. Erickson, who served from 1925 to 1933, was born in the Norwegian town of Stoughton, Wisconsin, during the Civil War. His family moved to Kansas where he grew up, was educated, and admitted to the bar in 1891. In 1894 he went to Montana, became a county attorney, district judge, and finally governor for two terms, after which he was appointed United States Senator to fill the vacancy caused by the death of Senator T. J. Walsh. In more recent years, another Erickson of Norwegian stock has figured prominently in Montana's public life. Leif Erickson, chief justice of the Montana Supreme Court, was born in Cashton, Wisconsin, in 1906, educated at the University of North Dakota and North Dakota State College, received his Ph.B. and J.D. from the University of Chicago, and was admitted to the Montana bar in 1934. After serving as a county attorney for two years, he became an associate justice of the Montana Supreme Court, received the Democratic nomination for governor in 1944 but was defeated, and in 1946 won the Democratic nomination for United States Senator from Burton K. Wheeler, but was again defeated by his Republican opponent.

10

The Far West

THE STORY OF the settlement of Norwegians in the Far West is very like a play within a play. There is the overarching action of the intercontinental migration, spanning the century from 1825 to 1925. Beneath it are the smaller continental migrations: New York to Illinois, Illinois to Wisconsin, Wisconsin to Minnesota, Minnesota to the Plains, a pause, and then the long jump over desert and mountain to the Pacific Ocean. It is this last migration that curiously parallels the larger in the similarity of the causes that produced them.

In the first migration Norwegian Quakers in search of religious, economic, and political freedom led the way to the new land, settling in the wilds of New York, the "West" to them. In the last migration Norwegian Mormons, seeking the same things, marked the path to the Far West in their march to Utah in the 'forties. Then came the discovery of gold in California in 1849, to many Norwegians in the Middle West and in Norway as tantalizing and as luring as the discovery of the rich black soil of Illinois had been in the early 'thirties. Nor was the decision to journey across the blazing plains, deserts and rugged mountains less momentous, requiring, as it did, the same courage and endurance as setting out across the Atlantic in a small sailing vessel.

As the generations of the 'forties, 'fifties, and 'sixties were stirred into action by the "America letters" and advertising from Illinois, Wisconsin, and Minnesota, so the later generations during the 'eighties and 'nineties, both in Norway and in the upper Middle West, responded to the call that came from California, Oregon, Washington, and western Canada in letters from settlers there, in newspaper articles and railroad advertising. The wonders of the Pacific valleys and waterways sounded like tales of a fabled land to many farmers of the upper Middle West who had fought a losing battle with drought and high costs. Generally, it's probably true that one of the main factors in the background of this migration was the acute agrarian discontent of the 'eighties and early 'nineties. When the Granger and Populist movements failed, many of the disillusioned packed up and headed west.

I have referred repeatedly to the constant westerly shift of the Norwegian immigrants. Most of them knew at least two homes, many three, in their lifetimes, and always they went west to cheaper and better land. With the mass of them this was not primarily restlessness, a romantic urge to follow the sun that drew them westward. These migrations were but a corollary to the devastation of the midwestern farm lands, of the grazing lands on the Great Plains, and of the northern forests that took place on such a gigantic scale in the half century after the Civil War. As long as cheap good land lay to the west, scientific farming and conservation seemed unnecessary. The same grains were planted year after year in the same fields. When the soil was exhausted, the settlers simply moved on from Illinois to Wisconsin, from Wisconsin to Minnesota, from Minnesota to the Dakotas, planting and reaping again until rains washed away the top soil, drought and dust drove them to Montana where their plows bared the grazing land to the mercy of wind and rain, where year after year enormous herds of cattle and sheep cropped the lush grass to the roots until the plains turned desert dry. Thus the North repeated, in its own way, what before the Civil War, when the cotton planters moved forever west in the search of new soils, had been one of the tragedies of the South.

Nor must one forget the profound economic changes that affected our agriculture during this period. The pioneers of Wisconsin and northern Iowa were subsistence farmers, using but few implements and no labor, except that of their sons and daughters. As they acquired machinery, they began to supply the domestic market. When the Dakotas were reached, our extensive agriculture, using a great deal of machinery on its far-flung acres, fed the world. The farmer then found himself struggling, often helplessly, in the larger currents of economic life. Mechanization was expensive; transportation costs were high, particularly with the government in the hands of the railroad tycoons; yet Argentinian, Canadian, and Russian competition had to be met. Everybody knows what happened. In 1866 a midwestern farmer made more than a dollar profit on a bushel of wheat; in 1894 he sold it for slightly less than half a dollar. Many of those who in the depression of 1893 lost their heavily mortgaged land inevitably pushed onward to the Pacific frontier.

To Benedikte Steffensen, stumbling beside the hand cart her husband and his partner were pushing laboriously over sandy hillocks and clumps of sagebrush, the journey had come to be a nightmare. For weeks the Mormon party they were with had been walking, on slowly decreasing rations, across the burning plains and wastelands. Many had died on the way. Fortunately the longed-for Valley of Zion was just over the mountains from Bridger's Fort, which they hoped to reach by nightfall. This thought alone kept Benedikte from faltering. Until she met and married Christian Steffensen, Benedikte Krogh had lived a life of ease in the home of her wealthy father, captain of a large ship, in Arendal, Norway. But when she was converted to Mormonism in the early 'fifties her family turned against her. Only her joy in having found the true Church and her desire to reach the New Jerusalem, soon now to be realized, had carried her through the years until their departure from Norway in the spring of 1859. Sick and exhausted, the party entered the valley in the fall of this year to join the few thousand Saints who had already begun to turn the desert into neat patches of farmland guarded by rows of high poplars. Some years later Beneditke's parents accepted the new Gospel and in 1875 joined their daughter in Utah. Coming from a large home where servants had cared for their needs, they were appalled to find their daughter and her children living contentedly in a crude two-room adobe house. But they stayed, and the family, with its many descendants, remained steadfastly in the faith of the Church of Jesus Christ of the Latter Day Saints.

The story of the Norwegian Mormons forms a strange and fascinating chapter in the history of the group. It must be seen against the background of religious and economic uneasiness that prevailed in Norway during the middle decades of the century. Specifically, it ties in with the Haugean movement, which upset the orthodox Lutheran thinking of many Norwegians. Among the first to be attracted by the golden tablets and the words of wisdom were the early settlers in the Fox River settlement. Away from the restraining hand of the old state church, they drifted off in different religious directions. Though a majority remained Haugeans or orthodox Lutherans, some became Methodists, some Baptists, some Episcopalians, and others Mormons. A few even voiced agnostic opinions. Several who entered the Mormon Church had been Haugeans, at least two of them, prominent lay preachers. They became officials in the Mormon Church, one of them a bishop. The Norwegian Mormons who stayed in Illinois had their own church, which at the end of the century numbered 140 Saints.

The Sugar Creek settlement in southeastern Iowa, across the river from the Mormon capital, Nauvoo, was almost entirely converted to the Mormon faith. Most of them later moved to Utah.

But strangely enough, it was not the Norwegians already in America who were most influenced by the prophesies of the Second Coming and the promises of material glory. It was Norway's dispossessed who listened with the greatest eagerness to the fiery words of the messengers from the Valley of Zion. For those who didn't have the money, the church provided passage from its Perpetual Emigration Fund, and when they had crossed America to the outfitting quarters at Iowa City, they were given hand carts and supplies for the march to the Valley. Marching, they sang "The Hand Cart Song":

> "Some must push and some must pull
> As we go marching up the hill,
> As merrily on the way we go
> Until we reach the Valley, oh!"

In the 'seventies there was again a zealous drive for converts in the Scandinavian countries, as well as in England and on the Continent. England and Denmark furnished the greatest number of Saints to be gathered into Zion, and Sweden several more thousand than Norway. Because of the missionary success of the Mormon Church in these northern European countries the dominant cultural tone of Utah has been Anglo-Scandinavian. Since 1900 the number of Norwegian-born residents in the state has been roughly around two thousand, dropping by 1940 to slightly over one thousand. In 1930 when the Norwegian stock numbered about six thousand, the Danes counted about eleven thousand, the Swedes nine. By 1940 there were a little over four thousand Norwegian immigrants and children of immigrants.

Although the Norwegians are scattered throughout the cities and towns of Utah, they have concentrated in Salt Lake City. Most of the five hundred Norwegians there belong to a Norwegian Church of Jesus Christ of the Latter Day Saints, and for thirty years or more a group of them have maintained a vigorous Norwegian literary society largely for the purpose of preserving their language.

One of the group's most active leaders is Martinius A. Strand. He had been a skier in Norway, and, upon coming to Utah some forty years ago, he set out to make his new home a winter wonderland for the devotees of the snowshoe. By 1915 he had organized and was president of the Norwegian American Athletic Club, later called the Utah Ski Club. In the years that followed he became president of the United States Western Ski Association, the Rocky Mountain Ski Association, the Intermountain Ski Association and vice-president of the National Ski Association. Through his efforts national tournaments, Olympic tryouts, and international meets have been held in Utah, and Sun Valley, Alta, Brighton, and the Snow Basin became famous names in the skiing world. His contributions have not been confined to the realm of sport. As an electrical engineer he was in charge of numerous large installation projects at Boulder Dam; helped build the naval ammunition depot at Hawthorne, Nevada, substations and transmission lines for the Southern Nevada Electric Company, and many buildings in Utah. Some of his inventions have been adopted by the Bell telephone system; his patent for an automatic phonograph stop was bought and widely used by the Edison Company.

One of the leading architects among the Latter Day Saints is Ramm Hansen, who was born in Norway and received his training at the Royal Arts and Handicrafts School. Like Strand he came to Salt Lake City after his conversion, and in 1916 entered into partnership with a descendant of Brigham Young. Among the many buildings designed and constructed by the firm of Young and Hansen are the Mormon Church Offices Building and the Federal Reserve Bank Building in Salt Lake City, the Mormon Church in Washington, D.C., and the temples at Mesa, Arizona, Idaho Falls, Idaho, and at Westwood, in Los Angeles. They also planned the Central Building at the University of Utah.

A few Latter Day Saints of Norwegian stock or birth have attained positions of leadership and renown in their church and in the nation. Reed Smoot, prominent United States Senator for over quarter of a century, had a Norwegian-born mother.

The Council of the Twelve Apostles of the Church of Jesus Christ of Latter Day Saints is, as everybody knows, the highest body of the Mormon hierarchy. One of its present members, John Andreas Widtsoe, was born in Norway and came to Utah as a lad in the 'eighties. He received his early education in the church schools, later on went to Harvard, and studied in Germany and Switzerland. After his return to Utah he taught chemistry, then became an administrator for various Utah educational institutions, finally serving as president of the University of Utah from 1916 to 1921. In 1912 he was president of the International Dry Farming Congress, in recognition of his scientific leadership in this field. In 1921 he was made an apostle. A glance at Widtsoe's bibliography will help us to catch the flavor of this peculiar career that led from dry farming to the portals of heaven: *Dry Farming* (1911), *Irrigation Practice* (1914), *Rational Theology* (1915), *Success on Irrigation Projects* (1927), *In Search of Truth* (1930), *Seven Claims of the Book of Mormon* (with F. S. Harris, 1936), *Program of the Church of Jesus Christ of Latter-Day Saints* (1936), *The Word of Wisdom* (with Leah Widtsoe, 1938), *Priesthood and Church Government* (1940), *In the Gospel Net* (1941), *Evidences and Reconciliation* (1943).

The news of the discovery of gold in California a century ago was like an electric shock to people the world over, the staid, the steady, the rooted, as well as the adventurous and the footloose. One would expect active response from young America, feverish with "manifest destiny," where every man dreamed of carving his future in the golden West. But one would scarcely expect scores of people tucked away in the mountains and valleys of Norway almost halfway round the globe to be so deeply affected that they undertook the physical hardships and financial risks involved in a journey to California.

Letters from California appeared in the Norwegian press, books about California were published. The newspapers reported that a shipbuilder from Arendal, who was in California at the time of the discovery, returned to Norway with a chest of money. "Gold" flashed into their thoughts like a sudden shaft of morning sun into a night-gray valley. An expedition was organized in 1850 and 160 passengers sailed from Trondheim for San Francisco by way of Cape Horn. The company disintegrated when it reached Brazil, where a few remained to form a Norwegian colony. Some found their way to California, others returned home. Many a gold seeker left Norway during these years; probably only a small percentage actually reached California and the diggings. One of the 'forty-niners who did make it was the grandfather of the late Evans Fordyce Carlson, commander of a Marine raider battalion in the Pacific, who inspired some of the most selfless devotion and daring enterprises of the Pacific war.

In the early 'fifties Norwegians in Illinois and Wisconsin, too, left their recently cleared farms and headed for Sacramento Valley. Most of them were young, unmarried men like Hans Christian Heg, later a colonel in the Union Army, and three companions who left southern Wisconsin in 'forty-nine. From his letters sent back to a Norwegian newspaper in his home community the people there followed his journey to the West. Another such record has been left by Tosten Kittelsen Stabaek, who with nineteen Norwegians and one Frenchman formed a caravan of seven wagons and sixty-eight head of cattle that left Wisconsin in the spring of 1852. Men and cattle died on the five months' march. But most of them reached the gold fields, spent a few years panning and digging, then returned to their families in Wisconsin and Illinois, richer, if not in money, at least in experience and in knowledge of America and her many peoples.

Although the prairies and farms called many gold seekers back to the Middle West when the gold dust in the gravel began to run thin, some remained on the coast and took up other callings. Jon Toresen, better known as "Snowshoe" Thompson, left the Fox River settlement in Illinois in the first rush to the mines and in a special sense came to belong to the mountains of the West. Mail service over the high Sierras during the winter months was then almost impossible. Thompson, reared in the mountains of Norway, made himself a pair of sturdy oak skis and volunteered to carry the mail regularly between Placerville, California, and Carson Valley, Nevada, a distance of over ninety miles. His offer was accepted and for the next twenty winters Snowshoe Thompson shuttled back and forth over the mountains with a seventy-five-pound mail sack on his back, as regular as a clock, two days going, two days coming back, no matter what the weather. Caught in blizzards, he would seek a rocky cave and dig himself out when it was over. When the warm sun made the snow sticky, he would rest by day and travel by night. He fought weather and wild beasts, saved lives in the hazardous mountains, yet his pay was irregular and trifling. When he went to Washington in 1874 to ask the government for $6,000 for his many years of service, officials shook their heads. Today his skis are in a museum in Sacramento, in tribute to this forerunner of the stagecoach and the railroad.

In the total picture of peoples that founded homes in California the Norwegians have not been numerically significant. From 1860 to 1940 the group increased from seven hundred to somewhat over fifteen thousand, giving California seventh rank in the number of Norwegian-born. Swedes considerably outnumber Norwegians in the state. Scandinavians have been an important group in the shipping industry as skippers, owners, and crewmen. For several decades the coastwise fleet has been known as California's Scandinavian Navy.

Just before the turn of the century a Norwegian sailing master by the name of Olson brought his family to California and continued there in his trade. His son, Oliver J. Olson, after a year of high school went to work as a bookkeeper for a paper box company. Not many years later he was operating a small line of ships that hauled lumber from the mills on Puget Sound to San Francisco. An Irish shoe salesman named Andy Mahoney, who had won the Louisiana lottery grand prize of $15,000, invested the money in Olson's enterprise. The Olson & Mahoney firm prospered in spite of the somewhat stormy relationship between the temperamental partners. In addition to their growing coastal fleet, they owned the Richmond–San Rafael Ferry and Transportation Company operating on San Francisco Bay, which is still run by Oliver Olson's sons. In 1916 Mahoney withdrew from the firm; Olson continued to prosper, became influential in San Francisco financial circles, built a mansion overlooking the Golden Gate, and took his sons into business with him when they had completed their college educations. When he died in 1940, they were capably operating a fleet of steel vessels in intercoastal trade.

Norwegian sailors frequently left their ships when they docked at San Francisco to take better paying jobs with such firms as Olson's or with fishing concerns. One such Norwegian sailor, Andrew Furuseth, came to California in 1880 and eventually became the founder of the International Seamen's Union. The notable career of this great leader of American labor will be told in a later chapter.

Although there are no distinct Norwegian settlements in California, the majority of the immigrant settlers and their children live along the coast in the San Francisco–Oakland region. Shipping, fishing, and lumbering have been their main occupations; many, too, are engaged in construction work, not only as laborers, but as engineers and architects. Ole Tobiason Versland, for example, left his ship at San Francisco in 1895, and entered Leland Stanford Jr. University to study civil engineering. When the Standard Oil Company chose the village of Richmond for the site of a large refining center, they engaged Versland to lay out the town. John Engebretson, who was born in Eker, Norway, in 1858, came to California in 1882 and lived to be referred to in newspaper accounts as the "widely known Southern California roadbuilder." The construction of several important highways, particularly around

Los Angeles, was under his supervision. His many years' service as deputy consul, acting consul, and vice-consul for Norway and Sweden and for the former after the dissolution of the union between the two countries also brought him the title of "dean of Pacific Coast foreign consuls."

S. E. Sonnichsen, who came to America in 1902 already a trained architect, worked his way, over a period of years, from New York to the West Coast. Since 1923, when he formed a partnership with the well-known theater architect, B. Marcus Pretica of Los Angeles, Sonnichsen has had under his supervision the design and construction of a large number of Pantages' and Warner Brothers' theaters in San Francisco, Los Angeles, Hollywood, and other California cities.

Many Norwegian Americans have been and are employed by railroad companies as engineers, machinists, and master builders, like Governor Earl Warren's father, Methias, who was born in Norway and as a lad came to the United States with his parents, settling in Iowa where they changed their name from Varran to Warren. Methias Warren, a carpenter, took a job with the Southern Pacific railroad in California, where he and his wife, the daughter of Swedish immigrants, reared their son Earl in a small cottage in a workers' residential district in Los Angeles. On California soil a number of people of Norwegian birth and extraction have made their contributions to science, education, and the arts, as will be seen later in this story of Americans from Norway, but the majority of those who settled there resemble the delightful family that Kathyrn Forbes portrayed in her book *Mamma's Bank Account,* which reached the stage, screen, and television as *I Remember Mamma.*

11

The Pacific Northwest

GROUPS OF NORWEGIAN newcomers stood around a tall case in the bureau of immigration of the Northern Pacific railroad in Portland, Oregon, looking at jars of grain, sheaves of wheat six feet high, oats ten feet high, red clover over six, and timothy grass almost eight. They could scarcely believe their eyes. When they went to the desk to ask questions of the attendant, in their broken English, faces brightened as he answered them in Norwegian, told the men from Hardanger or from Eide which part of the country was best suited for them, that they could grow crops there that would average thirty-five to forty-five bushels an acre. An eyewitness described the scene in an article in the *Atlantic Monthly*, January, 1883: "To see Swedes, Norwegians, Germans, Irish come in, stand wonderingly before the case, and then begin to ask their jargon of questions, was an experience which did more in an hour to make one realize what the . . . tide of immigration to the New Northwest [meant than] the reading of statistics could do in a year." He reported that most of the 150 immigrants pouring in daily were Scandinavians. In Washington the same thing was going on, even on a larger scale.

With the completion of transcontinental railways many of the twenty to thirty thousand Norwegians arriving in America each year during the 'eighties went directly to the new frontier on the Pacific Coast. Discontented older settlers from the Middle West, too, were drawn to the lands of milder winters, to the forests and waters of the New West. Those who settled in Oregon farmed on the pastured slopes and rich bottoms of Willamette Valley; fished for salmon in the Columbia River and for albacore tuna off the coast; planted orchards around Klamath Falls, where springtime was as lovely as in the southern valleys of Norway; worked in lumbermills, fish canneries, and construction companies in Portland, Astoria, Eugene, and other towns.

The high tide of migration into Oregon and Washington came after the turn of the century, after the effects of the depression of the 'nineties had worn off. Oregon has not been as popular a settlement area for Norwegians and other Scandinavians as Washington. In 1910 the Norwegian-born and the native Americans with both or one parent born in Norway numbered about 13,500, or about 5.6 per cent of the foreign stock of the state, while Washington at the same time had over fifty thousand first and second generation Norwegians, making up over ten per cent of its foreign-stock population. By 1930 Oregon had over twenty thousand and Washington between seventy-five and eighty thousand first and second generation Norwegians. In 1940 Oregon ranked eleventh among the states in the number of Norwegian-born, while Washington ranked third. And, as in California, the majority were urban rather than rural dwellers. Why this is so, we shall see as our story unfolds.

Among the earlier arrivals in Oregon was Simon Benson, whose activities there began in the days of ox-team logging and ended ten months before the Liberty Ship *Simon Benson* was launched at Portland in June, 1943. He had spent his childhood on a 1½-acre farm in Gudbrandsdalen, Norway, where his father, Berger Bergersen, was a carpenter. After the Civil War his oldest brother, who had been working in the Wisconsin pineries, brought the family to America. They settled in Wisconsin and changed their name to Benson. In 1879 Simon Benson came to Oregon. Three times he went broke in the logging business before he got hard-boiled enough to make it pay. After he had become a millionaire, people called him, not unaffectionately, that "son-voggon of a Swede." He seems to have been a curious mixture—tough lumberman, strict prohibitionist, a do-gooder in a businesslike way. In some circles he was respected far more for his poker playing than for his millions. Liquor he abhorred, and in an effort to redirect the drinking habits of the lumberjacks who came in from the camps for the weekends, he studded downtown Portland with ornamental bronze drinking fountains, a striking feature of the city's streets. He built the Benson Hotel and the Columbia Gorge Hotel; gave $100,000 to a Portland school district, making possible the construction of the Benson Polytechnical School. As chairman of the state highway commission he was a leader in the good roads movement, even to the extent of loaning money to the state of Oregon for the building of highways. At the Pan American Fair in San Francisco in 1915 he was honored as Oregon's first citizen, having been designated for this distinction by the governor of the state. In his later years he lived in California, where he died in August, 1942, at the ripe age of ninety.

A few Norwegians came into Washington before the Civil War and settled on Puget Sound, but not until the period from the 1890's to the 1920's did they, as well as the Swedes, swarm into the state. The Puget Sound region attracted the bulk of them, particularly Seattle, Tacoma, Everett, Bellingham. Many settled in the twin cities of Aberdeen-Hoquiam, a coastal lumber center. During the 'thirties its population of thirty thousand, heavily Scandinavian and Finnish, included about two thousand Norwegian-stock inhabitants. In the eastern part of the state Spokane became the center for Norwegian immgirants.

One almost entirely Norwegian settlement is the charming fishing village of Poulsbo and its environs, stretching along a fjord across the Sound from Seattle. Hillside farms slope down to the edges of the town, the heart of which is the waterfront with fishing craft anchored at the wharves, fishermen mending their nets, bringing in salmon from the Sound, halibut and cod from Alaskan waters. One of the early settlers on Poulsbo bay, John Storseth, has written a picturesque account of pioneer days and the growth of this settlement. He describes a Seventeenth of May celebration held, perhaps, shortly after the turn of the century:

> One year it was decided that Seattle and the Norwegian settlements around Puget Sound should celebrate the Seventeenth of May festival in Poulsbo, since the place was reputed to have the most numerous Norse population on Puget Sound. The Seventeenth of May that year turned out to be a grand day for Poulsbo. . . . It was as if all Norway had moved out to the Pacific coast.
>
> Poulsbo bay was filled with steamboats, sailboats, rowboats, and all kinds of other craft. People came overland through forests, over poor roads. They came also where there were no roads, they came in such a force that it was amazing to behold. . . . There were over seven thousand of them in Poulsbo that day.

Today they still celebrate with dances in native costumes, games and speeches in Grieg Hall, their Sons of Norway lodge quarters.

The Norwegians, although not the founders of the fishing industry of the Pacific Northwest, have, since 1900, come to play a dominant role both as fishermen and entrepreneurs in the field. The halibut and herring industries are principally in the hands of Norwegian fishermen;

they number about ninety per cent of the Puget Sound salmon trollers. Purse-sein salmon fishing is mostly done by Slovenian fishermen. Again, Norwegians dominate the dogfish and soupfin-shark fisheries of Washington and Oregon, form the bulk of the tuna and small sardine fishermen of the Northwest. In the higher brackets they own and manage packing companies, salmon salteries and canneries, codfish stations ashore, and many large fishing vessels and steamers on the sea. They have held responsible posts in the Association of Pacific Fisheries, in co-operatives and trade unions in the fishing industry. Also they engage in the allied occupations of fish brokers, boatbuilders, marine architects, inventors and manufacturers of fishing gear and canning machinery. There is no question that the fishing industry has been one of the major sources of livelihood for a large segment of the Norwegian population in the Northwest. A novel like *The White Reef* by Martha Ostenso, herself an American from Norway, portrays a typical Pacific Coast fishing village—Norwegians, Swedes, Scotch, old-stock Americans, their minds filled with the lore of the sea, which is their livelihood, their playground and, sometimes, their grave.

Inevitably, too, the Alaskan fishing waters drew permanent Norwegian settlers to the northern outpost of America. Gold lured a few, and others played a prominent part in the development of the reindeer industry. But it is the canning and preserving of fish, Alaska's leading industry by far, that attracted the largest number. Among the foreign-born residents Norwegians, for several decades, have been the most numerous. In 1920 the 2,169 Norwegians constituted 17.7 per cent of the foreign-born population, in 1930 there were 2,767 (27.2%), in 1940 there were 2,444 (27.8%). The second and third largest groups are the Swedes and Canadians, each of them with about fifteen hundred souls.

Peter Thams Buschmann was born in Trondheim and came to America in 1891 with his wife and children, settling first in the Puget Sound area. He tried different kinds of fishing, but, dissatisfied, went to Alaska, where he bought a piece of land on the southeastern coast. He built a house and called the place Petersburg. Salmon was abundant in the waters, but catching them, he soon found out, was not enough to make a living. They also had to be preserved and shipped. So, Buschmann built a canning factory, thus drawing more Norwegian fishermen and laborers to the little settlement. Later, as the business flourished, he built two more factories. His introduction of salmon trap fishing, replacing hand nets and seines, greatly increased the catch. In one season his haul was two hundred thousand to three hundred thousand more salmon than were caught in the whole of Norway at that time. His method and his product set a standard for much of the West Coast salmon industry. Crab, herring, and shrimp are also processed and shipped from Petersburg. Peter Buschmann's enterprise was carried on by his three sons after his death. By 1940 the town had some three thousand inhabitants, ninety per cent of them Norwegians. On the Seventeenth of May, when the old colors fly from the flagpoles, the strains of *"Ja vi elsker dette landet"* drown out the sound of the new tongue, and the smell of fish mingles with the fumes of gasoline from the boats bobbing in the harbor, Petersburg in Alaska looks and feels like many a village in Norway.

Early in the 1890's reindeer were brought to Alaska from Siberia and from Norway to provide a domestic industry for the dwindling Eskimo tribes. A young Norwegian American, William A. Kjellmann, of Madison, Wisconsin, who had spent his youth herding reindeer in his native Finnmark and had later been employed by a Norwegian firm that traded in reindeer and reindeer products, supervised the work of a few families of Lapps and Norwegians who instructed the Eskimos in the care of the animals. At the beginning, ownership of the herds was divided among the Lapp instructors, several church missions, the United States government, and the Eskimo herders; but, fairly early, private enterprise entered the field. The largest firm was Lomen and Company.

Gudbrand J. Lomen's parents emigrated from Valders, Norway, and settled near Decorah, Iowa, where he was born in the 'fifties. After graduating from Luther College and from the college of law at the University of Iowa, he practised law in the Middle West. During the gold rush he took a trip to Alaska and remained there, in the new town of Nome. Active in the political life of the territory, he was first mayor of Nome, then United States district attorney, and later a judge of the Federal bench. Meanwhile other opportunities could not be ignored. He operated the only photographic studio in Nome; he opened a pharmacy, founded a steamship company; and in 1914 he organized the business that made his son, Carl Lomen, who became president of the company after his father's retirement, the reindeer king of Alaska. As the Lomen reindeer business expanded to become the largest of its kind in the world, Carl Lomen established an office in New York. In addition to their huge herds, corrals, slaughter houses, and storage plants, the company ran an experimental station, owned stores, lighterage facilities, a fleet of motor ships, and held a half interest in a dredge and mining enterprise. The huge quantities of dressed reindeer meat they exported bore the tag "Lomenized Alaska." In about 1940 the Lomen business, by that time known as the Northwestern Livestock Corporation, owned about 250,000 reindeer.

Among a group of herders who came to Alaska in 1898, with a herd the American government had purchased in Norway, was a young man named Jafet Lindeberg. Once in Alaska, however, the gold fever caught him, and, granted release from his duties as a herder, he began to dig and pan in the Snake River, striking a rich vein in the middle of that summer. With his two partners he took out more than $200,000 worth of gold in ninety days, which was the signal for the rush of miners to the Cape Nome area. Two years later forty ships were anchored in the harbor and forty thousand men were crowded into the wooden shacks of the new town of Nome. Lindeberg and a few others started the Pioneer Mining Company with Lindeberg as president. By the time of the first World War, when he was thought to be the richest Norwegian in America, he was in the reindeer business with the Lomens, manufactured diesel motors in California, and had gold and oil interests in that state. Though he lost much of his fortune in the crash of 1929, his friends say that he salvaged or recouped a goodly portion. Be that as it may, his fabulous career from reindeer herder to multimillionaire has long been legend along the Pacific Coast.

Another Norwegian, Leonard Seppala, who came to pan gold, but did not strike it as rich as Lindeberg, became the most famous dog-sled racer in Alaska. For a moment, in the winter of 1925, the eyes of the world were upon him. A diphtheria epidemic that had broken out in Nome soon exhausted the supply of serum in the small hospital. Fairbanks, almost six hundred miles away, had enough serum but could be reached only by dog sled. So Seppala started from Nome; another Norwegian, Einar Kaasen, with the serum from Fairbanks. They met halfway, and Seppala, battling fierce arctic blizzards on his way back, returned a hero. When Byrd planned his South Pole expedition, Seppala was asked to direct the work of placing markers in the ice-bound wastes to guide the flyers to their landing places. Although he was fifty years old at the time, he undertook the task and carried it successfully to completion.

12

The Atlantic Coast

ACROSS THE CONTINENT on the Atlantic Coast there are over 115,000 first and second generation Norwegians, a group sometimes forgotten by those who think that our group belongs exclusively to the Middle West and the Pacific Northwest. True, the decades up through the 'eighties spilled Norwegians most lavishly over the great central valley of the American continent, but each year a few dropped out of the main stream as soon as they touched the eastern shore.

Ever since the time of the Dutch settlement there have been Norwegians in New York and in some of the other eastern ports. From 1825 up to the early 'fifties the majority of the immigrant boats landed at New York, a few at Boston, and always a sprinkling of artisans and sailors remained in the East to take construction jobs or to work in the harbors. During the next two decades, until 1870, the immigrant boats landed at Quebec, chiefly because rates to the Canadian port were cheaper and because the boats coming there could expect a load of lumber for the return voyage. Almost to a man these immigrants went directly west. But when the immigrant traffic shifted back to Castle Garden after 1870, the little Norwegian colony in New York began to grow steadily. Skilled laborers and business people gave the group a permanence and unity it had lacked as long as it was largely composed of sailors. Professional people, looking for more opportunity than tiny Norway could offer, came in increasing numbers toward the end of the century. They gave the colony its leadership. By 1940 New York ranked second only to Minnesota in number of Norwegians, and Brooklyn, where most of them lived, was the largest single settlement in the United States, between forty and fifty thousand of the first and second generations.

A few small Norwegian colonies with histories dating from about the turn of the century are to be found in Troy, Albany, Schenectady, where most of them are employed as engineers, foremen, and machinists by the General Electric Company, and in Corning, where they are connected with the Corning Glass Works. The arrival in 1903 of three expert glassblowers from Norway started a minor stream of these skilled artisans from the famous glasswork centers in Norway to Corning. For many years the most prominent Norwegian in this colony of two to three hundred has been Alfred Vaksdal, plant engineer at the glassworks. A Norwegian Methodist church is the cultural center of the group. Buffalo and Rochester also have small colonies, where active Sons of Norway lodges attest to a fairly energetic Norwegian life.

Over five thousand Norwegian-born people live in New Jersey, over four thousand in Massachusetts, and about fifteen hundred in Connecticut, the majority of them engaged in the shipping and building trades. Pennsylvania has some two thousand Americans from Norway, most of them engineers and skilled technicians in the industrial centers. At a ceremony in May, 1948, the Norwegian room, seventeenth of the nationality rooms in the University of Pittsburgh's Cathedral of Learning, was presented to the university by the Norwegian Society of Pittsburgh. Many of those who were most actively interested in the Norwegian Society and in the promotion of the Norwegian room, designed and furnished in a modern version of the eighteenth century Norwegian peasant style, are immigrant Americans who had come as engineers and designers and eventually established their own manufacturing concerns or became connected with the powerful utilities corporations, United States Steel, and other large industries. Stavanger-born Frederic Schaefer, inventor, manufacturer, and president of the Schaefer Equipment Company of Pittsburgh, is one of them. The Norwegian Society of Pittsburgh, co-operating with other nationality room committees, also established a Norwegian scholarship for summer study at the University of Oslo.

Washington, D.C., has a Norwegian Society that has existed since 1902 and has today an active membership of 150. A Sons of Norway lodge of one hundred members co-operates with the society to celebrate the Seventeenth of May. One of the most enthusiastic leaders of the capital's group is Peter Moe, who for twenty years has been a supervising architect in the Public Buildings Administration. If one pages through volumes of the *Official Register of the United States* over a period of years, one sees a surprising number of Norwegian-born Larsons, Johnsons, and Petersons who are janitors, carpenters, engineers, stenographers, and clerks in all departments of the Federal government. In a later chapter other, less humble, figures on the Washington scene will find their places.

13

The Century Mark

ON A CHILLY gray morning in June, 1925, our family—Mother, Father, my brother and I—drove the forty miles from our home in southern Minnesota to the State Fair Grounds in St. Paul. Cars from every part of the Midwest and even farther away were parked solidly for acres on the grounds. Thousands of people were streaming toward the huge grandstand. Frequently the ear caught Norwegian sentences from the jostling throng of old people, middle-aged successful farmers and businessmen, and children, thoroughly American youngsters eating pink cotton candy and carrying balloons. I was one of the latter. At the stands decorated with Norwegian and American flags Norwegian food, as well as hot dogs, buns, and pop, was being served. For three days the visitors had gone to *bygdelag* (societies made up of immigrants and descendants of immigrants who came from the same district in the old country) meetings, to religious services, had listened to Norwegian and English addresses by distinguished representatives of the government and the Church in Norway and in the United States, had seen historical pageants and athletic contests. The climax of the festivities was this particular day when the President of the United States, Calvin Coolidge, was to address the assembled thousands of Norwegian Americans.

I was so completely American a child that I was scarcely conscious of why we were at the celebration. To me it was another state fair. Yet, when I saw the President of the United States drive up to the flag-draped speakers' platform in a shiny black limousine, even my twelve years felt a moment's awe before I settled down to my popcorn. Then the Yankee spoke, with sober oratory and not without insight, of the millions of Europeans, Norwegians as well as others, the sum of whose plain, unsung lives had become "that magnificent and wondrous adventure, the making of our own America. . . . If fraternity and co-operation are possible on the scale of this continent among people so widely diverse," he said, "why not on the scale of the world? It is not a new thought, but it is a profoundly engaging one. I firmly believe it is more than a chimera. I feel it is possible of realization. I am convinced that our national story might somewhat help to guide mankind toward such a goal. Therefore I urge the deeply thoughtful study and teaching of our history."

The planners of the celebration arranged for the publication of a history of the Norwegian people in America. The Luther College professor, Dr. O. M. Norlie, whom they had commissioned, produced, indeed, a prodigious compilation of facts in time for the festival. Yet if—as I fear one must—one takes the tone of his book as representative, then it has to be admitted that after a century in America the group still bore marks of provincialism, not to say parochialism. Its official spokesmen at least wanted to believe that Norwegians in America and the Norwegian Lutheran Church in America were one and the same; that this church was the only institution through which all that was worth cherishing in their heritage could be preserved. It is true, there was some uneasy recognition of Norwegian life outside this pious pale; but much of it, if they were aware of it at all, they passed in silence. Later Norwegian American historians had to delve into these hidden areas and are now gradually piecing together a more complete picture. Thus, while Norlie's book will always remain an important source of information in a somewhat restricted area, one can no longer say that it has "for all time fixed the place of the Norwegian element in the making of the American nation," as the Centennial Committee of the Norwegian Lutheran Church of America naively wrote in the preface.

But let us turn from the historian back to history itself, the wide-flung spread of Norwegian-born people and of their children over the United States. In one hundred years they had dispersed from a small colony in New York to every state in the Union, had grown from a group of fifty to over a million. In 1925 men of Norwegian descent were governors in four states; fifteen sat in the United States Congress.

The Norwegian centennial almost coincided with the closing of the gates by the quota system. Except for a handful—the annual quota of our group is 2,377—immigration from Norway came to a halt. In the last two and a half decades there has been but a trickle of immigrant traffic from Norway and a few thousand returns during the years of the great depression. By and large the story of the great Norse migration to America begins in 1825 and ends exactly a century later.

PRAIRIE SOCIETY

14

Taking Roots

FAR IN THE north of Norway in a region of mountains and sea lies the island of Dönna. For centuries its people have "sailed the seas of Nordland in the company of sea gulls and cormorants, herring and cod," as one Dönna dweller wrote to his brother in America. The brother, Ole Edvart Rölvaag, had spent only the first twenty years of his life on Dönna, yet the tradition of its many generations was to stay alive with him and within him, articulately and personally his own. To leave what he thus knew and loved struck a deep wound. The wound healed, but a scar remained. The first entry of the diary he kept from the day of his departure reveals his sharp sorrow: "It is done; it is done. I have left home. If I had had but a faint notion of how hard it would be to leave Mother, I probably would not have decided to go. . . . And now I am going out into the world to seek my fortune, my happiness. I will not find it." Eventually he found as much contentment as is given to his kind; yet he carried a heavy burden of loneliness, a feeling of tragic loss, to the end of his life. As the youthful diarist cried for his mother, so the man, great and loyal American though he became, was to yearn forever for this other mother—Norway.

The familiar story of Rölvaag's life has been well told by his biographers, Theodore Jorgenson and Nora Solum. Only a few facts need to be recalled. He came in 1896, first worked as a farmhand in a Norwegian community in South Dakota; then, by selling books during the summers, he was able to spend four winters at the near-by Lutheran academy in Canton. In the fall of 1901 he went to St. Olaf College, the institution with which he was identified the rest of his life, first as a student, then as a teacher, and to which he brought fame. Here he felt as secure and as happy culturally as, perhaps, it was possible for him any place in America. Here he became the spokesman for the Norwegian immigrant, interpreting him to his own children as well as to the rest of

America. I know of no other national group that has had so articulate and honest a mediator as the Norwegians had in Rölvaag. In his magnificent novels he faced up to the basic problems: the painful transition into a new culture, the conflict between the first and second generations, the tensions arising from marriages between people of different national and religious heritage.

Rölvaag saw the immigrant essentially as a tragic figure, severed from one culture, never to be at home in another, living in the past emotionally and only physically in the present. Material success or even the great new symbols of liberty and justice for all under the Stars and Stripes could never still the nostalgia for familiar sights, for smells and sounds, for the feel and the rhythm of another way of life. U. V. Koren, one of the pioneer pastors, reports a revealing incident in his reminiscences. Once he asked a man from Halling if he ever longed for Norway. The answer came fast, with a sprinkling of English in the Norwegian: "No, sir, there were so many stones there." But then he sat for a while, deep in thought, and finally said, "You know, the *tyttebaeren* [blueberries] in the fall—those I remember. Well, sir, they were fine berries."

Others could not adjust that well to the strange and difficult circumstances of the New World. There was a rather high percentage of insanity among the immigrants, particularly the women. Among the foreign-born settlers in the Middle West, Norwegians and other Scandinavians had the highest incidence of insanity. Yet extreme physical strain, financial worry, loneliness, poor health conditions and lack of medical attention were equally trying for all pioneering immigrants. Was it, then, that the Norwegians' step faltered when, in the new freedom, their eyes turned back to the stern God of their youth? Did the change from a small, closed-in mountain community to the flat, sprawling, wide-open prairies make them feel helpless and unprotected? Were the unaccustomed extremes of temperature a source of strain? It is striking how many Norwegian-born mental patients in a Minnesota institution believed that the hot weather or a sunstroke had caused their breakdown. Be that as it may, many an immigrant would have echoed the complaint of one who returned: "In America the hot summer days caused the sweat to flow even when we sat still, so that our clothes were quite soaked."

Disturbing, too, was the change from a diet of fish, milk, bread, and potatoes to one that consisted largely of meat, especially pork. Letters and diaries frequently mention the ever-present pork. One writer in the 1840's even attributed to the "prodigal use of pork" the sickness rampant among the settlers. "This indulgence in pork," he propounds naively, "produces an excess of bile, and makes the eater susceptible to the dangerous bilious fever."

The lot of the women was particularly hard. While the men in the pursuit of their business got occasionally to the nearest town, to a mill, or to another settlement, the women stayed home, alone with their fears of Indians, wild animals, desolate nights. Fredrika Bremer vividly records the picture of a lonely Norwegian pioneer woman in the Kosh-konong settlement in 1850:

> The Norwegian pastor, Mr. P[reus] had only left Norway to come hither a few months before. His young and pretty wife was standing in the kitchen, where a fire was blazing, boiling groats as I entered. I accosted her in Swedish. She was amazed at first, and terrified by the late visit, as her husband was from home on an official journey, and she was here quite alone with her little brother and an old woman servant; but she received us with true Northern hospitality and good-will, and she was ready to do everything in the world to entertain and accommodate us. . . . She was only 19, sick at heart for her mother, her home, and the mountains of her native land, nor was she happy in this strange country, and in those new circumstances to which she was so little accustomed. She was pretty, refined, and graceful; her whole appearance, her dress, her guitar which hung on the wall, everything showed that she had lived in a sphere very different to that of a log-house in a wilderness, and among rude peasants. The house was not in good condition; it rained in through the roof. Her husband, to whom she had not long been married, and whom for love she had accompanied from Norway to the New World, had been now from home for several days; she had neither friend nor acquaintance near nor far in the new hemisphere. It was no wonder that she was unable to see any thing beautiful or excellent in "this disagreeable America." But a young creature, good and lovely as she is, will not long remain lonely among the warm-hearted people of this country.

Most novels of pioneer prairie life use the episode of the wife waiting, with increasing anxiety, for her husband's return from his trip to town, the weather deceptively warm when he starts out and the blizzard striking before he returns. Hackneyed as it is by now, this formula derives from a harsh, soul-trying truth.

Love between the sexes was brutalized by conditions that often forced several families with their children into one small cabin. Pregnancy and birth became traumatic experiences, and, more often than not, led to infections and painful disorders that darkened the gloom. Even the more fortunate had to suffer. Olaus Duus, a pastor, writes to his family in Norway about the recent arrival of a baby girl:

> Even though it is only two weeks since I wrote and told you of Sophie's good fortune in being attended by an Indian midwife, I mean to send you a few words today, too, to say that everything continues to go as well as can be expected both with the mother and with the young daughter. Sophie has this time been entirely free from after-effects of childbirth, praise the Lord.

Erick Berdahl, an uncle of Mrs. O. E. Rölvaag, wrote in his autobiography about the birth of his first child in a little sod hut on the Dakota prairie: "The anticipation of my wife to become a Mother in the winter in this wilderness caused all but a pleasant feeling but the same blessed providence that with his guiding hand had brought us here also gave us his protecting care during those dark hours of struggle and all went well." As more children came into the family, the young Berdahls, like so many pioneer parents, went through the agony of watching them die, helplessly, from diseases for which no remedy was to be had in the wilderness. In Erick's autobiography we read:

> On the 31st. day of Jan 1876 our family was increased with a baby Boy which was named Albert Oliver. he was Strong and healthy child, but at the age of 3 yrs 16 days he was stricken down with that dreaded Croup decease and passed away Feb 16, 1879 that brought our first great grief and sorrow. . . . On Dec. 10th 1877 Kari Olina our 2nd Girl was born and matured to be a strong and healthy child, but at the age of nearly 6 years old She was taken with that dreadful Diptheria Croup decease and died Dec 6th 1883. . . . On Feb 16th 1880 the 3rd Girl came to us Only to Stay with us for a short duration. . . . She had been getting along Very nicely for her age up to 3 years old About that time she caught the Measles and other complycations set in and on March 4th 1883 that arch enemy Death again made his appearance and left us to again mourn the loss of one of our dear ones.

Erick and Hannah Berdahl thus lost two of their children within ten months! Meanwhile another boy arrived. When he was no more than six months Hannah became bedridden with "information of the bowels," and while she was still desperately ill the oldest daughter, ten-year-old Christina, contracted inflammatory rheumatism and "had to be lifted around in a blanket. We had to maintain a Hospital the best part of the summer," wrote her father.

Is it any wonder that many an immigrant woman broke under the crushing burden of this life? Is it to be wondered that, in their desperate need, they became more deeply religious, anxious that churches be built and pastors brought to the wilderness to baptize the children, instruct them in God's Holy Word, keep them in the faith of their fathers? It was the men who acted in these matters, but it was the homesick, lonely women—the Berets of *Giants in the Earth*—who drove them on.

Yet, there is, too, the other side of the medal. The toil was hard, but the economic reward was greater than anything these people had ever known before. So, naturally, they did not remain alien to the spirit of optimism that flowed then through America. Whatever frontier they came to, they took part in the organization of townships and counties, in the building of roads and the founding of schools. Active participation in local government became their entranceway into the public life of the country. And they were proud of the part they played. Erick Berdahl's autobiography tells of his first experience in politics in Fillmore County, Minnesota:

So on Nov 6th 1871 having then passed my 21st year since Aug 8th I got my permission to vote. And my close neighbor and School Mate Jo Power who was a year or so older had already become quite a politician and got me started to help to work for a change in some of our Township Officials that seemed to have combined together not for the best interest of the Township, and our efforts resulted in their defeat on election day Very much to their surprise as it had all been worked on the quiet.

In the fall I had the honor of representing our Township as one of the Delegates to the County convention which was the first one I had ever attended and it looked to me at that time to be a great affair.

When the Berdahls and their neighbors moved westward to the Dakota frontier they already knew enough to elect members of their group to the offices of road overseer, sheriff, assessor; and they were represented when it came to the formation of a territorial government. Such experiences are basic. Whoever shares in them becomes, by this very fact, an American in his own right. From this point of view, the transition was easier for the frontier pioneer than for the later immigrant who, coming to an orderly community already well-established, remained an outsider to its affairs for a few years, or, perhaps, for his whole life, depending upon the circumstances of time and location.

And they had social affairs which, whether they lived among people of their own background, other European-born immigrants, or native Americans, must be counted on the brighter side. N. O. Nelson, whose parents settled on a Missouri frontier in the 'forties, wrote about his childhood there: "Social activities were abundant. We had dances, grubbing, and quilting bees, debating societies, protracted . . . camp meeting, and much visiting. . . . My juvenile farming is a delightful memory. Farming is real work, but the pitying wail about the grinding toil of man, woman, child, and beast on the farm is a mixture of ignorance, laziness, and morbidness. . . . School and chores in the winter, farm work suited to the age in summer, play and a variety of interest all the time." About a Wisconsin frontier in the 'fifties Nils Haugen later wrote: "I have heard much said about the dreariness, poverty, and homesickness of the early immigrants. My recollection does not bear that out. On the contrary, they were as a rule a happy, industrious, and cheerful lot. The hope of seeing their condition improve as time sped, naturally contributed to happiness."

From the Berdahl records we get a picture of the debating society organized in 1873 during the first winter of the little Norwegian settlement on the Dakota prairie. In a vacant sod hut belonging to Mrs. O. E. Rölvaag's father, lighted by two lamps and "seated with some planks and blocks," some fifteen young men gathered regularly around the stove and "had some pretty hot debates there." And we have the story of a "dinner dance" staged at the home of a Norwegian immigrant on the North Dakota frontier in the 1880's:

Kettel Aaneson sent word to his neighbors and relatives to come to his home on a certain Sunday to eat, drink, shake their brogans, and be merry. . . . After we had arrived, by ox team, there was hand-shaking all the way around and the cup of cheer was passed, containing some kind of homemade liquor with alcohol as the chief ingredient. Dinner over, the room was partly cleared. The fiddler tuned up in the corner, drinks were generously passed around again, and soon the room was in a whirl. The few girls and the elderly married women danced until the perspiration ran down their faces. One rather elderly woman smoked a cigar while she danced, and considering her capacity for drink also, I couldn't help marvelling at the way she could hold her balance. As the evening ran on, drinks were passed more and more often, and soon a fist fight between two young men was in progress. This inspired two of the old fellows to settle a score of long standing—something that had taken place over fifty years before, back in Norway where they had herded cows and goats on some sæter.

But all the while, through bad times and good, consciously or unconsciously, they were yielding to the new civilization. It began with the obvious, with material things, such as food, clothing, shelter, and the furnishings of the home. Then they felt their way into the English tongue. Finally they found themselves thinking American ideas. They yielded, but they also retained on all these levels, so that it might be more correct to say that they joined the new to the old. One wonders, for example, how long it took an immigrant, accustomed to thinking of a farm in terms of two, ten, or twenty acres, to accept completely the idea of a farm of 160, 240, or 320 acres. When did he shed his wonderment and accept such dimensions as natural? If we could trace such things, we would know much more about the intangible process of becoming an American.

Somewhat easier to trace is the acquisition of the new language. Of course, the tempo varied greatly with the pattern of settlement. In general it can be said that immigrants from the same district tended to settle together. Naturally in such circumstances the Norwegian language was retained longer and the dialects remained relatively pure. Where there was a mixture of dialects, certain common usages evolved. In both types of communities a gradual change took place from pure Norwegian to what has been called a "Norwegian American" language. What happened was that the immigrants were constantly doing, seeing, using things whose names had no Norwegian equivalent. So they adopted the English name, giving it a Norwegian ending and a Norwegian pronunciation. Dozen, breakfast, all right, whiskey, plenty, or squaw thus became døssen, braekfest, ål rait, viski, pleinti, skvå. Many children who grew up in these communities never suspected that words such as these were not really Norwegian. In this linguistic halfway house the immigrant dwelt for a while not too uncomfortably before he finally turned to English for the expression of his thoughts. Einar Haugen aptly put it when he described this phase: "The shell is still Norwegian, but the inward pattern, the spirit of the thing, is American. This is Norwegian American, the language of the Norwegian immigrant."

Most of the immigrants' children became bilingual quickly. Andrew Berdahl in his autobiography tells about conditions in a settlement in Houston County, Minnesota, in 1860:

> This Blackhammer Township . . . was settled principally by Norwegians, most of whom had lived in this country but a few years, and in their daily intercourse naturally would use their native language.
>
> Father had as yet learned very little English, so that when he went to town to do trading or other business, he would take me along as interpreter; for I had been at school a few months of each year of the 4 years since our arrival, and thought I was quite proficient in the language of the land.

In Missouri where N. O. Nelson spent his youth in the 'fifties there were a few Norwegian families in a predominantly American community: "We became Americans, we went to American schools and churches, we associated with American neighbors. I learned Norwegian and English, one at home, the other at school, and no one has ever detected an alien accent in either of my languages." Again, some children had the experience Kneut Kneutson (later changed to Neutson) relates from his boyhood on a farm near Faribault, Minnesota:

> Although able to speak hardly a word of English understandingly, I was sent to school where all subjects were taught only in that language, and where all the pupils except myself, my brother and sisters, talked English, as ours was the only Norse family in that school district. . . . My learning of this new language, so far as words were concerned, ran ahead of my understanding, for I remember well that I joined with the other children in singing American

songs, such as "Yankee Doodle" and "Nellie Gray," without understanding the words to any extent. . . . My other youthful days were spent constantly with English speaking people. It was not strange therefore, that through my childish and youthful carelessness, within a decade or so, I had in large measure, forgotten my mother-tongue.

Rölvaag was deeply concerned with the language problem. "The old he cannot let go because that would mean starvation of his soul. The new he cannot master because the process is beyond human power. Bear in mind, if you please," he often told American as well as Norwegian American audiences, "that acquiring a language doesn't mean merely picking up words and phrases enough to get along in trade and travel—that most people can do. I have in mind the mastering of a new language so intimately that one's emotional life can express itself freely and naturally through the new idiom." Such mastery the bulk of the Norwegian immigrants—except the children, of course—who came in the half century following the arrival of the "sloopers" in 1825 were unable to achieve. They were simple, uneducated people for the most part. They settled together in rural areas where, until travel became easy, *they* dominated the local culture pattern and the *Americans* were outsiders. So what Rölvaag says is abundantly true for these immigrants, many of whom never felt at home in English.

For those of the later era, whose assimilation took place largely in urban centers, it is true to a lesser degree. I have in mind a statement in the diary of a young immigrant who came to Minnesota in 1919 knowing no English. Yet, in 1924 he wrote in his journal, where he recorded his innermost thoughts and emotions: "Now I don't know whether to write in Norwegian or English—it's getting easier to write in English." From that day on there were no Norwegian entries. These people faced a different set of problems. Catapulted into wholly American environments, they were forced to make a quick change; their pains were sharper but passed more quickly. Also these people were for the most part better educated than the earlier immigrants; and, there is no doubt, of course, that the wider one's knowledge and understanding, the more easily one enters a new civilization. But in the era of the Berets, who epitomize immigrant psychology in Rölvaag's mind, the curse of the tied tongue hung over whole lives.

Up to a point Rölvaag believed whole-heartedly in assimilation. In his mind there was no question of the immigrant's first duty: to learn the English language, to learn about American life. But he was equally convinced that the heritage of the forefathers must be preserved for its own sake and permanently, not just in order to forestall a vacuum while acculturation takes place. For, in his romantic vision of history, "a people can grow only so far as they are organically one with their soil and their own historical background." So he was afraid that in shedding their language, the customs and precepts of their youth in Norway, his people would become cultural tramps. He was appalled at what he considered the cultural barrenness of the second generation Norwegian homes he saw when he came to America toward the turn of the century. The children knew nothing of the history, the literature, the lore and folkways of Norway. Even the language spoken in these homes bore little resemblance to the Norwegian of Norway.

The longer he lived in America, the more Rölvaag became convinced that the Norwegians in the Middle West had to be roused to an awareness of what he thought of as the hidden America, their own native culture, that lay beneath the Anglo-Saxon surface. So while others were preaching the "melting pot," Rölvaag preached preservation. From his hilltop college classroom, on lecture platforms, through Norwegian American religious and secular publications he called upon the people, the churches, the schools, and the press to see, to value, and to preserve their heritage.

If one raises such a torch, one must, as Rölvaag did, seize it with both hands and work hard if one wants to affect the course of the silent forces. Rölvaag no doubt worked hard. But was he right? I, for one, do not think so. Rather, it seems to me that this business of preserving one's heritage can be overdone and that Rölvaag asked for more than is reasonable or wholesome to expect from a foreign element that has to make its way into a new environment. And, even more important, he asked for more than is desirable for, or even compatible with, the progressive growth of American civilization.

It is one thing to call the attention of historians and sociologists to the culture that came across the Atlantic in the immigrant chests, as Carl Wittke has so gracefully said, so that we can come to a better understanding of the ingredients in our civilization. This can be done; this should be done. It is fine to encourage the preservation of folk habits, crafts, food preparations, and dances to enrich our life. Who would want to live in an America without Hungarian goulash or kosher pickles? Who does not enjoy the French atmosphere of New Orleans or the German flavor of St. Louis and Milwaukee? But the moment such things become issues, the moment one accepts the doctrine of the "peculiar treasure" to be preserved, unsullied and undiluted, for future generations, one is headed toward obvious dangers, among which the fostering of a phony, pseudo-romantic nationalism, bad as it is, is not the worst.

Pride in one's background and a secondary kind of loyalty to its traditions are not only a normal, healthy part of one's cultural equipment; they can be of great therapeutic use in the acculturation of groups that suffer from inferiority feelings or have a background of persecution. But when emotional excess along such lines freezes defensively into the ideal of permanent apartness, into the unrealistic desire for ethnic subcultures within our American culture, that is another story again. The most charitable thing that I, today, could say about this aspect of Rölvaag's thought is that it rationalizes honestly and, in this sense adequately, the transition pains of his group.

To come down to brass tacks after all these generalities, let us for a moment consider that business of name-changing, so common in all immigrant groups. Whatever the variety of personal reasons, what it all comes down to is essentially a matter of convenience. Names are something that the people around should be able to pronounce, that the register of deeds should be able to spell without too much difficulty. Not many Norwegians went so far as the family who changed from Kruge to McCully when they noticed that nearly everyone called them Crudge.

Besides, most Norwegians had quite a few possibilities to choose from when they came to America. Surnames used by all members of the family and handed down in the male line were not the custom in rural Norway. Lars, the son of Anders, was simply Lars Anderson; his son Knut, Knut Larson; his daughter Trina, Trina Larsdatter. Only occasionally was a place name, or such, added by way of a permanent appellation. And since farm names, such as Bjelle, Flaam, Husebø, were difficult for American tongues, many immigrants shed them and chose the simpler patronymic. My own family is a case in point. My great-grandfather's name was Nils Bö or Boe, as it was often written, his son's name Christian Nelson Boe, but when the latter came to America he dropped the farm name of Boe because, having lived all his life in a small parish where there were many Boes, this name, ironically, seemed to him more common than Nelson. Only in the more strictly Norwegian communities were the farm names maintained because some of them implied social distinctions that their bearers would not allow to be forgotten. Even the custom of naming farms was continued by some of the immigrants, so that for a while the members of a family were known among them in this manner. Church records in some Wisconsin communities show that many families used such names among their Norwegian neighbors. But when it came to registering their property and dealing with Yankees they used their father's name with an often Americanized form of the traditional ending. Halfway house again!

The case of one Norwegian might illustrate the confusion that was brought about by this practice. In 1844 he was using the name Johannes Larsen Hollo, in 1849 Johannes Larsen Hedemarken, in 1850 John Larsen, and in 1860, not quite intelligibly, Johannes Johannsson. Gradually, however, a stabilization took place, the children usually adopting more anglicized forms, such as Olson, Johnson, or Anderson. Today, when the third generation has come onto the scene, Peterson and Anderson sound as American in our ears as Smith and Brown, and I hope, as Rossi, Vondracek, and Goldberg will sound tomorrow. Rölvaag and the other sentimental nationalists of his generation swam fervently against this stream. In their ardor for the old they urged many people, particularly students, to change back to the old farm names, such as Braaten, Gampehaugen, Mykklebust. One critic of this romantic nationalism tells the story, apochryphal perhaps but significant nevertheless, of how scandalized one mother was when her son returned from college with one of those "historically fit" names. "Think," said she, "what he has gone and done! Changed a good Norwegian name, Olson, to Vinje." In the letter she was wrong. In the spirit, I believe, she was right.

But whether Vinje or Olson, it usually took at least a couple of generations before a "Norwegian" family became easily and unconsciously American. Few have described this better than Eric Sevareid, news commentator and writer, whose grandfather came to the Iowa frontier from Norway. In *Not So Wild a Dream* he writes:

> For my father's generation, born in America though they were, the "old country," which they had never seen, still seemed close. He carried a faint Norwegian accent in his speech throughout his life, which came from his early boyhood when few around the farms spoke English. Christmas dinner was never right for him without *lutefisk* and *lefse,* and Pastor Reishus always preached first in Nor-

wegian, then in English. But there came a break with my generation, the third. It happened throughout that northwest country. Talk with visitors in the parlor about the old country bored my brothers and me. I hated the sound of the Norwegian tongue and refused to try to learn it. It meant nothing to me that my grandfather on my mother's side was one of America's most distinguished scholars of Scandinavian literature and life. The books in my classroom dealt only with the United States, and there lay the sole magnet to our imaginations. The thread connecting these northwest people with Europe was thinning out, and with my generation it snapped.

Left to sink into history, when this thread snapped, was a whole way of life, established by the first generation to fill the needs of aliens in a strange land; carried on by the spiritually double-rooted second; honored, if no longer supported, by a third generation that is naturally and unself-consciously American. To understand this way of life, both where it is good and where it is bad, we must trace it to the centers of its strength—church, school, press.

15

The Church

THE OVERWHELMING MAJORITY of the Norwegian immigrants who filed across the Middle West to build their homes in the knee-deep prairie grass had a sturdy faith in God and a deep attachment to the Lutheran Church. True, the early years of settlement, particularly on the Illinois frontier, were a period of religious chaos. Some settlers, enjoying the freedom of the new land after their escape from the watchful eye of the state church, kept aloof when opportunities for organized worship came to their community. A Norwegian lay preacher who travelled extensively up and down the frontier complained that no immigrants were more indifferent to religion than the Norwegians. Fredrika Bremer also reported the same thing when she visited the settlements near Chicago in 1850:

> I also heard it lamented that the Scandinavian immigrants not unfrequently come hither with the belief that the State Church and religion are one and the same thing, and when they have left behind them the former, they will have nothing to do with the latter. Long compulsion of mind has destroyed, to that degree, their powers of mind; and they come into the West very frequently, in the first instance, as rejectors of all church communion and every higher law. And this is natural enough for people not accustomed to think greatly; but is a moment of transition which cannot last very long in any sound mind.

Not a few among the early settlers who felt a need for some formal church connection responded to the friendly overtures of missionaries from the Methodist, Baptist, Seventh Day Adventist, Episcopalian, and Mormon churches. But by and large, there was in the Norwegian immigrants an inbred desire to worship in the Lutheran way and when the Lutheran Church was eventually established among them, they became members as quickly as any displaced creature finds his way back to his natural habitat. And it was natural, too, that coming as they did to an institutionless frontier the immigrants should build a social world along lines familiar to them from home; so the church they established in the New World, though accommodated to the principle of separation and the ideals of a frontier democracy, was a reasonable facsimile of the church they had known in the Old.

In the course of this transplantation the religious differences in Norway, particularly acute during the first half of the century, came to flourish on American soil, like the wheat and the corn, far more abundantly than they ever had in the old country. There the state church contained the differences within itself, gradually and cautiously adjusting to the various demands for change. In the New World everyone was free to choose what best suited him from among many shades of opinion and, if he so desired, to set himself up as the leader of a new body. Thus, the outstanding feature of Norwegian American Lutheran Church history throughout the nineteenth century was strife. And though this struggle signified in many ways a healthy, democratic development, the bitterness, acrimoniousness, and jealousy it engendered left scars that are faintly visible to this day.

It will be better to oversimplify than to burden the reader with a detailed account of ecclesiastic organization. So I shall give but a bird's-eye view. Two major religious forces came out of Norway: the pietistic Haugean movement, of low church ideals, emphasizing lay preaching, "awakening" and conversion; the state church, taking the high road, emphasizing orderly church life, the sacred functions of the ministerial office, and above all the authority of the church. A third tendency to steer a middle course of moderation was often represented by those who had come under the influence of N. F. S. Grundtvig, the Danish theologian. His was a joyous, practical, socially oriented kind of Christianity, and the life and warmth that he brought to the coldly rationalistic Danish Church made itself felt in Norway's university. The first three religious leaders on the immigrant frontier represented these three influences: Haugean, Grundtvigian, orthodox.

The Haugeans and the orthodox each organized their own church bodies, and from these two main stems sprouted the branches that represented varying shades of Lutheran opinion. In 1860 there were three synods; during the 'seventies and 'eighties more splits occurred, making, by the late 'eighties, five synods among the Norwegian Lu-

therans. In 1890, when three of these merged, the three remaining stayed
true to the underlying pattern. The high church group was known as
the Norwegian Synod; the broad church group called itself the United
Norwegian Lutheran Church; the low church group was the Hauge
Synod. Further divisions occurred; but in 1917 a major union of these
three synods finally led to the organization of one large body, the
Norwegian Lutheran Church of America, which in 1946 changed its
name to the Evangelical Lutheran Church of America. Thus, the year
1917 marks the end of the nineteenth century schisms, the formal break-
down of the synodical fences that had kept the bulk of the Norwegian
Lutherans separated for two generations. Only the Lutheran Free
Church, a group that had split from the United Norwegian Lutheran
Church in the 'nineties, is still independent.

During the early history of Norwegian Lutheranism in America
attempts were made to unite with the Swedes and Danes, but language
differences and other difficulties could not be overcome. Except for an
early experimental effort, the Swedes, though greatly outnumbering
the Norwegians, have had only one Lutheran body, the Swedish
Augustana Synod. The Norwegians, in their stormy history, had as
many as fourteen separate synods. Yet the percentage of Swedes that
remained in the Lutheran fold is smaller than the Norwegians'. One is
almost tempted to conclude that Norwegian Lutheranism thrived on
theological and ecclesiastical controversy. Indeed, the laity followed
the arguments of the clergy in the church papers and skirmished with
their neighbors over the subtler points of justification and predestination.
For, amidst the intellectual barrenness of the frontier, theological brooding and debate were among the few outlets for livelier minds.

Invigorating as these struggles were, they were also expensive. Each
new church body started its academies, seminaries, and colleges, poorly
equipped and staffed for the most part. Most of them withered and died
within a short span. The immigrants spent thousands of dollars building churches that need not have been built. Small communities often
tried to support two or three different synodical affiliations where one
would have amply sufficed.

I myself have lived in such a town in my youth. Madison, Minnesota,
then had about fifteen hundred inhabitants, sixty to seventy per cent
of whom, I would judge, were of Norwegian stock; yet, there were two
Norwegian Lutheran churches, even though it was post–1917 and the
official merger had already taken place. One had originally belonged

to the Hauge Synod, the other to the United Norwegian Lutheran Church. As far as co-operation was concerned they might have been a Jewish synagogue and a Roman Catholic church. The congregations each had a membership of, I suppose, about two to three hundred. The inadequately paid ministers served scattered country parishes as well as their town congregations in order to make both ends meet. Each congregation had its Ladies' Aid raising money for new altar furnishings or an organ, its Mission Society supporting China missionaries, its choir singing Lutheran hymns, its pastor preaching Lutheran doctrine at a nine-thirty service in Norwegian and at eleven in English. The social world of our parents was limited to members of their family church, but in school, where our teen-age gangs were half Hauge, half United, these barriers broke down. We each accepted the superiority of our congregation as a matter of fact and resented any slurs against it—as there were—but our parties and dates were completely mixed. As far as I know these two congregations, though now members of the Evangelical Lutheran Church of America, still cling to their separate ways. Tradition is stronger than common sense.

But we must again return to the beginning of our story. The majority of the first immigrants who retained their Lutheran faith, and there were many, held Haugean views; so, it was only natural that the first religious leader to arise among them came from the Haugean ranks. He was Elling Eielsen, who, after ten years of itinerant lay preaching in Norway and Denmark, chafed under the confining hand of officialdom and came to America late in the 1830's, going almost immediately to the Fox River settlement.

There, using the upper floor of the cabin he had built, he called the people together for religious services. Preaching mightily against the sects that sowed confusion in the minds of the settlers, he became the focus for the Lutheran impulses of the Fox River settlement. He provided books for the religious instruction of the children, even journeying to New York to see to the printing of an English translation of Luther's Small Catechism. He visited settlement after settlement to preach to the people who were hungry to hear the Word of God in the Norwegian tongue. Simple, thoroughly at home on the unsophisticated frontier, Eielsen was stubbornly attached to a somewhat narrow conception of what constituted a Christian—only one who had been "awakened," who had repented and had been converted.

And there was something else he, like most Haugeans, shared with the non-Lutheran evangelical churches of the nineteenth century: he was fanatically opposed to drinking, dancing, and smoking. The simple prayer meetings he and his co-workers held catered to most emotional needs of the early days; yet, as the people became settled and their lives more stable, the desire for institutional regularity again prevailed. They wanted someone who could rightfully baptize and confirm their children, marry them and administer the Lord's Supper, functions which were, strictly speaking, not within the competence of a lay preacher. Consequently, Eielsen's supporters prevailed upon their reluctant leader to let himself be ordained. A German Lutheran pastor performed the ceremony on October 3, 1843, thus making Eielsen the first ordained Lutheran minister among the Norwegians in America.

Meanwhile, other settlements were faced with the same problems. Lay leadership proved insufficient. In the summer of 1843 a fairly well educated young Danish immigrant arrived in the Muskego settlement in Wisconsin with the intention of becoming a schoolteacher. He was Claus L. Clausen, whom we have already met in connection with the early settlement of Minnesota in 1850. He had had some formal religious training, had been a lay preacher in Denmark, and while visiting in Norway, had been urged to go to the Wisconsin settlement as a teacher. Arriving there, he found that the settlers, instead, wanted him to become their minister and "assemble the scattered flock and feed them with God's true and undistorted word and the precious sacraments," as he wrote in his diary; so he, too, was examined by a German Lutheran pastor and ordained, two weeks and a day after Eielsen's ordination. Now there were two Lutheran pastors to serve the Norwegian immigrants, but as yet no formal church organization. Eielsen did not believe in it; Clausen, although he placed more importance on the ministerial office than Eielsen and did not regard the latter's ordination as valid, was too absorbed in missionary activities to trouble about the details of a formal organization.

Into this amorphous situation, a few months later, came a determined young university-trained, properly ordained clergyman from Norway, J. W. C. Dietrichson. He was as stubborn and uncompromising in his high church attitudes as Eielsen in his low church beliefs; with his coming the lines of the ecclesiastical battles to come were drawn. Clausen was more or less in the middle; he had mild Haugean sympathies, was very democratic in his outlook, but, like many others after him, did not find it possible to work with the adamant Eielsen. With Dietrichson he co-operated in spite of the latter's authoritarian ideas and demeanor. Although Dietrichson eventually returned to Norway—basically and very properly he disapproved of emigration—this efficient, imperious divine laid the foundation of one of the main branches of the church by organizing congregations according to a program, establishing a uniform church service, and building churches. Thus the Eielsen forces, too, if they wanted to survive, had to organize. The body they established in 1846 was known as Elling Eielsen's Synod, sometimes as the Evangelical Lutheran Church of America, or more colloquially as the Ellingians. It is this body that eventually came to be called the Hauge Synod. Representing the low church wing, it established schools and a seminary, but throughout its history it depended a great deal on lay preaching.

One young leader, Paul Andersen, who was present at the founding of the Eielsen Synod, later broke away from this group. At Beloit College, a Presbyterian institution in Wisconsin, he came under the wider influences of American life, and, finding Eielsen's nationalism and Lutheranism too confining, he joined with American, German, and Swedish Lutherans in establishing, in 1851, the Evangelical Lutheran Synod of Northern Illinois. Although the liberal Andersen urged co-operation among Lutherans of all national backgrounds and had closer contacts with American Lutherans than any other Norwegian leader of his day, the Norwegian element in the Synod of Northern Illinois eventually left this supra-national body and in the course of the next few decades became the "center party" in the ecclesiastical divisions among the Norwegians.

Meanwhile the struggle between the Dietrichson and the Eielsen forces was going on, the former being strengthened by the arrival in the late 'forties and early 'fifties of a few university-educated theologians, most of whom came from upper class families, the military, church, and government circles of Norway. By 1853 they had organized the Norwegian Synod, or, as it was generally called, the Synod, destined to become the strongest of the church bodies. Undeniably reflecting the state church attitude, the new organization yet made concessions to the American environment. The local congregations were allowed to manage their affairs as long as their acts were not contrary to the constitution of the synod, the highest authority. The majority of the immigrants, though they demanded some of the freedom they all felt was one of the blessings of their new country, were yet glad to have some authority to look up to, to turn to. They could not shed the awe they felt for the office of the pastor. The robes he wore, the white ruff, the solemn tone in which he chanted the liturgy gave them a sense of participating in higher things, brought a note of dignity and richness that was sorely missing in their crude homes and lives. There was in them a mixture of old and new ideals.

A story that well reveals this ambivalent attitude has been told by one of the pioneer leaders among the university-educated pastors. Ulrick Vilhelm Koren and his wife Elisabeth, both sensitive, cultured, educated people, came from Norway to the Iowa frontier in 1853. Koren organized and served congregations in the Decorah area for many years, was a stanch and significant friend of Luther College, which he, with its first president, Laur. Larsen, helped to establish. (During his university days in Norway Peter Laurentius Larsen began to sign himself Laur. Larsen, the form by which he ever afterward was known.) In his reminiscences Koren tells of one of the first church meetings he held.

"I had anticipated," he wrote, "that all would at once gladly assent to my proposal that we should join the newly established Synod. There I was wrong. Our people are cautious, and this was something new. 'Synod? What is that? Is it something that will shackle us?' they asked." Koren continued to argue for joining. But the parishioners obviously were suspicious. Finally, so Koren tells us, old Thrond Lomen, at whose home the meeting was being held, went outside. Young Koren followed him. Lomen gave the new pastor this sound advice: "I have been convinced that we should join the Synod, but it is a new idea to these people. Don't drive them into anything today, but let them think it over slowly and carefully and they will follow as you wish." They did.

And thus this conservative branch of the church grew under the strong leadership of these pioneer university-trained pastors, Preus, Stub, Koren, Larsen, Ottesen, Brandt—names and families that have played cardinal roles in the history of the church. They were the aristocracy among the Norwegian immigrants, and in their frontier homes, log cabins though they might be, the little amenities of life were preserved. Flowers bloomed, musical instruments—soon even pianos—were common, books by the standards of frontier days were plentiful, periodicals and newspapers arrived regularly in the mail. Laur. Larsen wrote to relatives in Norway in 1853, "I keep an excellent Republican paper, *The New York Tribune,* which keeps me fairly well posted, and at the same time I am making good progress in English."

Mutual affection united these pastors' families. Scattered over the frontier, they met for pastoral conferences once or twice a year at one of the parsonages; usually the entire family came, looking forward to the event with undisguised pleasure. The young wives exchanged news of mutual friends in Norway, revealed that a new baby was on the way and received the advice of all the other women; the men talked pastoral problems far into the night while the children slept on the attic floor above them. One of these children was Karen Larsen, the distinguished historian, who later wrote in her admirable biography of her father, "A close friendship bound the little group of ministers' families together in an intimacy that only the isolation of a few like-minded people in a strange land can produce. The grown-ups were 'uncle' and 'aunt' to all the children in their little circle of friends, and ties were formed that in many cases have lasted into the second and third generation."

The rush of Norwegian immigrants into the new West quickly created a dearth of ministers to carry on church work. Lay preachers had to be used, even in the Norwegian Synod which opposed lay ministry; but most of the settlements wanted trained pastors. Enthusiasm for service on the American frontier was not great among theological candidates in Oslo. Many who did come returned to their homeland after a few years. Nor did the Norwegian Synod have money to carry on a training program of its own. So, after looking over the field of existing Lutheran seminaries, the Synod leaders finally made an arrangement with a German Lutheran institution, Concordia College, in St. Louis, Missouri, whereby a Norwegian professorship was established, allowing Norwegian students to have the advantages of a fully equipped college and at the same time to be trained by one of their own people in the Norwegian language. This connection with a vigorous yet not always orthodox center of German theological speculation lasted from 1859 to the middle 'seventies. The laity always regarded it with some suspicion and it probably did give rise to many a theological argument that might otherwise not have troubled the Norwegian Lutheran mind in America.

One of the longest and most nerve-shattering of the controversies that vexed the councils of the godly was the question of slavery. As a group the Norwegian immigrants condemned slavery. When rumors filtered North that Laur. Larsen, the first man sent by the Synod to hold the Norwegian professorship at Concordia Seminary, shared the faculty's southern sympathies, the editor of *Emigranten,* leading Norwegian American newspaper of that day, asked, in the spring of 1861, for a statement from the professor. The dust Larsen's answer stirred up did not settle until 1869, four years after the North and South had ceased fighting. His position, and that of the majority of the Norwegian Synod clergy, that "according to the Word of God, it is not in and by itself a sin to keep slaves," was opposed by most of the laity and some clergymen led by Claus Clausen, whose democratic and humanitarian sympathies would not permit of such a strictly biblical view toward an institution that was in their opinion a present evil in these United States.

Nor was the opposition content to keep the argument on the level of an academic discussion among theologians. Polemical articles, parodies on the polemics, diatribes from both sides kept the atmosphere in the Norwegian settlements electric with excitement. The heat of this battle over slavery, at a time when the Norwegian settlers did not yet fully participate in American affairs, is understandable only if it is seen as an episode in local ecclesiastical politics, a reflection in the new context of the old struggle between commoners and officialdom in Norway. Even so the whole curious controversy smacks of unreality, has an air of fighting windmills. Among the clergy Laur. Larsen's orthodox insistence on the strict interpretation of the Scripture eventually prevailed. The Synod accepted his view; Clausen left and affiliated with another Lutheran body. The political sympathies of the typical Norwegian settler, however, remained unchanged. He was a fervent northerner.

Just as violent and perhaps even more acrimonious was the prolonged struggle over the common school. For almost two decades the pastors of the Norwegian Synod fought for the establishment of parochial schools, while the immigrants themselves, in the main, favored the free common school system of America. Nor is this attitude of the Synod clergy difficult to understand. Those educated at St. Louis were impressed by the German Lutherans' well-developed and efficient system of parochial education, and their argument that these parochial schools were superior to the frontier common schools in this period from the 'fifties to the 'seventies was not easy to meet. The men trained in Oslo naturally shuddered away from a school that did not set itself the task of inculcating orthodox Lutheran doctrine. Moreover, the Norwegian Synod pastor of this period, no matter where he was trained, was for the most part a strong nationalist and saw in the parochial school the means to stem the tide of Americanization, to preserve the language together with all other things Norwegian.

Although Hjalmar Hjorth Boyesen, Norwegian-born professor at

Columbia University in the 'eighties and 'nineties, was, as an easterner, out of touch with the realities of prairie society, he recognized the basic issue when he wrote in 1891:

> The system of parochial schools, too, which the Scandinavian Lutheran churches are endeavoring to establish, is directly hostile to the settlers' best interests, being intended as a bulwark (and a most effective one) against the incoming tide of Americanism. For the public schools, with all their defects, have always served as a hopper into which all the mixed and alien grain is poured, to be ground into flour, the general quality of which is American. Parochial schools . . . are usually founded for the very purpose of perpetuating alienism and preventing the children of the immigrants from becoming absorbed in the dominant nationality.

Fortunately, the moment the Synod leaders began to criticize the common school and to promote the establishment of parochial schools they met with strong opposition. Left-wing Norwegian American newspapers called upon the people to break the control that the clerical clique tried to exert over them. These champions of the public school admitted its present inadequacy, but they argued that it was right in principle and that, therefore, it was the duty of parents to support it and to work for its improvement. Nor did they forget the argument, still familiar in American politics, that the support of religious schools increased the financial burden of the faithful. And not even the clergy dared to deny the value of a thorough foundation in English. So they concentrated their attack on the pernicious effects of the secular spirit in the common schools and the lack of discipline that allegedly went with it. But at least one immigrant parent commented stolidly that if the children misbehaved at home he could still exercise his privilege of thrashing them "in Norwegian." And the immigrants did, as a matter of course, send their children to the common schools, which in most settlements were the only schools available.

Erick Berdahl wrote of the school he attended in Winneshiek County, Iowa, in the winter of 1859:

> This being the only School House in the Settlement for Miles around we had as Meny as 60 Schollers in attendence and . . . a large part of the Schollars were full grown men and women who had Just come over from Norway and was trying to learn the lan-

guage of the country they had adopted. The Teacher was from Norwegian parentage which was of great help in cases of emergency but we were not allowed to talk Norwegian within his hearing but as soon as we got out of the School House you would never hear a word of English because every schollar was genuine Norsk.

Most of the parents were proud when their children came home using English phrases, soon speaking in English sentences. They wanted their children to enjoy what they themselves had been denied—a free education, open to all, rich and poor. Nevertheless, they welcomed the summer parochial schools where instruction was carried on in Norwegian, very often by Norwegian men teachers who had had a little special religious training in the old country. And in some communities the parochial schools did take the place of the common school. By 1870, it is safe to say, the victory of the common school could be foreseen; by 1890 the strife, that at its height drew many leading Norwegian Americans into debates far from friendly, had subsided. In the meantime the Synod leaders, accepting the facts, however reluctantly, began to turn their attention to education beyond the elementary level, to the establishment of Norwegian academies and colleges. Their first venture was Luther College in Decorah, Iowa, foremost among the pioneer schools.

During this period, while slavery and common school occupied the minds of the Synod clergy, the other Norwegian Lutheran bodies were gaining strength and experience as they brought the services of the church to the expanding frontiers.

As the older settlers moved into the Dakotas and Montana, they wanted pastors from the synods they had been attached to in Illinois, Wisconsin, and Iowa. Duplication and strife, consequently, marked the spread of Norwegian Lutheranism. A Dakota pioneer pastor of the 'eighties, J. J. Ringstad, wrote that oftentimes "one pastor, with his flock, would wait outside the schoolhouse where the meeting was to be held, while the other pastor concluded his services, and people would meet, while going to and from services." However, the doctrinal issues that clearly divided the Norwegian Lutherans close to the centers of the storms subtly degenerated, as they filtered to the edges of settlement, into petty differences and jealousies of a more or less personal kind.

The hardy men of God, sent out as missionaries by the church, served people in settlements scattered over as much as two western states. In its Annual Report for 1883 the Norwegian Augustana Synod recommended to its mission committee that a missionary be sent "to work among the fellow countrymen in Idaho, Montana, Utah, and Washington territories." For these pioneer pastors who travelled, on horseback or in a wagon, from settlement to settlement there were days of prairie or mountain between congregations, nights spent on a blanket under the stars. "I often ate only one meal a day on those trips," wrote one pastor, "for many people had brought an awe inspiring respect for the officials, with them from Norway, and considered their food too plain for a clergyman." In the Far West, where the railroad frequently preceded settlement, the missionaries often travelled, like Elmer Gantry, by hand-car and preached in section houses.

From the diary of the pastor who established the first Norwegian Lutheran church in Montana we get a vivid picture of how the church followed its people into the western wilderness. In 1885 the Norwegian Augustana Synod sent P. J. Reinertson as a missionary to Dakota and Montana. A group of Norwegians had settled on the mountain ranges of the Montana Sweet Grass region northwest of Big Timber. When Reinertson arrived there, about noon one October day, he expected to be met by someone from the settlement some distance over the mountains. Big Timber he found dreary, "only a few houses, stony streets, no Scandinavians"; also, he had but one dollar left, and though he was hungry he did not dare spend it on food, since, if no one came to get him, he might have to use it for lodging in the hotel-saloon overnight. As he sat gloomily on the bank of the Yellowstone River waiting for the man from the other side of the mountains his courage flagged. But then, the sight of those mountains turned his thoughts "to Him who is the Rock of Eternity" whose "promises stand fast." In the evening the man from Sweet Grass came. The servant of the Lord was abundantly fed, comfortably lodged and, as he takes the trouble to record in his diary, still had his dollar.

A few days later he conducted his first church service in a log schoolhouse. Men, women, and children, even some half-breed Indians, came riding down through the valleys from different directions. "This was something entirely new and they came to hear and see." Five children were baptized that day. After some days Reinertson and two men from the settlement rode over the mountains on ponies to the home of Martin Grande on the Musselshell River. In his home and in a schoolhouse, the missionary conducted services, most of the time in the English language, since there were also Indians, Scotch, and French in the audience. Here in the latter part of the month he and the settlers organized the first Lutheran congregation in Montana, laid out and dedicated a graveyard, usually, in the West, the first step toward the establishment of a church. He was commended for his use of English in the official organ of the Norwegian Augustana Synod, the *Luthersk Kirketidende,* which adopted a more liberal attitude toward the language question than did the Norwegian Synod church paper, *Kirketidende.* "Here is an extensive mission territory," wrote the editor of the former publication, "where English speaking Lutherans are scattered everywhere without minister or church. These are our brethren in the faith and we are in duty bound to be concerned about them. How important it is, then, that our young men who are being educated for the ministry be thoroughly instructed in the English language." But Reinertson was, apparently, an exception among the pioneer pastors, for on the whole the churches in Montana and elsewhere in the West were ministered in the Norwegian tongue, which caused the loss of many potential members to English-speaking congregations. This, as well as the fact that only a few pastors could be sent into the western states, is the cause for the relative weakness of the Norwegian Lutheran Church in these areas. Nor is it, perhaps, without significance that while the colonization of the Far West took place the attention of the older centers was once again absorbed by a theological battle.

Again the responsibility can be laid at the door of the older Synod leaders whose subservience to the Calvinistically inclined Missouri Lutherans came in for more and more unfavorable comment as the younger men accused them of Calvinistic views concerning election and predestination. Throughout almost the entire decade of the 'eighties this theological quibble engaged the minds, not only of the clergy, but also of the laity, finally producing a schism in the Synod. Congregations denied pastors, who had served them for decades, the right to continue in their pulpits. Other congregations split, entangling themselves in lawsuits over church property; families divided, some remaining with the churches that followed the Missouri doctrine, others joining with the Anti-Missourians, as the opposition was called.

Out of this strife another Lutheran school was born, St. Olaf's School, later called St. Olaf College, in Northfield, Minnesota. Started by one of the main leaders of the Anti-Missourian faction, B. J. Muus, it was at first hardly more than a high school for the boys and girls who wanted a pre-college education under Norwegian Lutheran teachers. Gradually, however, it rose to college level and the preparatory department was discontinued. The followers of the old Norwegian Synod called the new institution the "rebel" school, and between Luther College, the Synod school in Decorah, and St. Olaf College there developed a keen spirit of rivalry which lasted long after the synods were merged into one body in 1917.

Somewhat earlier another school, Augsburg Seminary, had been established in Marshall, Wisconsin, by one of the bodies that favored low church ritual and free congregational action. When the seminary was moved to Minneapolis in the 'seventies a four-year college and a four-year academy were added. Under the leadership of a few dynamic Norwegian-born and educated professors—in particular Georg Sverdrup, for many years president of the institution, and Sven Oftedal—Augsburg College and Seminary became a center of cultural activity for the Norwegian Lutherans in Minneapolis. Under the wing of the Lutheran Free Church it has maintained its low church ideals and a flavor of pietism even unto the present.

The increasing desire for higher education among the children of the immigrants, their reluctance to go to Presbyterian, Methodist, or Congregational colleges and academies, and, finally, the general scarcity of such institutions in the newly settled areas prompted the establishment of Norwegian Lutheran academies, normal schools, ladies' seminaries, and colleges in more than fifty communities between 1860 and 1890. Always a minister was installed as president and teachers, preferably with some theological training, were hired to teach algebra, Latin, Longfellow's *Evangeline* and the Gettysburg Address, in addition to numerous courses in religion. By present standards these schools and their staffs were dreary affairs, but to the rural youth of their day they were the entrance to a wider world beyond the farm. My own parents went to such a normal school. As the various synods merged and as public high schools increased in number most of these small institutions were either absorbed by the stronger ones among them or discontinued.

Today the Evangelical (Norwegian) Lutheran Church of America maintains two seminaries, the main one in St. Paul, a smaller one in Canada; five senior colleges, four of them in the Middle West and one in Washington, the latter jointly supported by three Lutheran bodies; two junior colleges, one of which is in Texas, the other in Iowa; and three academies, one in Canada, the other two in the Middle West. Three-quarters of the seven thousand students enrolled in these institutions are Lutherans. And not only through these schools but also by means of Lutheran student centers on the campuses of state colleges and universities does the church try to keep the youth from Norwegian American homes within the pale. Some thirty charitable institutions are under the control of this Lutheran body, as well as a dozen or more social work agencies. About two hundred missionaries are serving the church in foreign countries.

There is no question that the Lutheran Church has been a pillar of Norwegian American prairie society. But since the Federal census reports on foreign stock have never gone beyond the second generation and the religious census includes all generations, it is not possible to determine reliably what percentage of the Norwegian stock has remained within the fold. It is probably safe to say that among the descendants of the early immigrants in the Middle West church membership is higher than among the coastal urban groups whose parents came at a later period from Norway's cities. Of the 750,000 members of the Evangelical (Norwegian) Lutheran Church of America, for example, about ninety per cent live in the Middle West. Yet I would not go as far as one present-day historian who asserts that "most of the Norwegian immigrants and their descendants have either become unchurched or have joined non-Lutheran English-speaking congregations."

The Norwegian Lutheran Church in America has, of course, made outward concessions to the prevailing pattern. A quarter of a century ago almost half of the church services were bilingual; now only three per cent of the services are non-English. Yet it was only in 1946, after more than a decade of discussion, that, as I mentioned before, the largest single church body dropped "Norwegian" from its name. In its doctrine, however, this particular synod remains unyielding, unaffected by the liberalism that is slowly changing the complexion of American Protestantism. Indeed, some of the younger generation of pastors ride high on the wave of the new orthodoxy that proclaims its allegiance to such men as Kirkegaard and Barth. So they are more rigidly fundamentalist, more pietistic, and more hostile to all other intellectual currents than were some of their ecclesiastical predecessors. In rather ironical contrast to all this, outward conformity to the ideals of the market place leaves nothing to be desired. Like other "executives" these young prophets of doom hold office hours, keep secretaries busy, introduce Girl and Boy

Scout troops into their churches, organize basketball teams, write their annual reports of souls lost and gained in horrifyingly businesslike terms. The competitive spirit and the pecuniary instinct, to use Veblen's terms, are as highly developed in them as in other professional groups.

I once happened to see the annual report of one young pastor of Kirkegaardian leanings. Subtracting the number of deaths and those who had moved away from the congregation from the number of newly baptized, confirmed, and transferred members, he wrote down coolly that he had for the year "a net gain of 18 souls." As smoke indicates fire, such stylistic inroads of the materialistic spirit betoken, I fear, that not everything is well in the temple of the new orthodoxy. But let me tell another story from the life of this young man.

In the year 1940 he and his wife ministered to a small Norwegian community in Iowa. Their house was cozy, comfortable, and modern. They owned an electric refrigerator, a radio, a car. Their first child, a son, had just been born. On the Sunday morning that he was to be baptized his mother bathed and dressed him with added care, gave him his bottle and burped him. Just before they left for the church the infant began to scream, lustily and healthily. The nervous mother looked for a pin that might be sticking him. Everything was as it should be. So she patted him for another burp. Nothing availed. The baby screamed. And then the mother said, "There you see, there's nothing wrong with him. It's original sin that makes him cry like this."

Do we really think that mentally healthy citizens of today and tomorrow can be brought up by mothers whose minds are thus burdened by the sombre myths of the race? Isn't there a middle way between Kirkegaard and that shallow optimism which believes that the wickedness of the human heart can be conquered with a little "child psychology"?

As I have said before, the leaders of Norwegian American life through its various periods, the official spokesmen for the group, have tended to identify it with the Lutheran Church. This attitude seeped down to the masses and was further reinforced by the fact that until recently most Norwegian American history was written by authors who were in one way or another church-affiliated. Yet, there were countercurrents, some of them very articulate, which will be treated in a later chapter. And there is also enough incidental evidence to suggest that there were many others, less articulate, who did not feel at home in the church of their fathers.

Kristofer Janson, poet, writer, and Unitarian minister who lived in Minneapolis in the 'eighties and published there a religious magazine, has in his autobiography printed letters from his readers, most of them Norwegian farmers. Several of them said that they had been Unitarians for many years without knowing it, that in Janson's religious philosophy they found the peace they had sought in vain in the Lutheran Church. One Minnesota farmer wrote about his experiences at a Norwegian Lutheran church convention where, after listening for two days to the dialectical hairsplitting on theological issues like "justification by faith" and "atonement" and watching the cavilling minds of the Norwegian Synod preachers at work, he decided that it was all humbug, theological nonsense, and evil priestcraft.

Homesteading out on the Dakota prairie, Knute Steenerson spent his first bleak winter reading Darwin, Spencer, Ingersoll, and the writings of the Norwegian labor leader, Marcus Thrane. Many years later he wrote:

> After long study I moved out of the orthodox faith and into the faith of Robert Ingersoll, and I must say that it seemed a great relief to get rid of the fear of hell and damnation. It took a long time to free myself of the superstitions which had been instilled into me, but I gradually did so, and I felt like a bird getting out of a cage or a slave set free. I felt better and slept better, for it is horrible to think that some people's souls are tortured in eternity without end. After I changed my faith the world seemed different to me; and today, after forty years without an orthodox faith, I feel assured of a peaceful sleep in all future eternity.

In the 1930's one of the church leaders wrote to a friend about a mutual acquaintance: "He is a very independent thinker and is of the type that usually works his way out of our Church just because our preachers are a little bit hesitant when it comes to a man who does his own thinking. I noticed that even his own pastor was a little afraid of him. He has always taken a large interest in the Church but from time to time they feel almost as if he does not belong, as his way of thinking is not the usual obedient type that we have so much among us."

In the course of a correspondence in 1943 with a member of the administration of one of the Norwegian Lutheran colleges, a Chicago attorney, Olaf Ray, known for his wide interest in and devotion to

Norwegian American affairs, explained his attitude toward the Lutheran Church and its clergy:

> You compared me to Bjørnstjerne Bjørnson . . . regarding my attitude toward ministers. That I will answer a little more fully in a future letter, in the meantime be it said briefly: Our ministers, mostly Lutheran ones, are strangers to the message of Christ in the Sermon on the Mount; they advocate nothing for the betterment of our life here on earth; they are *callous* to the sufferings of our "Forgotten men and women" except for charity which the parishioners are to extend. They picture heaven as their refuge, taking their worldly interests away by illusions about a life hereafter, which no sincere man, with all his senses preserved, can truthfully describe to anyone. They make our people (in Chicago) absolutely indifferent to political matters and social advancement which must come through our government. They teach hell and torment like in the Middle Ages, when Huss and Luther rose in protest to church cruelties. The *Church* is a *business* institution and not one for public welfare. The churches are all out for free enterprise like in our commercial spoils system.

Such critical minds as this do play a role in the present-day picture of Norwegian American life. Ever increasing is the number of the descendants of the immigrants who view the church as the social agency that it is rather than as a custodian of eternal verities that are not.

16

Two Colleges

IN AUGUST, 1861, *Emigranten,* most important of the Norwegian American newspapers of that period, carried an announcement that the "Norwegian Lutheran School for the Education of Ministers" would open on September 1. The readers welcomed this news, for many of them had been alarmed by the articles which during the spring and summer had revealed the "southern sympathies" of the Synod leaders and of the German institution in Missouri where their future ministers then received their training. The hierarchy itself felt that the time had come when they could no longer be a burden to another church. The new school opened in temporary quarters, a vacant parsonage a few miles outside the town of La Crosse, Wisconsin. Two professors with their families, a handful of students, a caretaker and his family crowded into the house, which for a year was to shelter what was sometimes grandiloquently called the "Norwegian University." The next year the school was moved to Decorah, Iowa, the site originally chosen for it. There Luther College, or as it was known among the immigrants, *presteskolen i Decorah* (the preachers' school in Decorah), expanded steadily, training Norwegian young men in the strict classical tradition of the Old World *gymnasium* as well as in theology. Responsible for the tone and direction of the institution was its first president, Laur. Larsen, who during his forty-one years in that office built Luther College from a primitive pioneer school into a college of reputable, even high, standing in the Middle West.

The start was difficult. Wealthy Norwegian farmers were not numerous, and it was upon the farmers that the Synod depended for its financial existence. Nevertheless, they shouldered the burden, for, as Larsen later wrote, "there was so much Lutheran spirit among them that they knew it to be the duty of Christians, if at all able to do so, to provide for the propagation and preservation of the Word of God among them through their own efforts; and that under all circum-stances it is a sin to go to Jews and pagans or even to erring sects asking them to help in the building up of a church of the true faith."

To acquaint himself with the mechanics of running a college Larsen visited several American institutions, among them the University of Wisconsin, Beloit College, the University of Michigan, and Oberlin College, which he described censoriously as the very "pinnacle of Yankee humbug and conceit." Laxness of discipline, easy-going instruction, decline of classical studies, and the emphasis on natural sciences, par-ticularly in the universities, he viewed with horror. These were the trends he fought at Luther College. There an atmosphere of strict, paternalistic control prevailed, the students' days being regulated from six in the morning until ten at night. As one might expect, Larsen's attitude toward the larger forces that, as he saw it, threatened his well-ordered Christian universe was stiff-necked, uncompromising, and not without acerbity. In a series of articles, "Some Thoughts of Our Times," published in 1875 in the Synod periodical, *Kirketidende,* of which he was the editor, he denounced with restrained passion four major evils: the spread of Marxism, the growing intellectual and economic power of the Jews, the spirit of Enlightenment and the naturalism of science, and above all papal power, the pope being *the* Antichrist. To fight these evils was the responsibility of the Lutheran Church, which, more than any other branch of Christendom, had been vouchsafed a deep grasp of scriptural truth.

To protect the minds of the students and to steep them deeply in Christianity and the classics Larsen called to his faculty linguists and scholars from Norway's university; so, an Old World atmosphere hung oppressively over the college until well into the 'eighties. Perhaps the only dissenter was Andrew Veblen—brother of Thorstein and like him a graduate of non-Lutheran Carleton College in Northfield, Minnesota— who taught at Luther from 1877 to 1881. And even he had to conform outwardly as long as he stayed. At any rate, when, later on, he filled out a questionnaire that is preserved among the Veblen papers at the Min-nesota State Historical Society, he answered the question concerning church affiliation with a somewhat belated defiance: "Lutheran Church until 1881."

Andrew Veblen's unpublished biographical manuscript, "At Luther College, 1877–1881" is a rich source of information. He notes, for in-stance, that the Norwegian "Fru" was used in addressing pastors' wives and certain of the faculty wives, while others were mere "Mrs." "In some way," he wrote, "it was a gradation in which Mrs. was an undefinable degree lower than Fru." So the Veblens thought it somewhat singular that, though they were the only "Americans" on the campus, President Larsen introduced Mrs. Veblen as "Fru Veblen," thus setting a precedent that was followed during their stay on the campus.

Knowing the unfavorable opinion Synod people had of American institutions, Veblen was even a little surprised that he, a Carleton graduate, had been appointed to a teaching post at Luther. Of one of the most prominent members of the faculty, Professor Thrond Bothne, Veblen says that he was "an extreme case of the professional Norwegian of that time; the worst he could say of one was that he was 'Americanized.' Having come there as an American, or rather as *the* American of the faculty, I naturally enough wondered what judgment he made as a consequence of the hardly polite looking over he gave me when I was introduced to him." Of this thoroughly Norwegian professor, Veblen remarks further that "his constant criticism when questions of practice or policy arose, as in faculty meetings, was 'thus we do at home.' . . . Neither did he seem to accept as decisive what might be the practice or custom of the Germans [Missouri Synod], whose standards and opinions in those days counted for so much among the leading lights at the College, as well as among the theologians and laymen generally of the Synod."

Veblen's first assignment was to teach, in Norwegian and from a Norwegian textbook, first-year Latin. During his second year he taught English. "When I came there [1877]," he observed, "I think English and Norwegian were used to about an equal extent among the boys on the campus," except for baseball, which "could hardly be played except in English. It was the chief sport cultivated at L.C. and I believe one is justified in crediting the gradual Americanization of the College partly to the influence of this, the 'national' game." Even so, one is amazed to hear that when Veblen left Luther College only four years later, "English had practically displaced Norwegian as the language of the campus and largely so in the everyday intercourse between the students, as well as among those of the teachers who had been reared in this country. . . . But in many important matters the College continued long to be patterned on Norwegian (and German) practice and methods."

From the memoirs of an English farmer who lived in Decorah between 1869 and 1879 we see other aspects of the college life through the eyes of a non-Norwegian observer:

A fine Luther College . . . stood on a hill overlooking the town. It had a strong faculty, headed by a president of marked ability. They turned out well educated scholars, many of whom have made names for themselves in the literary and scholastic world. The students organized a glee club, giving public recitals, which brought forth generous applause, especially those parts which were rendered without instrumental accompaniment, in which they certainly did excel. . . . The professors of the Norwegian Luther College, with their wives, were constant visitors [at the town skating rink], skating perhaps with a little more sedateness than the students. . . . The students of course were in their element, and figures of eight, the outside edge backwards, and similar movements not easily acquired by the tyro, were executed by them as a mere matter of routine.

Undoubtedly the most graceful and daring skater was the daughter of the principal of the College. She was always the centre of attraction. . . . My wife used to call on her mother at the College, always meeting with a kindly welcome, accompanied by the appearance of cake and wine.

Gradually the college Americanized, revising its curriculum away from an exclusively classical and Norwegian foundation, including the study of English history and literature, and even some science. When the students started a college paper in 1884, the editors declared, very much to the discomfort of the older faculty members, that "English is now unquestionably the reigning language at Luther College. . . . We are citizens of America, and the more Americanized we can become the better." As these changes took place, the college became less and less a school for the training of prospective ministers and more and more an ordinary liberal arts college. And many of its graduates distinguished themselves in various fields: Ludvig Hektoen, world-famous pathologist; J. C. M. Hanson, founder of the Library of Congress catalog system; Laurits Swenson, during his long diplomatic career, United States Minister to Denmark, Switzerland, Norway, and Holland; John Granrud, Latin scholar at the University of Minnesota; Sigurd B. Hustvedt, scholar of balladry at the University of California; his brother, Olaf M. Hustvedt, Vice Admiral in the United States Navy;

Bryn J. Hovde, president of the New School for Social Research until recently and an eminent historian. This is but a random selection that could be tripled in length without straining.

After the first World War, some of the Luther leaders, realizing that the college was at a disadvantage in having to compete with coeducational institutions, urged that women be admitted. But the church body (Norwegian Lutheran Church of America) would not easily consent. Only in 1936, after the school had gone through some years of financial difficulty, was the change finally approved. Today, although it preserves its heritage, Luther College is as liberal in its curriculum and educational outlook as a school supported by a powerful and conservative church group can possibly be. Still, almost ninety per cent of its student body of nine hundred come from Lutheran homes, most of them Norwegian, in Iowa, Minnesota and Wisconsin.

St. Olaf College has not had on its faculty nor among its graduates as many distinguished scholars as Luther College, largely because it lacks the classical spirit—with its emphasis on scholarship in a few strictly circumscribed fields—which the Decorah college owed to its first president, Laur. Larsen. Rather, the pietistic inclinations of J. N. Kildahl, St. Olaf's forceful president after its pioneer days, diffused over the campus an aura of anti-intellectualism. But with the decline of the classical tradition at Luther, the balance of academic prestige gradually began to swing toward the expanding Northfield college, which had come under the hand of a vigorous, far-sighted president, Lars W. Boe. During his administration St. Olaf College made its bow to the world through the novels of Ole E. Rölvaag, head of the Norwegian department, and through its a cappella choir under the direction of Norwegian-born F. Melius Christiansen, for four decades head of the music department. Singing Bach chorales and reviving the fine old Lutheran hymns, this choir, travelling all through the nation, brought the Old World tradition of a cappella music to a country that, when Christiansen first began his work, knew only the glee club. The big cities of America listened in amazement to choristers from the little midwestern college they had never heard of. Christiansen's exacting standards, his unflagging patience with untrained voices, his vivid personality, and his fine musicianship year after year molded choirs of students that sang with a technical precision and a freshness of spirit which baffled and stirred to paens of praise—and I'm not exaggerating— even the most jaded of critics in metropolitan centers.

What kind of a college was this that could produce music more germane to the vaulted cathedrals of Europe than to the plush-curtained concert stages of America? Most of the credit goes, of course, to the individual, F. Melius Christiansen, who had spent his musical youth in Norway and, later, had studied in Leipzig with Gustav Schreck, the famous choir master of St. Thomasschule. But secondarily, at least, this unique musical achievement must be seen against the background of the cultural climate at the college. Christiansen himself has said, "You don't need to be a Norwegian Lutheran to sing Bach, Lindeman, Mendelssohn, and Brahms well." But, on the other hand, one cannot summarily dismiss the impact of a richly Lutheran influence upon the receptive personalities of eighteen- and nineteen-year-old youths who are constantly told by their president that they are "bringing a religious message to the world through song." Religious idealism, closely tied in with other campus activities, was, indeed, one of the choir's marked characteristics year after year. This was still so when, between 1933 and 1937, I was a member of the choir.

As I see it, both good and bad cultural influences have emanated from St. Olaf. No doubt the college has earned our gratitude for having nursed and promoted the genius of a Rölvaag and of a Christiansen. But then, this was first done for the sake of nationalist and fundamentalist propaganda. Only after America at large had responded to these two men as artists, without any hyphen or axe to grind, did the college authorities follow suit. Lars W. Boe, in particular, during whose long presidency both artists developed, was broad enough to see that Rölvaag and Christiansen made significant contributions to the larger stream of American culture. And he stood firm in the defense of Rölvaag when his realistic novels aroused many conservative Norwegian Lutherans to cries of blasphemy. In return Rölvaag and Christiansen rescued St. Olaf College from the mediocrity that is the fate of the overwhelming majority of sectarian educational institutions. Nevertheless, more than a decade after Rölvaag's death, when his novels had long been translated into many languages and his name secure in the history of American literature, there was still a stubborn, narrow-minded, pious group who fought the proposal that a newly erected college library be named after Rölvaag. A vote of the alumni, whose contributions had financed the building, was necessary to settle the issue. Finally the new library, as well as the college, was honored by the name of the great novelist.

The nationalistic spirit at St. Olaf, strong though it was, has never been quite so intense as at Luther, largely because the majority of its teachers, even the Norwegian-born of the earlier years, received their training in America. Until very recently the students of Norwegian ancestry were required to take a year's work in the Norwegian department, either a course in the language or one in Norwegian literature in translation. The study of the language, formerly enforced in tribalistic fervor, is now merely regarded as desirable. Ibsen and Bjørnson are produced regularly under the auspices of the Norwegian department, not only, I like to think, to keep Norwegian alive in the campus community, but also to educate the public's taste for what is good in the world's dramatic literature. Even so, the majority of the students of the late 'twenties and of the 'thirties would have preferred to be indifferent to their background, but since that was difficult at St. Olaf, they chose to be somewhat scornful. More recently, under the impact of Norway's war experiences and of post-war exchanges of students and professors, that mood has given way to one of appreciation. Completely secure in their Americanism, the present-day students discover the pleasure of acquaintance with a rich, old civilization, a pleasure enhanced, I daresay, by the knowledge that their forebears were part and parcel of it.

The college itself, like the church, has remained fundamentally conservative and refractory to the more liberal currents in American religious thought. Several courses in religion, taught, of course, within the pale of Lutheran doctrine, are required of each graduating student unless his affiliation with another church body prevents him from accepting religious instruction outside his own church. Among the seventeen hundred students in 1947–1948 only two hundred were non-Lutherans; sixty-seven were Methodists, twenty-seven Presbyterians, twenty-two Congregationalists, fourteen Catholics, eleven Episcopalians, eleven Baptists, and the rest scattered.

Not many years ago a student in a religion class stirred the fury of the professor by venturing the mildly heretical question that so long as people believed that Jesus was the Son of God and the Savior of mankind what difference did it make what sect they belonged to. Scenting the threat of defection, the professor, pacing in front of the class in glowering agitation, staccatoed a warning, "Beware, beware, you are getting on dangerous ground, you are getting on dangerous ground!" There are degrees of conservatism certainly, and this professor represents the extreme right in the faculty, but the distance between the right and the left at St. Olaf is not great.

No doubt the strong strain of Haugean piety that runs through Norwegian Lutheranism accounts for some of the taboos that still exist on the campus. Dancing, smoking, and drinking are frowned upon; only men students may smoke in their rooms and off-campus. Needless to say, the students hanker after the forbidden fruit and many a rule is broken. All this cannot but create an atmosphere of petty friction, which, in fact, helps to destroy what it so ineptly tries to preserve. Sometimes the height of the ridiculous is reached, such as when a woman faculty member addressed the girls of the choir, about to leave on one of its tours, reminding them that the rules of the college went with them. "No woman who smokes can sing, 'Blessed is He Who cometh in the name of the Lord,' without being blasphemous," she piously concluded.

The members of the college staff are carefully selected, primarily for their religious and national backgrounds, only secondarily for professional training and achievement. Non-Lutherans have taught in the physical education, language, home economics, and a few other departments, but they are a small minority. Most of the faculty are themselves graduates of Norwegian Lutheran colleges, many from St. Olaf, having returned after a few years of graduate study. Broader ideas they may have acquired at the universities are soon obliterated by the dominant conservative current. But it is only fair to say that there are a few of scholarly distinction. The administration, grateful for the prestige they give to the institution, is not likely to bother with their orthodoxy as long as they observe the forms and do not give offense.

Yet on the whole, even Boe's forceful personality—and St. Olaf for a generation was Boe—could not stem the tides of Americanization and secularization. When he once sought to bring to his faculty the brilliant son of an outstanding pioneer churchman, the young man courteously declined. Apparently he did not feel, as Boe put it to him, that he owed it to "his people" and "his church" to be one of them. Financially Boe was often more successful. Once he got ten thousand dollars for the college through Olaf Ray, the Chicago lawyer I mentioned before, who referred to himself as "an old radical" and was as a rule more impressed by labor than by church leaders. But then in such cases the appeal was humanitarian rather than religious, and nationalistic only in a harmless and sentimental way.

17

The Press

Two Norwegian farmers and a Scotch Norwegian immigrant in the Muskego settlement were the fathers of the Norwegian American press. They scraped together two hundred dollars for equipment, set it up in one of their log cabins, and hired a Norwegian typesetter who had worked on the *Chicago Tribune*. Edited by the talented Scotch Norwegian, James Denoon Reymert, the newspaper, *Nordlyset* (*The Northern Light*), first appeared on July 29, 1847, in the village of Norway, Racine County, Wisconsin.* On its front page was a Norwegian translation of the Declaration of Independence. Politically it was "Free Soil."

Since the publication of *Nordlyset* over a century ago the Norwegian American group has not, except for a few weeks in the late 1840's, been without a newspaper of its own. More than five hundred different newspapers and periodicals have found their way into Norwegian American homes, a number of them, to be sure, only a sheet or two and short-lived. These newspapers served and influenced the immigrants in three important ways. They taught the first generation the American way of life through the easier medium of the native language; they were a clearing house for many social and religious convictions stoutly held and hotly debated among the immigrants; they kept alive memories and knowledge of Norway, and, in doing this, were one of the conservative forces that helped to maintain the identity of the group. It is not surprising then that the peak in the number of such publications and, presumably, in circulation and influence was reached in the decade of the 1880's. By now there is only a remnant left. Such decline is only natural, and, as I see it, desirable.

* In January, 1847, the newspaper *Scandinavia* appeared in New York City. Sponsored by a Scandinavian society there, it published news from the Scandinavian countries and about Norwegians, Danes, and Swedes in America, using both the Danish and Swedish language. Although it had some eighty subscribers among the Norwegian settlers in Wisconsin, it did not gain much of a foothold in the Middle West.

Nordlyset, which from lack of funds was forced to discontinue before it was two years old, was followed by *Democraten,* edited by Knud Langeland, one of the striking figures in the history of the Norwegian American press. Langeland bought the printing apparatus of the defunct *Nordlyset* and for a year and a half issued his paper. In the meantime the church leaders were not idle. As early as 1847 the dynamic Clausen appealed to the congregations for support of a church paper. *Maanedstidende (Monthly Times),* which appeared first in January, 1851, later changing its name to *Kirketidende (Church Times),* was the official organ of the Norwegian Synod. This stirred the Haugeans into action. Still in the same year, as part of their campaign in defense of lay preaching, they launched a rival paper of their own.

Meanwhile, Clausen was organizing a Scandinavian Press Association to direct the publication of the church paper, of a secular paper, and of other safe and sound reading material for the immigrants. During its first year this association was almost entirely in the hands of the clergy, albeit the majority of the shares were owned by laymen. Clausen was the first editor of the secular paper, *Emigranten,* which as one would expect voiced the attitudes of the Synod clergy. Politically it started out as an independent Democratic paper, for a time in the middle 'fifties was a Whig organ, then with the organization of the Republican Party took up the anti-slavery cause, becoming more and more pro-abolition. Although other papers were started in the 'fifties to counteract the influence of *Emigranten,* they soon languished and this leading pioneer paper had no serious competitor until *Faedrelandet (The Fatherland)* began to appear in 1864 at La Crosse, Wisconsin.

From 1857 to 1868 *Emigranten* was under the editorship of C. F. Solberg, one of the ablest of the pioneer editors. Born in Norway and educated at a select school in Denmark, he was every inch a young gentleman wearing broadcloth and kid gloves when he came in 1853 with his family to the primitive surroundings of Ole Bull's Oleana colony in Pennsylvania, his father having been engaged as its director. The failure of the project sent young Solberg west and into the newspaper profession. During the Civil War period *Emigranten* had close to four thousand subscribers, but when one remembers that papers very often passed from family to family it seems safe to say that Solberg's editorials found fifteen to twenty thousand readers. In 1868 he sold *Emigranten* to *Faedrelandet* in La Crosse.

Of the nine or ten Norwegian newspapers in the Middle West up to the end of the Civil War, all but two were published in Wisconsin, then the center of Norwegian activities in the New World. The old columns of this press are a fine record of the variety of political opinion as well as the changing political temper among the pioneers. There were Free Soilers, Democrats, and Whigs among the editors; verbal battles were pitched, but from them the settlers learned something about the American political scene. Most of the early immigrants were sympathetic to the party of Jefferson and Jackson, but as the Democrats became more and more pro-slavery allegiance began to shift to the newly founded Republican Party. In the late 'fifties the swing to the Republican ranks became so outspoken that the few Democratic papers either closed shop or quietly turned color. By 1860 there was enthusiastic support for the Republican candidate, Abraham Lincoln. C. F. Solberg was an ardent Lincoln supporter; Knud Langeland, who wrote persuasively in the columns of *Emigranten* and elsewhere, perhaps did more than any other single individual to lead his countrymen into the Republican camp.

Most of the editors conscientiously tried to educate the immigrants about their new country. During political campaigns biographies of the candidates were printed and histories of the United States were run in serial form. Information about new states was constantly supplied to the readers; letters from the California gold fields and western territories were printed. Editors sometimes turned roving reporters themselves and travelled through the settlements to get first-hand information on frontier conditions. Thus did Johan Schröder of *Faedrelandet og Emigranten* and Svein Nilsson, editor of *Billed-magazin* (Madison, Wisconsin), the first magazine published among the Norwegians. Although the latter existed only during 1868 and 1869, it is important historically for the series of interviews with pioneers which Nilsson published after visiting numerous settlements. *Nordisk Folkeblad,* a Minneapolis paper, printed Paul Hjelm Hansen's glowing reports of his scouting trip, thus helping to direct the immigrant stream into the Red River Valley. From articles in their press the immigrants also learned new methods of farming, what kind of crops to raise, what kind of machinery to use. And in the advertisements they were not only encouraged to buy stoves and furniture for their homes, they were urged to cure their ailments with chill tonics, stomach bitters, and "family" pills, guaranteed to relieve physical distress at all ages.

After the Civil War three newspapers, *Skandinaven* in Chicago,

Decorah-posten, and *Minneapolis Tidende* emerged as the principal organs. *Skandinaven,* founded by an energetic Chicago immigrant, John Anderson, in 1866 had the strongest political policy of the three, taking a stand-pat Republican course throughout its career, except when the influence of the elder La Follette on the Republican Party gave it a Progressive tinge. Under the guiding hand of Knud Langeland, its first editor, it took a vigorous stand in support of the public school in opposition to those demanding a parochial school system among the Norwegian Lutherans. In recognition of this stand one of Chicago's public schools perpetuates Langeland's name. In the many squabbles that arose among the Norwegian Lutherans *Skandinaven* did not take a strongly partisan stand though it tended to favor low church ideas over the high church inclinations of the Norwegian Synod. Svein Nilsson, Peter Hendricksen, a professor of Greek, and Nicolay A. Grevstad, who had been editor of *Dagbladet,* leading organ of the liberal party in Norway, before coming to America and who during his career was American Minister to Uruguay and Paraguay, were among the outstanding editors of this newspaper which served the Norwegians faithfully for three-quarters of a century. It ceased publication in 1940.

Decorah-posten, started in 1874 by Brynild Anundsen in the stronghold of the Norwegian Synod, was independent and moderate in its political outlook, tranquil about the social and ecclesiastical problems that were forever disturbing the Norwegian Americans, and the most literary of the big three. Immigrants welcomed its supplement, *Ved Arnen (By the Hearth),* which had reading material for both old and young, and games and puzzles. So it came to be the "family" newspaper throughout the rural communities of Iowa, Minnesota, and the Dakotas. Writing about pioneer days in a North Dakota community, J. P. Hertsgaard observes: "I do not recall what English language newspaper was first taken in our house, but everyone read one or more of the Norwegian papers published. Quite a number took *Amerika* published in Madison, Wis., by Rasmus B. Anderson. . . . Perhaps the most read paper was *Skandinaven.* . . . Father always took *Decorah-Posten,* because as he said, it was such a peaceable paper; no politics and nothing controversial." Among its editors have been Johannes B. Wist and Kristian Prestgard whose literary talents set the tone of the paper. Today, under the editorship of Einar Lund, it is the only midwestern Norwegian newspaper of any significance.

Founded in 1866 by Thorvald Guldbransen, a North Dakota newspaperman who saw that Minneapolis was becoming the center of Norwegian life, *Minneapolis Tidende* grew steadily, absorbing other publications in the area until it became the largest newspaper in the upper northwest region. Under the editorship of able and thoughtful men like Sigvart Sorenson and Carl G. O. Hansen, who is now editor of the monthly magazine of the Sons of Norway, the paper "gave particular attention to the cultural life of the Norwegian Americans," writes Blegen, "and was noted for its articles and reviews in the fields of literature and music and for its admirable weekly 'summary of the political, social, literary, artistic, and intellectual life of Norway.'" In 1935 *Minneapolis Tidende* fell victim to the depression; its subscriber lists were taken over by the *Decorah-posten.*

On the West Coast many newspapers appeared as the Norwegian population there grew, but *Washington Posten,* established in Seattle in 1889 and long the favorite of western Norwegians, is the only one still in existence. For many years it was edited by Gunnar Lund, who took a leading part in Norwegian American affairs in the Pacific Northwest.

Since 1891 eastern Norwegians have read *Nordisk Tidende,* published from the heart of the Norwegian colony in Brooklyn. Under the management of its long-time owner, Sigurd J. Arneson, and its successive editors, A. N. Rygg, Hans Olav, and Carl Søyland, it became the largest of the Norwegian newspapers, a distinction it still holds.

Although the Norwegian American press has been overwhelmingly a Republican press, there were occasional defections from the line. A few newspapers in the Red River Valley region like *Normanden* (Grand Forks, North Dakota) and *Nye Normanden* (Moorhead, Minnesota), both under the editorship of the Norwegian American novelist, H. A. Foss, during the late 'eighties and early 'nineties became organs for the Populist Party. But the newspapers, like the farmers of the region, settled back into the Republican Party when good times returned, if they did not cease altogether.

Like many American newspapers of the nineteenth century, the Norwegian American papers had, as a rule, a literary section for poetry, essays, and novels. Bjørnson, at the height of his popularity in Norway, was being read eagerly on the American frontier in weekly installments. Also, Bjørnson wrote in 1873–1874 for the Chicago *Skandinaven* a special series of letters in which he discussed the current social and political issues of Norway.

Many immigrants and their children owe their first acquaintance with America's classics to translations that appeared in these news-papers. Agnes Larson, professor of history at St. Olaf College, still remembers how an older sister read Irving's story of Rip Van Winkle to them aloud in Norwegian from the literary supplement of *Decorah-posten*. Another historian, Laurence M. Larson, who was president of the American Historical Asociation at the time of his death in 1938, recalls in his reminiscences, *The Log Book of a Young Immigrant,* his mother's interest in Cooper's *Deerslayer,* which ran serially in their Norwegian weekly. He himself first came to know one of his favorite authors, Charles Dickens, when *Oliver Twist* appeared weekly for several months.

Some of the newspapers operated book departments, providing for the scanty literary needs of their readers. John Anderson, publisher of *Skandinaven,* had such a department, described by Birger Osland in his reminiscences, *A Long Pull From Stavanger.* In his first year in America, Osland, like many another newcomer, was befriended by the kind-hearted Anderson who gave him a minor clerical position.

> Anderson not only imported books from Norway and Denmark but he frequently reprinted them in his own establishment, which included a book bindery. He also published original works by Norwegian Americans. The latter were usually of a religious, linguistic, or agricultural character, more suitable for Norwegian-American folks and their living conditions than similar books pub-lished in Norway. In 1889 the manager of the book department told me that his best sellers were the Bible; Norwegian hymnbooks; *Troens Harpe (The Harp of Faith)*; *Gjest Baardsen,* the story of a master thief; *Svarteboken (The Black Book),* dealing with witch-craft; and *Farming med Hoved og Haender (Farming with Head and Hands),* which was written by the editor in chief of *Skandi-naven,* Professor Peter Hendricksen, the only member of the paper's staff in my time who was born and educated in the United States.

In addition the newspaper conducted a kind of mail order business, which Osland also describes:

> In connection with renewals or new subscriptions, the paper offered, at reduced prices, many useful articles. Among them were harvest-ing machines, house organs, lawn mowers, watches, books, and

pictures, articles which the paper bought at factory prices and sold to subscribers at less than current retail prices. The manufacturers delivered the articles direct to the purchasers. This extra business created considerable income for the paper, for all payments were made in cash in advance.

Thus the newspapers, to mutual benefit, took their place in the practical as well as in the intellectual life of the first generation.

In addition to its favorite newspaper each family subscribed to the weekly or monthly religious periodical published by the church synod of which they were members. These magazines were a powerful influence in keeping the Norwegian Americans abreast of and vitally interested in Lutheran affairs. Religious tracts, too, were published by several of the newspaper establishments, the huge sale of which undoubtedly helped to keep the concerns on a sound economic footing.

Norwegians in America also had their own literary magazines and illustrated monthlies, the first of which was *Billed-magazin,* founded in 1868 in Madison, Wisconsin, and designed to instruct as well as to entertain. Others like *Ved Arnen,* the literary supplement of *Decorah-posten,* and *For Hjemmet (For the Home),* another Decorah publication, were particularly popular during the 'seventies and 'eighties. On a higher level was *Symra,* a later literary venture of *Decorah-posten's* editors, Wist and Prestgard. Simultaneously a similar magazine, *Vor Tid (Our Time),* was appearing in Minneapolis, one of whose editors was the gifted Peer Strømme. Among several children's magazines *Ungdommens Ven (Young People's Friend),* published in Minneapolis and edited by N. N. Rønning was long a favorite of the younger generation. As the twentieth century advanced more magazines appeared, brave and glossy for a few months or at best a few years, and then were seen no more.

The distinctly Scandinavian tradition of issuing illustrated Christmas periodicals became a feature of the Norwegian American magazine world after 1910. Gayly decorated with peasant art or religious motifs, they contained colored illustrations, stories, poetry, travelogues, and even music for Christmas songs. The outstanding one among them was *Jul i Vesterheimen (Christmas in the Homes of the West)* which was started in 1911. Through the years one sees among its contributors such well-known Norwegian American literary names as Waldemar Ager, O. E. Rölvaag, Simon Johnson, Dorothea Dahl, Georg Strandvold,

Johan and Helen Egilsrud, and Carl G. O. Hansen. Since 1926 one of these periodicals, *Christmas,* published in English by the Augsburg Publishing House in Minneapolis and edited by Randolph Haugan, has achieved great success and a wide circulation beyond the Norwegian American group.

Yet another type of publication came off the printing presses for the Norwegians in America: the *bygdelag* periodicals. The *bygdelags* were organizations of immigrants who came from the same *bygd* or district in Norway, who through the publications of their organizations kept alive the dialect and local traditions of their native communities and preserved the personal histories of members of their clan. The earliest example of this type of publication was *Wossingen,* a sort of newspaper made up of letters from a society of people who had emigrated from Voss and settled in Chicago. Through these letters, published in the late 'fifties and sent back to Norway, they encouraged others to emigrate. However, not until after the turn of the century did the *bygdelag* movement get into full swing and the groups begin to publish yearbooks or magazines. Andrew A. Veblen, often called the "father of the *bygdelag* movement" founded in the 'nineties the first of these, *Valdris-Helsing,* for the people from the district of Valders; he later edited a monthly magazine, *Samband,* which dealt with the affairs of all the *bygdelags.* These and dozens of others like *Telesoga, Halling-Minne, Trønderlagets Aarbok,* and *Nordfjordlagets Aarbok* have been a valuable source of immigrant history. Some of them still exist.

From pioneer days to the present the Norwegian press has attracted some very able, even brilliant, men to its editorial desks, some of them far more enlightened than their countrymen for whom they wrote. An Englishman living in Decorah, Iowa, in the 'seventies remarked that the Norwegian weekly there was "edited by a man of far more than ordinary talent, and one well worth while to know." In the 1920's Nils P. Haugen, toward the close of a long career of public service both in the nation's capital and in his native state of Wisconsin, observed that the Norwegian press seemed to him as well, and in its editorials frequently better informed than the American newspapers of comparable circulation. "Editors of the foreign-language papers were and are, as a rule, men of a more liberal education than the majority of the English [language] press." Some like Peer Strømme, Waldemar Ager, H. A. Foss, and Kristian Prestgard were literary figures in their own right. Others like Rasmus B. Anderson, Thrond Bothne, and Peter Hendricksen were language and literature professors. Nicolay A. Grevstad and Gunnar Lund had taken law degrees in Norway before emigrating to America. Carl G. O. Hansen has long been known as an accomplished choral conductor and music critic. In addition he, as well as others like A. N. Rygg, have delved into the history of the Norwegians in America and made valuable contributions. Obviously it is impossible to do justice to all the individual talent and character devoted to the Norwegian American press. Perhaps the story of one editor, Kristian Prestgard of the *Decorah-posten,* will give us a picture of how many currents of American life met in the office of one professional Norwegian in the new country.

18

An Editor and His Friends

On a shelf in the archives of the Norwegian-American Historical Association in Rölvaag Memorial Library at St. Olaf College there is a section of several dozen large brown envelopes labelled "Kristian Prestgard Correspondence." The index sheet reads like a Who's Who of Norwegian Americans; but there one finds also the names of prominent Norwegians; Johan Falkberget, the novelist, C. J. Hambro, president of the Storting, Halvdan Koht, statesman and historian, Sir Karl Knudsen, Norwegian-born British industrialist and financier.

Kristian Prestgard was born in Gudbrandsdalen in 1866, and, as a correspondent for a Norwegian newspaper, came to America in 1893 to cover the Columbian Exposition. He stayed and lived here the rest of his life. In 1897 he went to the little Iowa town to work on the *Decorah-posten,* becoming co-editor with Johannes B. Wist after a few years, then in 1923 editor-in-chief until his death in January, 1946. On a hilltop site in Decorah he built himself a lovely home, which, whimsically, he named Troldhaugen, the hill of the trolls. American and Norwegian flags rippling in the breeze welcomed the many visitors from the old country and the new who came to see the master of the house. In the spacious and well-kept gardens of Troldhaugen, Prestgard devoted much time to his beloved gladioli, a hobby which almost became a second profession. Requests for his annual "glad" catalog and orders for his bulbs poured in from all over the country, and when the flowers were in bloom people came from great distances to admire them. Henry A. Wallace, when he was Secretary of Agriculture, visited Prestgard and became so interested in his hybridization and inbreeding experiments that a "gladiolus correspondence" was carried on between the two men for several years. The hobby had really developed into a business, a single block of bulbs one year bringing him $6,000. Finally unable to take care of what had become a big enterprise, Prestgard sold his entire stock of bulbs to a commercial concern, continuing, however, to receive a royalty on the varieties he had developed.

Gladioli notwithstanding, the center of Prestgard's life always was his newspaper and the problems of the Norwegian American group. His overriding purpose, to maintain centers of Norwegian culture at least here and there in middle America, brought him into close contact with Rölvaag and the circle of his friends at St. Olaf, with professors in the Scandinavian departments at midwestern universities, with historians, and with church leaders. He was the guiding spirit in the organization of a club whose chief purpose was the publication of a literary periodical, *Symra,* co-edited by the editors of *Decorah-posten.* Published from 1905 to 1914, *Symra* was by far the best literary magazine ever to appear among the Norwegians in America. The editors, in their desire to build cultural bridges, invited contributions from Norwegians as well as from Norwegian American authors. Yet *Symra* shared the fate of most little magazines, which is dubious at best, even if they do not represent a particularist interest.

Prestgard was an ardent supporter of the Norwegian American museum in Decorah, working with the Luther professors and with other Decorah citizens on a project for housing the pioneer relics. When, as an outgrowth of this work, the time seemed ripe for the organization of a Norwegian American historical society, the Decorah group met to discuss the founding of such an association. Professor Knut Gjerset of Luther College sent the records of this meeting to O. E. Rölvaag in Northfield, and during a few summer weeks visited leaders in the Norwegian centers of the upper Middle West trying to interest them in the project. When it was decided that invitations for an organizational meeting be sent out for October, 1925, Prestgard shrewdly advised that it be held in Northfield the day before an important two-day conference of the Norwegian Lutheran Church was scheduled to be held in Minneapolis, thus insuring the presence of several interested churchmen. The Norwegian-American Historical Association was founded at that meeting on October 6, 1925. Appointed to the board of editors, Prestgard threw himself into work that was very close to his heart. His voluminous correspondence with Theodore C. Blegen, managing editor of the association's publications, and the other officers— Rölvaag and J. J. Thompson of St. Olaf, D. G. Ristad, a Wisconsin Lutheran pastor, Birger Osland, a Chicago investment banker, and Laurence M. Larson, professor of history at the University of Illinois—

testifies abundantly to his great concern for the success of the association.

One can also through these letters follow the development of other projects being carried on within the Norwegian American group. For many years Professor Gjerset of Luther College had been compiling material for an encyclopedia of Norwegian Americans, which at the time of his death in 1936 was uncompleted. Realizing the historical interest of such a publication, Prestgard continued collecting *vitae*, hoping to keep the work going until someone could take it over. So far the project is still unfinished.

Prestgard was well aware of the cultural difference between the group his newspaper served and that served by the Brooklyn *Nordisk Tidende*. In a letter written during the war years to the Norwegian historian, Halvdan Koht, he touched on this subject. *Decorah-posten* still used old-fashioned Gothic type and the old Dano-Norwegian spelling. Yet, Prestgard envied the *Nordisk Tidende* its modern garb; the difference between the two papers, he felt, exactly mirrored the difference between the two groups. *Nordisk Tidende's* readers came over "last year," he wrote figuratively, making Brooklyn really a suburb of Oslo and a near neighbor to Stavanger, while *Decorah-posten's* readers have been on the prairies over a hundred years. The second, third, and even fourth generations learned their Norwegian from the *Decorah-posten;* so their language was the Norwegian of a hundred years ago. Things reached the point, Prestgard said, that when he tried to use clippings from Norwegian papers, "the editor complained, some of the readers complained, and the typesetters were ready to start a revolution."

Prestgard's realization that he fought a losing battle also comes out from time to time in the correspondence with his friend, L. W. Boe, president of St. Olaf College. At the opening of the school year in 1935 Boe made a statement in which he noted the decline of the students' interest in the Norwegian language. When Prestgard printed an editorial on the subject, Boe thought that Prestgard attributed to him a defeatism he didn't feel. Prestgard's reply to this gentle reprimand is noteworthy. Reassuring his friend first of the communality of their feelings, he goes on to say that the inevitable must be faced. Citing his own family as an example, he mentions that one of his daughter's children, whose father was an Irish Catholic, knew nothing of Norway and its language. Yet, he is not, he says, "scolding the young people into speaking Norwegian." Boe's long reply to this letter throws light on the complex awareness of the older leaders in a disintegrating group whose youth is crossing the threshold to complete assimilation. I shall quote from it generously.

America is a country made up of minorities, religious, racial, and otherwise. It has been settled, and I think should be accepted by all who come to the United States, that our civilization is to be English, or Anglo-Saxon, fundamentally. I have little patience with those who speak of it as still being an open question. . . .

You ask if it would not be fine if, when we go into American life, we could carry with us a knowledge of the Norwegian language. There is very little of what the folks brought with them from the old country that I would not like to take with me into American life. But we know that we are not going to be able to take it all. I want to take with me everything that I consistently can. What I fear is, that without intending it the Norwegian Press and the older generation may create here a Norwegian colony, a Balkan situation, in which case our fate will simply be to be crushed under the juggernaut and thus have nothing to give. We make the mistake of not taking the time to understand nor paint the background over against which whatever development takes place must take place. We simply think of the objective values the folks brought with them, forgetting that the essential factor, which under all circumstances must be taken into consideration, is our own American national life. . . . Has the time come when we should call a meeting of men like yourself, the presidents of our colleges, the men at the head of the departments of Norwegian, the men in the young people's work in our Church, the men in the universities who are interested in Norwegian, to face this problem: in what form must and should the future Norwegian work in America be done. We cannot afford any longer to go on quarreling, as at heart we all want the same thing. Sober realities are at stake.

That nothing seems to have come of Boe's suggestion is, as I see it, just part of that "sober reality" both he and Prestgard had to face, the one as a church leader, the other as the representative of a national culture. Even so, Norwegianism among Norwegian Americans received a new impetus when the old homeland was stricken by the Germans. This tide, too, left its mark in Prestgard's correspondence, which during these years deals to a large extent with the affairs of Norwegian Relief,

Incorporated. In this he found a faithful helper in Mrs. Lucius Boomer, Norwegian-born wife of the president of the Waldorf-Astoria Corporation, an old friend whose letters had over the years added a pleasantly cosmopolitan flavor to Troldhaugen as she wrote from New York, or Norway, or from a yacht on which she cruised in the Mediterranean in the company of the Sloans and the Chryslers.

But the center of all these far-flung activities and contacts was always the *Decorah-posten,* as Halvdan Koht, Prestgard's long-time friend and correspondent, wrote in a letter published in that newspaper, April 26, 1945, on the occasion of Prestgard's seventy-ninth and last birthday.

But it goes without saying that *Decorah-posten* is your greatest work. I remember the first thing I noticed about this newspaper, the rich collection of local news from Norway which I found there. No Norwegian paper at home had anything like it. . . . Only in *Decorah-posten* could we find news of our entire country. As an old newspaper man myself, I know very well how much effort and thought and how wide a knowledge of the country is needed to gather and put in order such materials. It was love for Norway which carried the work forward. And it created love for Norway. . . . You like work and research, and what you do must be well done. That stamp you have placed on *Decorah-posten.* That is what has made the paper what it is.

THE CITIES

19

Chicago

In the autumn of 1948 the *Saturday Evening Post* ran a series of stories on families representing various ethnic groups in America. The Percy Offerdahls, a large, successful farm family living in the strongly Norwegian community of Stoughton, Wisconsin, were presented as, one must suppose, a "typical" family of Norwegian origin. In this thrifty, hard-working family the rich opportunities of modern American rural life are sketched against a background of Old World traditions— *lutefisk* church suppers, Sons of Norway meetings, *kvindeforening* (Ladies' Aid society in the Lutheran church). In the sense that it is a true portrait of a large segment of midwestern Norwegian American life I have no quarrel with the story; yet it is unfortunate that it fixates in the public mind the stereotype of the Norwegian American as a midwestern farmer. A representative picture should also include the apartment dwellers of Chicago, San Francisco, Seattle, or Brooklyn, which, incidentally, has the largest settlement of Norwegians in the United States. And because this city dweller came out of a later and changed Norway—very likely from one of her cities—to the complex life of urban America, his habits and general outlook are quite different from that of his kinsfolk in Goodhue County, Minnesota, or Stoughton, Wisconsin. The farmer immigrant found an inchoate society upon which he set his stamp; the urban immigrant found an established society which set its stamp upon him. Nevertheless, the newcomer who lived in a cheap boardinghouse in Chicago was just as much a pioneer in his way as the immigrant who lived in a sod hut on the Dakota prairie. His story, submerged in the swirl of urban life, is only now coming to the surface and taking shape. Social historians are beginning to study the less familiar urbanites, but until more data are accumulated on such groups as the Norwegians their stories will remain fragmentary.

Let us, for a moment, look in on a scene of the gay 'nineties in

Chicago, the first urban center that attracted Norwegian newcomers in large numbers. A cab, wheeling through January's icy slush, grinds to a halt in front of one of the downtown hotels and deposits a man and woman who enter the foyer, splendid in bright lights and red plush. As the couple ascends the carpeted stairway to the second floor they exchange greetings and pleasantries with others bound for the banquet room, where small groups are standing about. Conversations are carried on in Dano-Norwegian, though now and then one hears an English phrase. The women are stately in pale satin and glowing velvet gowns; the men impressive in black tails, white shirt fronts, and coat breasts studded with medals signifying their rank in this social order. The Norwegian Quartet Club, the upper crust among Chicago's thirty thousand Norwegians, is having its annual banquet and ball. Most of the men, who had come to Chicago from Norway's cities in the late 'seventies and during the 'eighties, are now successful entrepreneurs and professional people; the head of a large exporting and importing firm, a glove manufacturer, doctors, lawyers, musicians, bankers, engineers. When the banquet speeches and toasts are over, the party moves to the ballroom where the president of the club and his wife lead the dancers in the polonaise that traditionally opens the ball. Later in the evening they dance the courtly française, remembered from youthful days in Norway. As they return to their comfortable homes in Wicker Park, which among themselves they call "Hommansbyen," after the fashionable residential suburb of Oslo, they feel they have once again for an evening recaptured their dimming memories of faraway Norway.

Sixty years before this, the first Norwegians had settled in Chicago, then swampy, malaria-ridden, ugly, but full of potentialities. As caravans going to the Fox River settlement passed through the young city, some of the immigrants inevitably found its hustle more attractive than the lonely prairie toward which they were headed. Perchance, several immigrants from the district of Voss in south central Norway were among the first to stay in Chicago late in the 'thirties. This colony of Vossings grew and exerted some influence on emigration through a correspondence society and an emigration society which they established in the 'forties and 'fifties.

To counteract reports circulated by dissatisfied immigrants who had returned to their native land, the Vossings systematically wrote letters to friends giving detailed and favorable accounts of their fortunes. One correspondent wrote that Ivar Larsen Boe, who later Americanized his name to Iver Lawson, had by 1848 "acquired a considerable amount of real estate in the city and a fine home. Besides, he and his brother are half owners of a sailing vessel which he and another Norwegian bought for eighteen hundred dollars, and he is employed at the post office and has now a wage of twenty-five dollars a month." To encourage people from Voss to emigrate Lawson and a few other prosperous Vossings from Chicago visited their home district, even extending financial aid to some.

Lawson also threw himself energetically into Chicago affairs, helping to organize the Republican Party, serving on the city council, and taking a seat in the state legislature. The sizeable fortune he accumulated in real estate was wiped out in the disastrous fire of 1871. With a fellow Vossing, John Anderson, he founded the Norwegian newspaper, *Skandinaven,* in 1866. The paper was distributed to Norwegian newcomers when they arrived at the railway station in Chicago, and it was a familiar sight to see a young man carrying a suitcase walking away from the station with *Skandinaven* stuffed in the pocket of a crumpled coat. Knud Langeland, for many years editor of *Skandinaven,* was an uncle of Iver Lawson's wife. Continuing the family interest in newspaper publishing, Iver Lawson's son, Victor, bought the *Chicago Daily News* and through his business genius made it a power in the newspaper world.

Another young immigrant, Christian Jevne, came to Chicago in 1864, clerked in a store and in a few years was running his own grocery business. By the late 'seventies he owned the largest wholesale and retail firm in the city and supplied Chicago's society tables with the finest of imported wines and delicacies. His name, sometimes mistaken for French and pronounced Jevné, prompted him to employ French floor-walkers in his establishment, greatly adding to the delight of his well-to-do lady patrons. The first electric lights used in Chicago were installed in 1880 in the Jevne store, attracting street crowds night after night to witness the illumination.

Until the 'eighties and early 'nineties Chicago was the mecca of city-bound Norwegian immigrants coming west. Young girls found domestic employment in the homes of prosperous Americans until they married a machinist or bookkeeper whom they had met at one of the Norwegian social clubs. Young men followed trades, worked for other businessmen, often eventually setting up their own shops, small manufacturing plants, or, after a few years of attending night school, professional offices. Bankers, doctors, and lawyers were solidly taking root and building homes in fashionable Wicker Park. The less prosperous of the thirty to forty thousand Norwegians were clustered on and around Milwaukee Avenue, known in the 'nineties as the "Norwegian" street of Chicago. Later there was a westward movement toward the Humboldt Park neighborhood.

The Columbian Exposition of 1893 drew hundreds of Norwegians to Chicago. Construction workers were in great demand and the new-comers, many of them skilled in the building trades, found jobs at the fair. Better educated and trained than the average immigrant were the engineers, graduates of Norway's excellent technical colleges, many of whom came to Chicago during this period. Kenneth Bjork's *Saga in Steel and Concrete,* a comprehensive study of Norwegian American engineers, shows that these able young men soon made their way into top-ranking positions with the large companies which designed and constructed the transportation systems, factories, steel mills, banks, hotels, and museums that made Chicago the metropolis of the upper Middle West. The Illinois Steel Company, for example, was a distinct gravitation center for young Norwegian engineers, particularly when Norwegian-born and trained Leonard Holmboe was the company's assistant chief engineer from 1889 to 1898, to become chief engineer until his retirement in 1931. Several of these technicians held municipal positions, the most brilliant work probably being done by Thomas Pihlfeldt, who, after receiving his training in Norway and Germany, arrived in Chicago in 1879. In the 'nineties he entered the bridge division of the engineering bureau and from 1901 to 1944 was chief engineer of bridges for the city. He was most widely acclaimed for the design and construction of the double-leaf bascule type of moveable bridges, which replaced the old swing bridges over Chicago's waterways. So successful was this modern development of the medieval hinged leaf over the castle moat that the Chicago bridges became the model for bridge engineers the world over.

Dozens of Norwegian engineers have been prominently identified with the planning and erecting of many of Chicago's notable buildings: the Field Museum, the Continental and Commercial National Bank, the Railway Exchange, the Chicago Opera House on Wacker Drive, the Merchandise Mart, the Chicago Post Office, and the Field Building in the heart of Chicago's Loop. This is but a brief glance at the con-tribution Norwegian immigrant engineers have made to the physical development of one large American city.

Like all immigrant groups the Chicago Norwegians soon organized social clubs and debating societies that bound them together in the hubbub of a strange city's life. Churches, of course, were founded almost at the outset, but though practically all the immigrants had been reared in the Lutheran State Church, not all remained with that Protestant body. Some joined with their Danish friends to form a Norwegian Danish Methodist church group, while others organized Norwegian Baptist groups. Some, like Iver Lawson, were active in church work during their early immigrant years, but later, as they prospered and moved more easily in American circles, left the church. On the basis of two hundred and fifty biographies of Norwegians in Chicago to be found in Strand's *History of the Norwegians in Illinois* (1905) the religious situation at the turn of the century looked like this: fifty-one per cent had no church affiliation, thirty-three per cent were Lutherans, and sixteen per cent were members of other denominations, the greatest number being Methodists. As one might expect, church circles often provided the initiative for the establishment of Norwegian institutions: homes for the aged, orphanages, homes for working girls, and a Norwegian hospital.

No picture of Chicago from the middle 'sixties through the 'eighties would be complete without a sketch of one of the leading intellectuals among the Norwegians—Marcus Thrane. He came from an upper class family and, following the tradition for young Norwegian intellectuals of the early nineteenth century, studied theology. But a career in the church was not to be his life. Without taking his examinations he left Norway to visit the Continent, where his receptive mind came under the influence of such early Socialists as William Weitling, Etienne Cabet, and Louis Blanc. When he returned to Norway in the late 'forties, he took up a journalistic career in Drammen. Stimulated by the 1848 revolutions, he not only vigorously urged liberal reforms of the agrarian system and of urban working conditions; he went a step further and organized a labor union in Drammen, the first in Norway. In two years' time Thrane had some twenty thousand supporters, and, we are told, the national congresses of labor representatives he called in 1850 and 1851 almost competed with the Storting. Alarmed by the rapidly growing strength of this movement, the government in 1851 arrested Thrane and some of his co-workers.

The labor movement in Norway was thus broken, not to be resuscitated for thirty years; for Thrane personally the eight years he spent in prison destroyed whatever prospects he might have had in his native land. In 1863 he arrived in America, bitter but still full of zeal to right wrongs and dispel the fog of ignorance and falsehood. Soon active in Socialist circles, he helped organize sections of the First Socialist International; and when he settled in Chicago about 1865 he started a newspaper, *Den Norsk-Amerikaner,* through which he continued to voice his political and social beliefs. The paper had two to three thousand subscribers when he sold it in 1866 to the newly founded *Skandinaven.*

To encourage the cultural life of his countrymen in Chicago Thrane organized in 1866 a dramatic group that performed Norwegian, Danish, French, and German comedies and song pieces, as well as several plays written by the talented Thrane himself. Even here his concern with social justice found expression, particularly in a later play—his best known—*Konspirationen,* which was based on the Haymarket Riot in Chicago in 1886. The interest Thrane's troupe had stimulated led in 1868 to the organization of the Norske Dramatiske Forening. For a few years this group of amateur players—succeeded in later years by other Norwegian dramatic societies—brought to the American West an echo of the European theater. In fact the world première of Ibsen's *Ghosts* took place in Chicago in 1883, at a time when the play was still banned in all the Scandinavian countries. It was even taken to Minneapolis and other towns to the west.

In 1869 Thrane was again publishing, this time a philosophical-religious monthly, *Dagslyset (The Light of Day),* which became the organ of the Scandinavian Freethinkers' Association, founded by Thrane and another Norwegian immigrant, Dr. G. C. Paoli, one of Chicago's leading physicians during his day, one of the founders of the first woman's medical college in the city and twice elected president of the Chicago Medical Society. When *Dagslyset's* printer, Christen Westergaard, moved west in the late 'seventies taking his press with him, Thrane turned to an old friend, another exile from Scandinavia, Louis Pio, the founder of social democracy in Denmark, and with him began to publish *Den Nye Tid (The New Age).* During the 'eighties he worked as a land agent for the Great Northern railroad, and while travelling through the Middle West helping immigrants find land, he lectured and wrote, trying to enlighten the common people.

The thorn in his flesh always was the Norwegian Lutheran clergy and against them he lashed out continuously. His scorn reached its peak

in *Den Gamle Wisconsin Bibelen* (*The Old Wisconsin Bible*), a scath-
ing satire written in biblical style. In its twenty-four chapters he intro-
duces the prophets and high priests among the clergy, singling out the
Synod leaders for special sarcasm. Their attitude toward slavery, their
scholastic quibbles over doctrine, and even personal matters such as the
Muus affair are grist for his mill. His account of Bjørnson's visit to the
Middle West in 1881, which roused the collective fury of the clergy,
gives a good idea of the spirit of the book.

Out in the West, he writes, there is the great city of Chicago, which,
like Babylon, is full of people, ungodly people who would not heed
the word of the Synod prophets. And it came to pass under the reign
of Caesar Ulysses that the Lord's patience was at an end and he sent
the Angel of Death with a flaming wind and brought fire to the city
which burned three days and three nights so there remained scarcely
stone upon stone of Chicago's walls. And the Lord thought that the
city would never rise again, but Satan was stronger than the Lord and
brought many people there and the city rose up out of its ashes greater
than before. When the Lord decided Chicago must be destroyed, the
high priests, Muus and Preus and Stub and Oftedal and others, asked
the Lord to spare the city. But the Lord lifted his hands and said: "I
cannot spare the city. There are three thousand saloons, swarms of
Freemasons and Oddfellows and fortune tellers and socialists and ni-
hilists and aldermen and county commissioners." Again the high priests
begged him to spare the city. So the Lord answered: "All right, I will
spare the city if you can find one hundred Philistines and one hundred
faithful Synodists." The high priests counted the people and found
over two hundred Philistines, but not one faithful Synodist, not a single
one. The Lord was so full of wrath that He decided to send to Chicago
a mighty false prophet, one who would corrupt the people and make
them believe falsehood. So he stepped up on the tower of Chicago's
waterworks and with a trumpet in his hand called in a loud voice,
"Bjørnson! Where art thou?" And Bjørnson fell on his knees and
answered: "I am here in Massachusetts,* what do you want?" The Lord
telegraphed him asking him if he wanted to work for Satan and make
six thousand silver shekels. Bjørnson answered, "Certainly," and when
the Lord told him to come immediately, Bjørnson telegraphed back:

---

* Bjørnson came to America in 1880 primarily to visit in the East where he was a
guest of Mrs. Ole Bull in Cambridge, Massachusetts. He visited the Middle West only
after repeated urging by some of his admirers there, notably Rasmus B. Anderson, the
Madison, Wisconsin, professor and editor.

"To Jehova Zebaoth, Esq.! I am coming before Christmas. I am, Sir, Yours most respectfully: Bjørnstjerne Bjørnson." So Bjørnson came to Chicago and stayed at the Palmer Temple.

The Synodists and the Philistines, among them *Skandinaven,* the champion of the Philistines, greeted him with veneration, prepared a banquet in his honor and celebrated with harp and psalter, drum and fife and wine. But when Bjørnson began to lecture he spoke such heresy about Moses and the Prophets that Sven Oftedal's breast began to heave,* and *Skandinaven* got such a pain in the stomach that all "Stomach Bitters" were in vain. The Lord at last permitted a Delirium Hypocriticum to come over them so they went around in sackcloth and ashes and swore by Moses and the Prophets. But Bjørnson went out through the West and all the people were driven by Satan to go and hear the mighty false prophet for half a dollar. And they heard his word and laughed and applauded. And the pastors were angry and called him an Antichrist and said it was a freethinkers' conspiracy that brought Bjørnson into the West, and they had many meetings in which they denounced him to the people. But the people followed after Bjørnson and heard his word and his word was spread over the whole West from Chicago to Fargo and from the holy cities of Eau Claire and Albert Lea to the borders of Kansas and Iowa. And afterward Bjørnson went back to Chicago where he held his last lecture outside Aurora Hall and there came Gog and Magog, and Jews and Greeks, and Synodists and Socialists, and Conferencers and reverends.†

Thus, with corrosive humor does Thrane record Bjørnson's memorable visit to the Middle West. The great writer had been the idol of the Norwegian Americans largely because of his romantic novels, *Synnöve Solbakken, A Happy Boy,* etc. Even though he had begun to attack orthodox religion before he came to America in 1880, the immigrants still admired him as a "Christian author" and were eager to have him visit the West. Had he confined himself to the subject matter of his

* The lecture that roused so much antagonism among the clergy was one called "The Prophets" in which Bjørnson said that the patriarchs were nothing but heathen gods with Hebrew names and similar flowers of higher criticism. Sven Oftedal, professor at Augsburg College, Minneapolis, was the most outspoken opponent of Bjørnson during his visit. Many pastors enjoined their parishioners not to attend Bjørnson's lectures, some going to absurd lengths in denouncing him.

† The literary quality of this passage is lost in translation. The original reads: *Og der kom Kreti og Pleti, og Jøder og Graeker, og Synodister og Socialister, og Konferentser og Reverentser.* "Konferentser" are members of the Danish Norwegian Conference, next to the Norwegian Synod then the largest of the Norwegian Lutheran church bodies. It was commonly referred to as "the Conference."

first lecture in Chicago, a historical account of the Scandinavian people, he would have retained their affection. But he could not refrain from expressing his atheistic attitude and berating the Norwegian Americans for allowing themselves to be led around by the clergy. Even stanch supporters like Rasmus Anderson were offended, and by the end of his lecture tour the Norwegians in the Middle West, which he had called "that hive of preachers," had turned against him.

The remainder of Thrane's book gives an equally devastating account of a gathering of pastors and lay leaders from various Norwegian Lutheran synods to discuss predestination and other doctrinal matters. His attitude toward these issues is clear from the following excerpt: "According to the scripture passage 'When one dies for all, so all are dead,' spoke Prophet [Laur.] Larsen beautifully and said, 'Therefore we conclude further: When one is raised up for all, so all are raised up.' (Then thought a saloonkeeper to himself: 'If this is true, then it must also be true that when one has drunk a glass of beer for all so all have drunk; but that is far from true.')"

No Norwegian Lutheran's brotherly love was great enough to embrace the author of *The Wisconsin Bible*. But a year after his death in 1890 a memorial service was held in Chicago's Aurora Hall under the sponsorship of his close friends, particularly Olaf Ray, Chicago lawyer and also an immigrant from Norway, who had long admired and supported Thrane. The auditorium overflowed with people, and messages of appreciation from leading figures in Norway and Norwegian America were read. Newspapers in many parts of the country reported the ceremony.

Norwegian American historians have consistently ignored Marcus Thrane. Theodore Blegen devotes a few pages to the Thrane movement in Norway in its relation to emigration, but says nothing of Thrane's activities in America. One of the longest accounts (two pages!) is found in Johannes Wist's article on the Norwegian American press after the Civil War, in which he treats Thrane as an "agitator, nothing more, nothing less," a fanatic who engaged in wild and hopeless battles against orthodox religion, to dismiss him with the comment that "his adherents were not numerous, and nothing of importance resulted from his activities." A few of Thrane's letters have been translated and published in *Studies and Records,* as well as some material on his dramatic activities in Chicago. Strand's very lengthy history, including about five hundred names, of the Norwegians in Illinois does not even mention Thrane, nor does Norlie's centennial history, which is as close to a directory of Norwegian Americans as there is in existence.

Had the talented Thrane worked for instead of against the interests of the Norwegian Lutheran Church he would almost certainly have been treated differently by some of the historians. As it is, he has been regarded as a man with radical and dangerous ideas and therefore unimportant. He was outside the main current of Norwegian American thought; thus his influence on his countrymen was necessarily limited, but that in no way diminishes his stature. And he may have had more admirers among the Norwegian Americans than we shall ever know. Even so, a few records of appreciation have been preserved. We have, for example, a picture of Knute Steenerson sitting in a shanty on his Dakota claim reading Darwin, Spencer, Ingersoll, and Thrane's *Dagslyset,* to which he subscribed. "It was an eye opener to me. It was a free thought paper and hit the nail on the head every time." Many decades after Thrane's death his friend, Olaf Ray, established memorial memberships in the Norwegian-American Historical Association for Thrane and for another great Norwegian American democrat, Andrew Furuseth. In a letter to the secretary of the association, Olaf Ray calls Thrane "the Norwegian apostle of the . . . 'Forgotten Man' " and refers to the Norwegian Danish Jeffersonian Democracy, a society which he, Ray, organized in the early 1890's, whose membership of over a thousand was largely recruited from the "many of our people who had become aware of the things Marcus Thrane had stood for." Today Thrane's native land, under a Labor government, has recognized him as a pioneer fighter for the common man. Under the auspices of the Norwegian government Thrane's remains were taken from Eau Claire, Wisconsin, to Norway and buried with honor in Olso in 1949, a century after his abortive attempt to found a Labor party.

Many of the Norwegian clubs that were founded lived for a time, withered as their members were absorbed into American life, revived as new generations of immigrants arrived with the same need for finding a place where they could speak their native tongue and carry on their customs from home. One of the most active leaders in Chicago's Norwegian American affairs from the 'nineties up to the present has been Birger Osland, an investment banker, whose reminiscences, *A Long Pull from Stavanger,* is a valuable document in the story of Norwegian urban society. His intimate connection with Norwegian club life from the time he joined his first group in 1890, a workingmen's organization in which he did not feel at home and which he soon left to join a group of young intellectuals in a debating society, through the heyday of Norwegian social life in the 'twenties when the Chicago Norske Klub entertained European royalty, world-famous explorers, and statesmen in its beautifully appointed rooms is testimony to the cohesive character of the Norwegian segment of Chicago's population. Though the number of clubs has declined since the depression, a few, like Sons of Norway and the Normendenes Sangforening are still vigorous enough. Space does not permit a detailed listing of the half a hundred clubs that have existed in this metropolitan center, but perhaps a character sketch of a few such organizations will suggest the larger picture.

Purely social clubs were legion. Perhaps the most outstanding was the Chicago Norwegian Club (Chicago Norske Klub), organized in 1911 by the fusion of two already existing clubs, the socially elite Norwegian Club of older immigrants and the Norwegian Club in Chicago, a group made up largely of engineers of a more recent vintage. Its purpose was to promote social intercourse among its members and to advance Norwegian cultural interests. A two-story brick clubhouse was built on North Kedzie Boulevard during the years of the first World War, designed and artistically decorated in proper Norwegian style by talented members. Meals were served regularly in its dining room; newspapers, periodicals, and books, both American and Norwegian, were plentiful in the library; those interested in singing, cards, dramatics, and athletics formed small groups within the club; art exhibits were held; national conventions of Norwegian American engineers were sponsored; famous visitors were entertained. Without question it held a significant place in the lives of the young engineers who sought professional contacts, who yearned for the kind of companionship they had known through their youth and student days in Norway. A women's auxiliary provided romance for many of them. For all of them it was a cultural oasis in the business-minded bustle of American life. Membership has declined as older members have died and immigration virtually ended. In 1917 there were 276 members, in 1945 only 196.

A few minutes' walk from the Norske Klub on Kedzie Boulevard brings one to an old brick mansion with neat hedges bordering the walk and a flagstaff topped by the American and the Norwegian flags. This is the home of another of Chicago's Norwegian clubs, Normendenes Sangforening (Norsemen's Singing Society), founded in 1870. Singing societies have been a feature of Norwegian American life the country over, particularly in the urban centers, and the Normendenes Sangforening has been one among many such clubs that brought a distinct Scandinavian note into the musical life of Chicago. Here in its clubhouse the sixty members of the chorus rehearse one evening a week and sometimes Sunday mornings, for concerts in Chicago, for *sangerfests* (singing festivals) in other parts of the country, and for their tours. Twice the group has taken concert tours to Norway, in 1924 and in 1938, not "with the expectation of making a great artistic triumph," we read from the introduction to their 1924 program, but "as the expression of our devotion to our fatherland and its traditions." Although the main function of the club has been to provide an organization for singers, the group includes many more members than those in its chorus. In 1945 it had a membership of about 235. From 1872 until 1938 the society maintained a sick benefit fund; during the depression the society and some of its well-to-do members gave financial aid to members who were unemployed. A ladies' auxiliary of a hundred and a junior club of sixty make the society a family affair. The latter was organized in 1933 because the older members saw that "the Club could not perpetuate itself without young people, and they saw need for a place for their sons and daughters to gather and meet others of Norwegian descent." This naively avowed purpose points up two features of Norwegian urban society: the amazing strength of the tribalistic feeling, and the minor role of the church, as compared with rural and small town communities, as a social center for the Norwegian American group.

The Dovre Club, a Norwegian American political organization, existed between 1909 and 1929. The preamble to its constitution states the purpose: "to uphold American ideals in order to stimulate patriotism and advance the cause of good citizenship; to inculcate the political principles on which the Republican Party is founded; to interest in political matters, all citizens, especially those of Norwegian birth or descent residing in the city of Chicago; to assist in procuring the privileges of citizenship to those not yet naturalized and in general, to work for the betterment of the body politic through the agency of the Republican Party and its principles." The leading spirits in this club of some thousand members "strove seriously to make the Dovre Club an influence for good in city, county, and state politics," writes Birger Osland, its president for four terms. Circulars were sent out during campaigns supporting certain candidates; mass meetings held once a year, oftener during campaigns, were addressed by United States Senators, Congressmen, or men prominent in state and city government. In city politics the club gradually became identified with the Brundage faction which opposed Mayor "Big Bill" Thompson, so that even candidates with Norwegian backgrounds if they had connections with Thompson and his henchmen, did not enjoy the support of the club. The Dovre Club played no major role in Chicago politics, but it did influence the Norwegian American element by making it conscious of its duties as citizens in the American body politic.

20

Minneapolis

TOWARD 1890, AS Norwegian migration spearheaded into the Northwest, Minneapolis replaced Chicago as the main destination of urban newcomers. Not only was it the marketing center for a vast agricultural region densely peopled by Norwegians, but there, too, were the central offices of their most powerful institution, the Norwegian Lutheran Church of America. Inside the city and within easy reach out on the prairies its colleges, academies, hospitals, old people's homes, and orphanages had been founded. All lines, economic and cultural, led to the city of the mills. Small wonder that laborers and technicians from Norway's factories came there to work in the white dusty air of the Pillsbury and Crosby mills, for construction companies, the streetcar companies, and the Great Northern; that ambitious young immigrants worked hard for an education in the city where they knew they could later prosper as doctors, lawyers, editors, and teachers; that the sons of pioneer farmers, yearning for urban life, should seek careers there.

There too, the new life brought them together in Norwegian societies and clubs. But on the social life in Minneapolis the church had a distinct influence. Here, more of the people than in Chicago were members of both church and club. Thus, there were fewer for whom the clubs were the only contact with the culture of the old country. The attitude of the church toward drinking, dancing, and card playing kept a number of immigrants out of the social affairs of the "worldly set," as the club addicts were called. Moreover, the church disapproved of the rituals that were part of the initiation and burial ceremonies of a few of the orders. Carl G. O. Hansen, the historian of the Sons of Norway, a fraternal organization, commented on its relationship to the church in the period around 1910: "A great many within the church . . . were inclined to look askance at Sons of Norway. Wasn't it a 'secret' society? According to a deeply rooted prejudice it therefore must be an instrument of evil." And when the order, as a gesture to that segment of opinion, abolished the burial ritual, the president of the Norwegian Synod commented favorably on the action and expressed the hope that further revision of ritual in the "right direction" would be undertaken.

The Sons of Norway is the largest and most active of the Norwegian secular organizations in America. In 1895 eighteen Norwegian-born Minneapolis residents, who had long felt a need for a society for mutual aid, organized the Sons of Norway, stating that its purpose was not only to provide benefits for its members but "to create and preserve among its members interest in the Norwegian language, in so far as compatible with the loyalty which they owe their adopted country" and "to educate its members socially, morally, and intellectually." As the years went on these aims were expanded and clarified, but essentially the society's goal, aside from its insurance program, was to unite Norwegian Americans through the preservation of their common cultural background.

Times were propitious for the success of such an organization. Thousands of Norwegians had come into the country during the peak years of immigration in the early 'eighties (almost thirty thousand in 1882); after a slight drop another surge of immigration in the first decades of the new century (over twenty-five thousand in 1905) brought new life into Norwegian circles. Dissolution of the union with Sweden in 1906 produced in America a rising spirit of nationalism among the older immigrants, who threw themselves fervently into the affairs of organizations like Sons of Norway. And the new immigrants of the period, still excited by events they had lived through and often intending to return to Norway after a few years of American prosperity, joined their compatriots in clubs where they could honor the old country in song, dance, and speech. Enthusiasm continued unabated when plans for the centennial celebration of Norway's independence in 1914 got under way.

Meanwhile interest in Sons of Norway was spreading throughout the Middle West. Additional lodges were started in Minneapolis, in other parts of Minnesota, then in surrounding states. At the end of its first decade the organization numbered close to three thousand members. Lodges were first started on the Pacific Coast by a separate organization, but in 1910 they consolidated; in 1911 the first lodge on the Atlantic seaboard was organized in Brooklyn. After a decrease in membership during the first World War Sons of Norway again went forward, growing steadily until the depression forced many lodges to discontinue. By the end of the 'thirties, however, interest revived with increasing economic stability; now, in its sixth decade, the order, including its auxiliary, Daughters of Norway, numbers some thirty-three thousand members. Its assets total over five million dollars; it has about fifteen million dollars' insurance in force. Large, modern clubhomes have been built in many cities, particularly on the West Coast. The lodges bear such names as Thor, Valhalla, Bjørnson, Ibsen, Nidaros, Oslo, Roald Amundsen, Peer Gynt.

The order has been composed largely of farmers, shopkeepers, and the average worker in the trades. At the outset, states Carl G. O. Hansen, "leaders were selected from among the common folks." Nevertheless, as time went on many professional people, particularly lawyers, doctors, politicians, editors, and university professors assumed leading roles. There was much rejoicing in the offices of the supreme lodge when governors of states, Congressmen, and United States Senators were inducted. Among the twenty-three initiates in one Minneapolis lodge in 1932 there were such prominent men as Governor Floyd B. Olson, Mayor William A. Anderson, District Judge Lars O. Rue, and Municipal Judge Luther W. Youngdahl (now Governor of Minnesota).

A typical career of one of Sons of Norway's supreme presidents was that of Olaf I. Rove, who came to America in 1884 at the age of twenty, studied law at the University of Wisconsin, became legal counsel for the Northwestern Mutual Life Insurance Company of Milwaukee, served for twenty-eight years as Norwegian vice-consul for Wisconsin, and for three decades was a leader in Sons of Norway affairs.

But a better picture of the membership can be gleaned from an analysis of the obituaries published in the order's monthly magazine. In the 122 obituaries listed in the 1947 issues the occupations of some sixty-five of the deceased are mentioned. Although it is not easy to classify them accurately, e. g., "he has been an employee of the Robinson Manufacturing Co., Everett, Wash.," one gets a rough idea of their economic status: The largest numbers—eleven in each classification— were farmers and owners of small business establishments such as clothing stores, barbershops, drycleaning shops; one was the owner of a large bakery company in Wisconsin. About eight were employed by the railroads as workers, machinists, and section foremen. About half a dozen were engaged in the construction trades as carpenters, plumbers, painters, two of them as contractors. About the same number were employed by the lumber industry as ordinary workmen, foremen, and superintendents. Again about six could be listed as skilled workers in factories, particularly as machinists and mechanics; one of these was a highly skilled instrument maker. Three were shoemakers, three sailors, six were in some form of government service on municipal, county, state, and Federal levels, as postal clerks, grain inspector, etc. The professions were represented by one lawyer, one dentist, one probate judge, and a miscellany of other occupations is mentioned. The conspicuous absence of the clergy bears out the earlier statement of the church's attitude toward such secular organizations. Among the fifty-eight whose birthplace is given all but twelve were born in Norway.

The nationalistic tendencies of the society express themselves in such affairs as the solemn commemoration of anniversaries significant in Norwegian history, the dedication of memorials and statues, a vigorous sponsorship of the movement for the recognition of Leif Erikson as the discoverer of America, and, most important, in attempts to preserve the Norwegian language. Members were urged to promote its introduction into the curriculum of public schools from the elementary through the university level. In this they were quite successful, at least in states and communities with large Norwegian populations. A 1914 Sons of Norway convention report refers to "the study of Scandinavian languages in 35 American universities, in 50 high schools in the Northwest and in 134 graded schools in Minnesota." Some of these advances were lost during the anti-foreign agitation of the first World War and never fully recovered. Today Norwegian is taught in the following institutions: in Illinois at the University of Chicago; in Iowa at Luther College, Decorah; at the University of Michigan; in Minnesota at Concordia College, Moorhead, St. Olaf College, Northfield, Bethany Lutheran College, Mankato, and in Minneapolis at Augsburg College, the University of Minnesota, South High School, Roosevelt High School, North High School; at the Bay Ridge Evening High School, Brooklyn, New York; at the University of North Dakota; at Pennsylvania State College; in South Dakota at Augustana Academy, Canton, and Augustana College, Sioux Falls; at the University of Texas; in Washington at the University of Washington, Pacific Lutheran College, Parkland, and Everett High School, Everett; and at the University of Wisconsin.

The problem of language within the Sons of Norway is also of interest. Until about 1914 Norwegian was used in meetings, in all reports, and in all publications. In 1914, the centennial year of Norway's independence, when the Sons of Norway historian felt that "Norwegianism in America seemed to have reached a climax," a request came from

Chicago, the first of many to follow, to form an English-speaking lodge. Not surprisingly the request was refused, since, as a convention committee stated it, the "greatest efforts should be centered on conserving the Norwegian language." Yet, in spite of directives issued by the supreme lodge changes occurred, slowly but irresistibly, as second generation Norwegians who could not adequately express themselves in the old language entered the local lodges. Gradually through the 'twenties the use of English spread, and when after the depression the order regained its strength the majority of the new lodges were English-speaking. In March, 1935, *Sønner af Norge,* the official organ, first published the minutes of the board of directors' meeting in English. In 1942, finally, all reports of the supreme lodge officers to the convention were for the first time given in English, which was also made the official language of the monthly magazine, now *Sons of Norway,* with the understanding that space be given to articles and communications written in Norwegian.

As Americanization has prevailed on the language level, so have the social activities of the order been adapted to the American pattern. Naturally, the Seventeenth of May still arouses a great deal of enthusiasm, and October ninth, Leif Erikson Day, is celebrated pretty generally throughout the order. But, except for the drive to raise money for the Leif Erikson monument recently erected on the grounds of the Minnesota State Capitol, the zest for memorial days and monument raising has spent itself. The lodges are primarily social clubs, not unlike the Moose, the Elks, and others. To be sure, native costumes are worn by gymnastic teams and dancing groups. Norwegian food is served, and Norwegian songs are not forgotten. But the main interest is by now in the picnics, the dances, and in the bowling and rifle teams. Bowling, especially, has become a favorite sport throughout the order. America, one sees, has put its levelling stamp on the Sons of Norway.

While social life in Norwegian American circles flourished in Minneapolis through the Sons of Norway, countless athletic clubs, the always popular male choruses, and other groups with more intellectual aspirations had their centers there, too. Two brilliant young Augsburg College professors, Sven Oftedal and Georg Sverdrup, both from distinguished families in Norway where they were educated, were the intellectual leaders of the religious circles.

In Kristofer Janson, poet, novelist, and Unitarian minister, who held court during the 'eighties for the liberal-minded Norwegian intellectuals of the city, Minneapolis had its counterpart of Marcus Thrane. Like Thrane he came from an upper class family, his father a merchant and consul in Bergen, his mother the daughter of Bishop Neumann of Bergen, whose famous letter against emigration was mentioned earlier in this story. Again like Thrane he studied theology and, after taking his examinations, travelled in Holland, France, and Italy. A crusader for liberal causes, an ardent champion of the new language, a friend and disciple of Bjørnson, and a writer of merit, Janson was by the 'seventies one of the leading literary figures in Norway, one of the first to receive an author's stipend from the government.

In 1879 he made his first journey to America. Already a Unitarian in belief, he stayed at Harvard for a time, reading Channing and Parker, and then under the auspices of the Unitarian Church went to Minnesota to lecture in the Norwegian settlements. He delivered some eighty lectures and returned to Norway. But an invitation from the American Unitarian Association to establish a mission in Minnesota brought him back to America in 1881. He organized Unitarian societies in Minneapolis, where he lived, in St. Paul, Hanska, and Underwood, Minnesota, and in Hudson, Wisconsin. Like Thrane he tried to break the spell the Lutheran clergy had cast over the minds and emotions of the immigrants, and, though Unitarianism made no significant inroads in the dense thicket of Lutheranism, it did offer to some a less exacting religious refuge.

Without doubt Janson was one of the most widely known Norwegians in America in the latter part of the century. We see, for example, the Stavanger student, Birger Osland, shortly before he emigrated to America, in 1888 writing to Janson, whom he knew only by reputation, asking for advice. One Sunday in a small town in southern Minnesota, Janson relates in his autobiography, he met a tall, erect young man with gold spectacles and an aristocratic, intelligent face. He spoke Norwegian and in the conversation that followed Janson learned that the young man's name was Knut Hamsun and that, to keep body and soul together, he was clerking in a hardware store there. Janson offered him a job as his secretary to help him with the editing and publishing of his religious magazine *Saamanden* (*The Sower*). Hamsun, though he had no interest in religion, consented, and for a year lived in the Janson household in Minneapolis. From the reminiscences of Andreas Ueland, a Minneapolis lawyer who had come to America in the 'seventies, we have a glimpse of the intellectual circle in which Janson and his wife Drude, also a novelist, were the leaders. "He and his gifted wife," writes Ueland, "received every Thursday evening and entertained by Janson's talks on literature and art and by songs from Schubert, Kjerulf, Grieg, and others, accompanied by the wife on the piano. On these occasions my wife and I often met a young Norwegian with hair *à la* Bjørnson in somewhat threadbare clothes, who was intensely interested in what Janson had to say about literature. We understood he was working for the street-car company, but of that I have no personal knowledge. . . . It was Knut Hamsun." Kristofer Janson returned to Scandinavia in 1893 where he lived in Oslo and Copenhagen until his death in 1917. Two of his sons, Ivar and Eiliv, became successful doctors on the West Coast.

As Chicago Norwegians had a chronicler in Birger Osland so the Minneapolis group had one in Andreas Ueland, whose *Recollections of an Immigrant* record life in that center. His father was Ole Gabriel Ueland, for more than three decades the leader of the farmers' bloc in the Storting and the first of his class able to stand his ground against men of higher education. He was a figure of more than ordinary stature, significant enough for Ibsen to caricature in *The League of Youth* and for Bjørnson to eulogize as the finest product of the soil. One of his sayings has become an adage in Norway: "Religion and the constitution are the twin pets of the Norwegian people." After his father's death in 1870, Andreas Ueland decided to emigrate, in spite of the opposition of his mother and friends, who, like most members of the ancient land-holding class, disapproved of emigration. Arriving in Minnesota in 1871, he worked as a farmhand in a community south of Minneapolis, then went into the city and worked as a laborer, earning enough in the summers to attend school in the winter. In 1877, after studying for some years in a law office, he was admitted to the bar. Since Scandinavian lawyers were scarce in this period, he soon had a large clientele among his people, and, consequently, saw many sides of Norwegian American life, personal and institutional. Involved in the legal affairs of some of the church synods, he was often led to be rather critical of the men of the cloth.

One of his first cases was that of Oline Muus, whose husband Bernt Muus, the revered founder of St. Olaf College, tried to claim his wife's inheritance under the laws of Norway after the death of his father-in-law. Ueland describes the two figures in this case that shook the pious and impious in Norwegian American circles.

She was highly gifted, well educated, an accomplished pianist,

well read in Norwegian literature, and she aspired to many things
outside the parsonage of those sturdy but uneducated Norwegian
farmers. He (the Reverend) was of a stern unbending character,
imbued with the Scripture that wives should be subject to their
husbands and the husband a god in his own house.

The American court permitted Muus to keep some of the inheritance,
"because she had not sued in time," explained Ueland. But Oline Muus
then received a divorce and obtained alimony for more than the remainder of the inheritance. She went to Alabama to live; Bernt Muus
returned to Norway in 1899. On both sides of the Atlantic critics of the
clergy were sharp in their disapproval of Muus, none more so than
Thrane in his *Wisconsin Bible*. From Norway Bjørnson wrote to Ueland
in April, 1880: "I have followed with disgust the case of Mrs. Oline
Muus; I have seen with regret how she is captured in the foolish dogma
of these ignorant priests (which they call spiritual liberation!), how she
sprawls in the net without being able to emancipate herself from twenty
years' imprisonment." Eventually the affair was forgotten. Generations
of St. Olaf students have come and gone without ever suspecting that
the founder of their alma mater was anything less than a "tall and noble
son of the Lutheran Church," to use the phrase of a Norwegian American historian.

Ueland's cultural and intellectual interests were wide. In the 'eighties
he helped organize the Norwegian Art Association for the purpose of
bringing the works of Scandinavian artists to the attention of the
American public. From letters written during the 'twenties to his children we get more intimate glimpses of his life and his attitudes. To his
daughter Brenda he wrote in 1920:

> I read evenings (or rather reread) Darwin, Huxley, Kelvin,
> Faraday, Fiske, William James, and other authors on scientific sub-
> jects, not hard, but sort of skim them lazily. For even in that way I
> learn *something,* and it gives me more pleasure than a good novel.
> It does one good to be impressed with the immensity of things, how-
> ever vaguely.

In a later letter he wrote that another daughter, Anne, "sent me a *Study
in Magic and Religion* [*The Golden Bough*] by James George Frazer,
thereby giving me another English bedfellow." That his interest in religion was rather marked comes out in a letter to Anne: "Have promised

to give a talk on the 26th to an organization here called the Norwegian Society on Higher Criticism, and shall therefore have to brush up a little on the subject and hope that many good orthodox Norwegian Lutheran ministers will attend."

Although Ueland had married an American girl, Norwegian Christmas customs were observed in their lovely home on the shores of Lake Calhoun. To Brenda he once wrote, "there can never be such Christmas in this country as there was in the Old, because there the enjoyment came largely from the Christmas food and drink and here the food at least is that way every day of the year." And to Anne he wrote a few days before Christmas in 1921: "I have spent the day browsing through the illustrated Christmas publications of past years, which Mother has already brought out—American, English, and Norwegian. It is *her* way of preparation instead of the butchering, brewing and baking of my boyhood." Again to Brenda he wrote in 1925: "We spent Christmas as usual; the big Norwegian dinner the evening of the 23rd, with lute-fisk, rullepölse, rice pudding, goat cheese, etc. etc., and the more American grub the 24th, with Christmas tree, the children, children's children, children's friends and their children."

Proud though Ueland was of his Norwegian background, he was not an uncritical admirer of his national group. Ardently in favor of assimilation, he again and again criticizes organizations whose purpose it is to maintain a strong Norwegian national sentiment among the immigrants and their descendants. He believed that the Norwegian Lutheran Church more than any other single agency retarded assimilation to the American environment, keeping its flock distinguished, even unto the third generation, as hyphenated Americans. That he regarded himself as a detached observer becomes evident in his reflections on the centennial celebration in 1925:

When so many people come together to commemorate their achievements an observer may learn to know them very well. In what is said and written he will of course find no criticism, but he will find that some things are passed over in silence, other things by faint praise, and many things vaunted with great pride. This will help him to understand the celebrators' stage of culture and the influence affecting it in one way or another.

The 1925 centennial marked the peak of Minneapolis' reign as the urban center of Norwegian American life.

21

Brooklyn: Suburb of Oslo

THE BAY RIDGE area in Brooklyn, sometimes facetiously called a suburb of Oslo and Bergen, has the largest concentration of Norwegians (first and second generations) outside of Norway. In 1930 there were almost sixty-three thousand and in 1940 about fifty-five thousand. From the 'eighties up to the present time Bay Ridge has been the seat of a closely knit Norwegian life. Literary and musical organizations, sport clubs, sick benefit societies, and charitable institutions such as a Norwegian hospital and a Norwegian children's home were promoted enthusiastically in the 'eighties and 'nineties. One of the special concerns has been the Norwegian sailors. A sailors' home, providing many services to the seamen, was established in the 'eighties and is still in existence; the Lutheran Church founded seamen's missions. Norwegian newspapers were started, but only the *Nordisk Tidende,* established in 1891, has continued to the present. The largest of the Norwegian American papers, it is, probably like the majority of the foreign-language press, nationalistic, comfortably conservative and middle class. There is, of course, a great deal of news from Norway, plenty of social gossip about the colony in New York, shipping and import-export news of interest to Norwegian Americans, Lutheran church and religious news and, usually, a serialized Norwegian American novel.

Quite naturally, ties to Norway are, in the New York group, much stronger than elsewhere. It is a fairly simple matter for a Brooklynite Norwegian, many of whom are twentieth century immigrants, to take a trip to the old country. Then, too, New York has had a constant stream of Norwegian visitors—royalty, government officials, writers, explorers, sports figures, artists—whose frequent appearances on the programs of Norwegian organizations, whose very presence in the city, has given these people a sense of participating in the life of Norway. The residence of Crown Princess Martha and her children in the East during the war years strengthened these sentimental ties. One outstanding Norwegian-born woman leader in the New York group referred to Crown Princess Martha in a personal letter to a friend as "our Princess." The invasion of Norway, of course, united Norwegians down to the third generation the country over and resulted in the splendid work of the American Relief for Norway, which was particularly active in New York.

Although the children of Bay Ridge are gradually moving to the suburbs and the inevitable slow disintegration is taking place, one still finds grocery stores and delicatessens where Norwegian is spoken by both owners and patrons. Most of these shops have the words *Norske Varer* (Norwegian Merchandise) printed on their windows. Non-Norwegians who live there have often picked up a little Norwegian in order to communicate better with their neighbors.

The Bay Ridgers are substantial middle and working class people, officers of vessels, lighter captains, shipbuilders, carpenters, painters, and plumbers, with savings accounts, well-kept apartment homes, cars, and college educations for their children. The tribute by Dr. Anne Tjomsland, which *Nordisk Tidende* published when Julius Olsen, a master mason, died in May, 1948, has been deserved by hundreds of his kind:

> When crossing the Brooklyn Bridge at twilight, traveling from east to west, and looking at the thousands of lights making lower Manhattan look like a magic mountain, I can't help reflecting that there is scarcely a large building that has not known the hands of Norwegian workmen: masons, steel construction workers, or carpenters, and many of them the designs of Norwegian engineers. . . .
>
> Julius Olsen, master mason . . . was born in Haugesund. . . . [He] was tall, muscular, lean, fair-haired and blue-eyed. His great strength and honest workmanship brought steady work on important construction jobs. I have never known him to be idle through lack of employment—even during the depression. He prospered, came to own real estate and houses, but kept on working until his heart warned him to keep away from lofty places. . . . After a week's illness he died in his sleep at 3 o'clock on the morning of Norway Day, May the seventeenth.

In 1941 the *Nordisk Tidende,* conducting a survey of Norwegians in Brooklyn, found that sixty-two per cent, or three out of every five, were occupied in the harbor or at the building trades. A large number of engineers were among the eight per cent listed as professional men; only eight and one half per cent were unskilled laborers; four and one half per cent were merchants and sales clerks. More than sixty per cent of the laboring group were unionized, mostly in the carpenters', bricklayers', painters', and international seamen's locals. Most of the business people are in some way connected with the shipping trade, as brokers, exporters-importers, and chandlers. The large volume of business between Norway and America led to the establishment of a Norwegian American Chamber of Commerce.

One of the most successful of the Norwegian business concerns, however, is the Larsen Baking Company, founded by C. W. Larsen who came from Oslo about 1890. His company, which specializes in Norwegian baked goods, employs about five hundred people and has some two hundred delivery trucks. During the early days of the Brooklyn colony, from the 'fifties to the 'eighties, several Norwegians, for some reason or other, went into the piano-making business, and, there being no factories other than Steinway and Chickering, found it a lucrative business. H. Gulbransen from Stavanger was the founder of a firm which eventually moved to Chicago and still turns out one of the finest pianos on the market.

Looking at the 1941 survey once again, we find that the large majority of the New York Norwegians have had no more than an elementary school education. This probably has a bearing on another piece of statistics. In one third of the homes Norwegian was spoken exclusively, in one fourth only English. In the rest both languages were used. Over half of the Bay Ridge people do not belong to a church, society, or club; one third are church members; seven per cent belong to a club or society such as Sons of Norway. Less than one in ten contributes both to the church and a national society; however, nine out of ten children attend Sunday school. Also interesting are the figures on intermarriage: forty-one per cent of the children of immigrants married Norwegians, twenty-nine per cent old-stock Americans, four per cent Irish, four per cent Swedes, the remaining twenty-two per cent being made up of other nationalities. As to religion, fifty-eight per cent married Protestants, five per cent Catholics; for thirty-seven per cent the religious affiliation of the partner was not known.

From this survey as well as from other reports one is led to conclude that the church is no longer dominant among the Norwegians in the East. In 1944 the Norwegian Lutheran Church claimed 10,211 members in its *entire* Atlantic Coast district (which extends as far east as Wisconsin), while the Atlantic seaboard Norwegian stock then numbered about 109,000. Remembering that we deal here predominantly with a highly unionized laboring group, one can perhaps say that among the eastern Norwegians the labor unions tend to take the place of the church and the national societies. Professional people, too, are drifting away. The Norwegian American engineers are a case in point. Bjork picked at random fifty biographical records from his files and analyzed them for such factors as church affiliation, memberships, and intermarriage. Though most of them were born into the Lutheran Church, only twenty-seven of these fifty had any church affiliation at all, and among these again only seventeen were Lutherans. The reasons they gave for non-affiliation or change ranged from complete indifference to a preference for an "American" church. Yet, twenty-six were still members of Norwegian American technical societies; and thirty-two had married Norwegian-born women.

Until recently not many links existed between the Norwegians of the East Coast and the Middle West, except for a few Norwegian Lutheran pastors who, born in the Middle West and educated at the seminary in St. Paul, took parishes in the East. Very few eastern Norwegians sent their children to the midwestern church colleges (the East has none). In the 1920's, however, some of the church leaders woke up to the fact that Norwegian America was no longer confined to the farm belt of Minnesota, Wisconsin, Iowa, and the Dakotas. In other words, they discovered what they considered a natural mission field; for, naturally, from their offices in Minneapolis the East looked like a neglected vineyard. One of the reasons for sending the St. Olaf Choir into the East on its first national tour in 1920 was to establish a community of interest with Norwegians in that section. Lars W. Boe, president of the college, gave public expression to this attitude in the letter printed in the official program of the choir tour: "The choir comes as a representative of the Lutheran congregations of the West with greetings to the Lutherans of the East. It is hoped that through its presentation of our common heritage we may become more conscious of our spiritual ancestry and of our common faith."

At the 1925 centennial the church, which played a leading role in the preparations, tried to stimulate interest in the East. Thus slowly over the years, some ties were built up. By now children of some of the Bay Ridge families are to be found in the church colleges of the Middle West, particularly at St. Olaf, and many graduates of these colleges try to locate in the eastern coastal cities.

22

The West Coast

MEANWHILE THE WESTERN cities, too, received their share of the twentieth century immigrants. Shortly after the organization of the Norwegian American shipping line, Birger Osland, one of its leading promoters in America, wrote in 1912 to the managing director in Norway suggesting that the line be extended to the West Coast through the Panama Canal, which was soon to be opened. Since "immigration from the Scandinavian countries to the United States in the last decade has gone more heavily to the extreme West Coast than to any other part of this country," he wrote, ". . . there will be plenty of freight on the West Coast, going back to Norway." Then, too, the migration from the Middle West to the West was going on simultaneously. By 1930 the West Coast population exceeded that of the East Coast. In 1940 there were about 143,000 first and second generation Norwegians in the Pacific states, while the Atlantic had 109,000. Together the coastal groups comprised a little more than twenty-seven per cent of the total Norwegian stock in the country.

To what extent the westerners identified themselves with organizations having a national flavor can be seen, at least partially, in the reports of the Evangelical (Norwegian) Lutheran Church and the Sons of Norway. Like the Atlantic Coast immigrants of the twentieth century the Pacific Coast newcomers came from urban centers where the anti-clerical attitudes of the late nineteenth century, stemming from leaders like Bjørnson and Ibsen, had become twentieth century indifference to the church. When in America they needed a minister for marriage or for burial they often sought out a Lutheran pastor, but the ties to the Lutheran Church were tenuous. Those who did join churches, both among the newcomers and the older generation from the Middle West, were often drawn into other denominations, particularly the Methodist and Baptist churches. What Lutheranism came to the West was brought largely through those who had previously lived in the church-dominated Middle West.

The 1944 annual report of the Evangelical (Norwegian) Lutheran Church shows that between four and five per cent of its then six hundred thousand members lived in the Pacific Coast region, which had at the same time over fifteen per cent of the first and second generation Norwegian stock in America. That the majority of these members were probably second and third generation Norwegians can be inferred from the fact that in the congregations there, only four to five per cent of the services were "non-English," in other words, Norwegian. By comparison, in the Atlantic Coast district, which constituted less than one per cent of the total membership of this church body, twenty-five per cent of the services were conducted in Norwegian, indicating a larger first generation membership.

Relatively weak though Lutheranism was on the West Coast, there was in the late 'nineties a movement to found a Pacific Lutheran university. This failed; but here and there a college and an academy were established. One of the academies, Pacific Lutheran, at Parkland, Washington, has now become a four-year college with a student body of about a thousand, sixty per cent of whom are Lutherans. Three synods, including the Augustana (Swedish) Synod, maintain the college, but its principal support comes from the Evangelical (Norwegian) Lutheran Church, which in 1948 had over forty thousand members living in the three coastal states.

Membership reports of the Sons of Norway show that by far the largest of the five districts in the order is the one covering the West Coast area with about thirteen thousand members. The second largest is the East Coast district with six thousand. Together they constitute almost sixty per cent of the total membership. At the 1948 supreme convention the president spoke of the migration of hundreds of their members to the industrial centers, particularly on the West Coast, and indicated that in general the growth of the city lodges had been most noticeable.

So far we have accounted for only a minority of the Norwegians living on the West Coast. Another thousand or two perhaps are identified with the popular Norwegian male choruses, ski clubs, and other smaller organizations. But I think it is safe to say that the majority of the immigrants and their children have lost their identity as Norwegians. Already typed as honest, orderly, and conscientious people, the immigrants who came as skilled fishermen, shipbuilders, lumbermen, and mechanics, readily found employment. Most of them counted every penny, like the San Francisco Hansens in *I Remember Mamma,* and eventually bought or built their own homes.

Highly unionized like their cousins on the Atlantic seaboard, the West Coast Norwegians have been fairly active in labor affairs, the outstanding figure, of course, being Andrew Furuseth, who became president of the International Seamen's Union. Many of those who came from the Middle West during the period of agrarian unrest in the 'nineties brought with them strong Populist sympathies, which provided a foundation for later support of the New Deal. But the coastal urbanites have not yet entered as actively into the political scene as the older generations in the Middle West.

Those who have become prominent politically have had their roots in the Middle West, like one of Seattle's mayors, Ole Hanson, who came to Seattle in 1902 after getting a law degree in his home state of Wisconsin. In 1918 he was elected mayor. His decisive action in meeting and overcoming a general strike in the city in February, 1919, brought national attention to him, and apparently he knew well how to ride the anti-labor wave that then swept the country. For soon we find him lecturing in manufacturing centers all over the country on "Americanization" under the sponsorship of the Citizens' General Committee, an organization of businessmen whose purpose was to educate the foreign-born to an understanding of American ideals and institutions. Mayor Hanson was also the author of a book, *Americanism vs. Bolshevism.*

A present-day political figure is Governor Arthur B. Langlie who was born in 1900 in a small Norwegian American community in Minnesota but grew up in Washington. From Seattle councilman and mayor he rose to the governor's chair, serving from 1941–1945; in 1948 he was again elected governor of the state. Among those in Congress is the New Deal Democrat, Henry Jackson, whose Norwegian-born father, a cement contractor, was active in labor circles in Washington for a half century before his death in 1948.

23

In Great Waters

FROM THE VERY beginning of our story there has been a group of Norwegians who have plied their business not on the prairie nor in the city but in great waters. Some lived here, others were transient Americans. When they came sailing in from the high seas to dock at Atlantic ports they learned that wages were higher and conditions better on American vessels. Furthermore, they found captains eager to sign up Norwegian sailors. The crews of the American clipper ships in the China trade were made up largely of Scandinavians, some even becoming captains and mates. In his book, *Norwegian Sailors in American Waters*, Knut Gjerset quotes Captain Robert Adams, who, choosing a crew in the 1850's for a voyage from Boston to the East Indies, told the shipping master to send him any good man, but preferably Norwegians and Swedes, "these being in my opinion, both in seamanship and docility, the best class of sailors that man our vessels." Many were masters of schooners, brigs, and barks in the coastwise trade, in the grain trade between America and Europe, and in the lumber trade of the southern states. They had little competition from native Americans, for the sea did not beckon the young of the nineteenth century. The inland empire offered more riches. "The history of men before the mast on board American merchant ships," wrote an American captain in 1910, "is not a history of American sailors, for strictly speaking there have never been any American merchant sailors as a class."

The replacement of sailing vessels by steamers, scorned by many a tar, brought a goodly number of Norwegian sailors to land where they became longshoremen, ship chandlers, brokers, yacht sailors, divers, and lighthouse keepers, settling all around the edge of America from Maine to Washington. Others who stayed on the water and adjusted to the new conditions were soon in almost every branch of American shipping: in the coal, oil, and especially the fruit trade, which rose to importance after 1880. It has been estimated that in the year 1893 there were twenty-three thousand Norwegian sailors in the American merchant marine. Some became American citizens; others continued to sail on American ships until the United States government in the 1920's passed laws requiring citizenship for seamen employed in the merchant marine. But by this time several thousand had established their homes along the seaboards and had become as thoroughly a part of the American scene as the larger group of Norwegian American farmers in the Middle West.

Among many distinguished Norwegian American sea captains one of the most prominent was Hans Didrik Kjeldal Doxrud, who after sailing under the Norwegian flag for many years came to America in 1880 and entered the service of the Red Star Line. He rose steadily from third officer to officer in command of the largest vessel of the line, the passenger steamer *Lapland,* and then to commodore captain, the highest rank that could be reached in the merchant marine. When the Norwegian America Line was established in 1912 he became its vice-president and director. The Norwegian government made him a knight in the Order of St. Olav and the Belgian government gave him its Order of Leopold; President McKinley personally presented him with a gold watch in recognition of his rescue of the crews on two American schooners. Captain Doxrud died in 1930. His daughter, Maria Johanna, was married to Joseph Stransky, Bohemian-born musician who came to America in 1911 and succeeded Gustav Mahler who had been guest conductor of the New York Philharmonic Orchestra.

In yachting circles Norwegian seamen have been prominent. As early as 1871 Captain Niels Olsen became superintendent of the New York Yacht Club, a position he held for many years. In addition to sailing in important regattas, helping organize the Norwegian American Seamen's Association, and the Norwegian Sailors' Home in New York, he was for some years yacht reporter for the *New York Herald* and editor of *The American Yacht List.* As a rule Norwegians were not members of clubs and owners of the expensive racing vessels, but their able seamanship, heritage of their viking past, has helped keep the famous Challenge Cup in America since the middle of the last century. Reporting the closely contested race between the victorious American yacht *Resolute* and Sir Thomas Lipton's *Shamrock IV* in 1920, the *Literary Digest* commented: "For many years American cup defenders have been manned by Scandinavian crews." The *Resolute* was no exception.

Its captain, Charles Francis Adams, was assisted by Norwegian-born Captain Chris. Christensen, sailing master, one of the most competent men in yachting circles in the 'twenties; John Christensen was first mate and Gust. Olsen second mate, both Norwegians. Of the crew of thirty, twenty-two were Americans from Norway.

Although it is impossible to tell accurately the number of Norwegian Americans who have served in the United States Navy, records indicate that seamen of Norwegian birth or descent seem to be as well represented there as in the merchant marine. One of the grand old men of the navy and the only Norwegian-born person to attain the rank of rear admiral was Peter Christian Asserson, who was born in Egersund, Norway, in 1839. He emigrated to America before the Civil War, became a civil engineer, served as a volunteer officer in the navy during the war, and in 1874 with the rank of lieutenant was stationed at the Norfolk navy yard where for some years he directed the building of drydocks and other important naval construction work requiring high engineering skill. Most of the seven children born to Rear Admiral Asserson and his American wife have been connected with the navy in one way or another. One son, Captain William C. Asserson, graduated from Annapolis in 1897, served in China in the Boxer Uprising, was an instructor at the United States Naval Academy before the first World War, and during the last months of the war served as chief of staff to the commander of the United States Patrol Squadron in the Mediterranean Sea. Another son served in the medical corps and was promoted to commander. A third son became a civil engineer and the father of Raymond Asserson, lieutenant in the United States Navy. One of his four daughters married Rear Admiral Fletcher; another married Colonel W. F. Spicer of the Marine Corps.

A later career is that of Olaf M. Hustvedt, son of a Lutheran minister in Decorah, Iowa. After graduating from Luther College in 1906, he went to Annapolis, served as an officer in the first World War, in 1940 became captain of the 35,000-ton battleship *North Carolina,* and during the second World War, as a rear admiral, was awarded the Legion of Merit for services rendered as chief of staff for the commanding admiral. He was retired in 1945 with the rank of vice-admiral.

Meanwhile the tide of immigration into the West carried with it Norwegian sailors as well as farmers, and very early in the history of Great Lakes transportation we find the names of Norwegians. Many a sailor on his way to a farm in Illinois or Wisconsin in the 'fifties and 'sixties stayed in Chicago or Milwaukee when he heard he could earn two dollars a day on the Lake, a fabulous fortune compared to the three dollars a month he had received sailing in Norway. Trade on the Lakes was brisk. The growing cities needed lumber from the forests of northern Wisconsin and Michigan; immigrant farmers were sending grain to the eastern markets; boats were hauling ore out of Michigan; the Lakes were full of fish. For the young man who wanted to earn his livelihood on the water countless opportunities lay waiting. Furthermore, the comforts of a home and family, from whom he need not be absent for long periods, were inducements for one who had known the loneliness of the high seas. Sailors who came inland to work on the Lakes for the summer season intending to ship out to sea and perhaps back to Norway for the winter months found conditions on the Lakes so agreeable they stayed.

Chicago, Milwaukee, Racine, Sheboygan, Manitowoc, Green Bay, and Sturgeon Bay became centers for the Norwegian sailors, and from the 'fifties through the 'seventies they all but dominated Lake Michigan. This era was characterized by two things—sailing vessels and the owner-captain type of seaman. Ideally suited by training for the one and by temperament for the other, the Norwegian sailor easily played his greatest role in this period, contributing significantly to the development of the sailing vessel trade on the Great Lakes. It has been estimated that in 1870, when sailing vessels were at the peak of their glory, fifty per cent of the seamen on Lake Michigan vessels were Norwegians. It was common practice for an immigrant, after he had sailed a few years, to buy part interest, perhaps a third or even half, in a vessel and become the captain of it. Later as the sole owner of this and other vessels he either bought or built, he made his own contracts with lumber companies, fishing concerns, and grain dealers.

Those who had been shipbuilders in Norway found work in the shipyards of the Lake cities, later perhaps establishing their own shipbuilding business. Andrew Johnson's career is typical. For six years after coming to America in 1870 he worked for others, then started his own yards at Green Bay, where, employing as many as thirty men, he built schooners, steamers, tugboats, and motorboats, accommodating himself to the changing conditions. And times did change as the 'eighties ushered in steam. Many a schooner captain retired, modestly well-to-do, gloomily to watch belching smokestacks herald the disappearance of the billowing sails; to see the decline of the small shipyards in his home town of Manitowoc, Green Bay, or Sheboygan as shipbuilding was concentrated in a few big companies in Chicago, Buffalo, and the other large Lake cities. When freight rates and wages began to drop in the 'eighties many sailors quit the Lakes. Owners of schooners found it unprofitable to compete with the new steamers that carried twice or three times as much cargo at greater speed. So they sold their boats and regretfully saw them stripped of masts and sails, piled high with freight, and attached to a string of other "has beens" behind an efficient steam tug that towed them swiftly through the waters. But the end of the era was most poignantly marked by the gray hulls of sailing vessels rotting in the harbors.

For many a Norwegian seafarer the thrill and excitement of life on the water was over. Those turned to the land. Others stayed on the Lakes and cheerfully met the new conditions. The steamers, too, needed captains and mates; wages went up again, and the high tides of immigration in the 'eighties brought fresh supplies of experienced seamen looking for a berth. Many who came in the 'eighties and 'nineties settled in Duluth and Superior, the shipping centers for Jim Hill's great northwest wheatland and, later, for the ores of the Mesabi range. Large numbers, too, became fishermen and even today we find the fishing industry off the coast of Lake Superior largely in the hands of the sons and grandsons of those immigrant fishermen.

Certain marked traits of the Norwegian seamen determined the role they played in the larger picture of American inland transportation. Coming from a land where a bare living was all they expected from the sea, they were satisfied with moderate financial success. Proud if they could do their everyday jobs well, they rarely looked beyond the tasks at hand in operating or building a ship. They built their ships well but along conventional lines. Their conservatism and faithful adherence to the old ways prevented them from adjusting to the new, from solving the problems that came with new forms of Lake traffic. As owners and captains they possessed every opportunity to exercise continuing leadership, but there is no record of any Norwegians attempting to organize a large company capable of operating a line of vessels. They had no dreams of empire; they lacked the vision and the spirit of co-operative enterprise that would have made them captains of industry.

24

Story of a River Captain

AMERICA'S RIVERS HAVE not, generally speaking, attracted Norwegian sailors. One finds them on the Mississippi, Missouri, and other rivers of the Middle West only as transient figures. Lumberjacks from the camps in Minnesota and Wisconsin, chanting the popular river songs in Norwegian dialect, were seen on the Mississippi. Young boys from large Norwegian immigrant farm families in Wisconsin and Minnesota often worked on the river for a season or two as raftsmen or deckhands, like Nils Haugen and Erick Berdahl, whom we have met before.

When the prairie schooners swept west into the Red River Valley some Norwegians found work on the steamboats running between Fort Abercrombie and Winnipeg in the 'seventies and 'eighties. A mate on one of these steamers was "an old Norwegian 'salt' whose name was 'Nels,' " writes Fred Bill, a historian of steamboating on the Red River. We can also assume, from the names of the people and of the steamer, that Norwegians were the directors of the Red River transportation company described by the same author: "The *Fram* * brought from above Crookston on Red Lake river in 1890, was taken over and rebuilt by the East Grand Forks Transportation Company, incorporated in 1900 by Anton O. Lystad, G. F. Peterson, James Elkington, E. Arneson and H. D. Anderson. The original capital stock of $25,000 was increased to $35,000 in 1903 at which time this company took over the Red River Transportation Company, the steamer *Grand Forks* and about a dozen barges and thus gained control of the local business."

Aside from isolated cases of such business interests and individuals whose love for boats have kept them on the river, the Norwegian group has played no significant role in this phase of inland water transportation. But I have personally met one remarkable exception from this rule.

* *Fram* (*Onward*) is a popular Norwegian ship name. The most famous ship carrying that name was Nansen's vessel in which he made his North Pole expedition in 1895.

He is Captain Louis Nyhammer, commodore and senior skipper of the three-boat Socony Vacuum Oil Company's Mississippi fleet and master of the flagship *St. Paul Socony.*

Born on an island in the long Sogn fjord on the west coast of Norway, Louis Nyhammer grew up in a world of fishermen and sailors, his only ambition to go to sea. He shipped out at the beginning of the first World War, serving in the Norwegian merchant marine until peace was declared. He first saw America when, after being torpedoed by a German submarine off the coast of New Foundland and spending twenty-six hours in a lifeboat, the members of the crew were rescued by a British ship and brought into Boston. After some days he left New York City on a ship bound for the Straits of Magellan. The war over, he returned to New York and in 1919 "came inland to Minnesota," as he said, to visit a brother and sister in Minneapolis. Back in Norway some months later, he persuaded another brother to return to Minnesota with him.

For the next three years he "learned America." Like most sailors he had kept a diary from the time he first went to sea. Intermittently he continued it in America, first writing in Norwegian, then haltingly in English. One significant entry of 1924, mentioned earlier, reads: "Now I don't know whether to write in Norwegian or English—it's getting easier to write in English." And he did from that time on. Excerpts from what he wrote the first few years reveal with personal freshness his reactions to the new land, his experiences, and his hopes for the future:

> *1921* Feel at home, find it easy to adjust myself to this new environment. Impressed by how many young men, my landsmen and others, seem to be just drifting along from one thing to another with little thought and plan for the future. They seem to follow in groups, what one does, or goes, the rest follow. This does not agree with me. Has been my nature to go my way alone in making decisions as to my present or future plans.
>
> *1922* Joined the Minnesota National Guard. Have attended public night school for aliens in Minneapolis.
>
> *March 1924:* Have gained in knowledge and experience as to the American way of life. Farmhand, lumberjack, roadworker, carpenter, and oil company worker. But not satisfied as to future prospects for betterment in the lines of work I so far have tried. Have therefore decided to take employment with a new-formed company which will operate river boats on Mississippi between St.

Louis and Twin Cities, Minnesota, in order to restore commercial freight transportation on the upper Mississippi. This new venture appeals to me, and above all, it is boats and water. From now on, little or no contact with my landsmen in my work, very few landsmen have tried their luck on these waters, so let me be a credit and honor to my native land in my work and conduct, so it may also here be said

"Hvor fartöy flyde kan, der er han förste man
(Wherever ship can float, he mans the foremost boat)." *

Knowing the fickleness of memory, the young immigrant recorded in his diary a history of his family, including many family stories, and minute descriptions of his parents and his home. When moods of home-sickness overtook him in the years that followed he reread these pages that took him back to the island settlement of Nyhammer, that brought to him the sound of his parents' voices, their familiar gestures, that led him to favorite spots overlooking the sea. Sometimes it cheered him, sometimes it saddened him to read thus of his home. But he had little time for moods. The first years on the river were difficult. "It took all my time, will, and effort," the Captain said, "to learn not only the river and my duties as master of a river craft but to learn and become an American, to go through the 'melting pot.' "

The River Transit Company, the "new-formed company" of Ny-hammer's diary, was organized in 1923 by a group of Minneapolis and St. Paul businessmen headed by J. M. Brodie, son-in-law of E. H. Hobe, who for many years was Norwegian vice-consul in the Twin Cities. Commercial traffic on the upper Mississippi had been practically at a standstill since 1915 as a result of railroad competition. The opening of traffic between Minneapolis and St. Louis in 1923 marked the beginning of a new era of transportation in the Northwest, the bridge between the packet boats and the streamlined diesels.

Young Nyhammer started as a cub pilot, an apprenticeship that customarily lasts three to four years. After one trip, lasting scarcely more than a fortnight, he was put in charge of a boat, a self-propelled barge of the stern-wheel type. His crew consisted of one man, an engineer. Standing atop the bunkhouse, guiding the vessel downstream by the use of long ropes attached to the tiller, the young pilot brought his first cargo, twenty restless horses, through the winding channel between wing dams, islands, and sandbars, safely to its destination, Dubuque,

* From Bjørnson's poem "Norwegian Seamen's Song."

Iowa. But he had to wait a year before his master license could be issued, enabling him to take boats from Minneapolis to St. Louis. Today Captain Nyhammer holds one of the most extensive master-pilot licenses on American rivers; it covers 3,200 miles of rivers from Minneapolis to New Orleans on the Mississippi; Pittsburgh to Cairo, Illinois, on the Ohio; Kansas City to St. Louis on the Missouri, and Stillwater, Minnesota, to Prescott, Wisconsin, on Lake St. Croix.

Since 1937, when the Socony-Vacuum Oil Company extended its inland water service to the Mississippi River, Captain Nyhammer has been master-pilot on one of its boats. He has made many records, and the one he cherishes most is that he has never lost a crew member and has never involved either man or vessel in a serious accident. Friendly rivalry as well as some jealousy among river men motivates them to get their boats quickly and safely over the river. Captain Nyhammer is considered one of the best. For three years in succession he fought through breaking ice, one of the biggest problems on the upper Mississippi, to make the earliest arrival of the season in St. Paul. In the spring of 1941 the *St. Paul Socony* with Captain Nyhammer in command brought a 10,000-ton tow of gasoline over the Chain of Rocks, bottle neck of the upper Mississippi. The cargo of three and a half million gallons of gasoline was equal to four hundred average tank cars, the boat and eight barges measuring the length of two and a half blocks. Not until 1945 was this amazing record broken. The sinking of oil tankers during the war and the diversion of many ships to the Pacific made rivers important highways for the transportation of petroleum products to the Atlantic seaboard. Captain Nyhammer's *St. Paul Socony* was the first in the fleet that brought oil from Texas to Pittsburgh. Most recently his boat has been active in towing cargoes of oil into areas suffering from petroleum shortages.

Captain Nyhammer is a tall, lean person, younger looking than his fifty some years. There is an atmosphere of Norway about him, in his friendly blue eyes, most certainly in his speech, in his gracious courtesy with its touch of the Old World. Thoroughly mixed with it is the ready response, the good humor and the generosity of life on the Mississippi. He has breathed the air of Mark Twain. It shows. He is the only Norwegian on the river, and known as such, but he has been welcomed into the closed fraternity of rivermen, enjoying their highest respect for his achievements, his character, and the soundness of his opinion on river matters. Rivermen and boat owners over a wide area come to him when they need advice and assistance.

He has belonged to the Sons of Norway for over a quarter of a century, but his devotion to his job has made possible only rare attendance at lodge meetings. However, he enjoys his circle of Norwegian friends and occasionally when he is in Minneapolis he joins a small group at some club for a meal of catfish, boiled potatoes, and aquavit (a popular Norwegian drink). He subscribes to Brooklyn's *Nordisk Tidende* and Norway's monthly publication for Norwegians the world over, *Nordmanns-Forbundet*. He is glad to support the Norwegian-language papers, for he wants to see it preserved among Norwegian Americans and thinks the contact with Norway through them is valuable for both countries. "My loyalty to America is undivided," he said, "but toward Norway I feel like a son toward his mother after he has established his own home and family." In 1947 he visited in Norway for five months, the first time he had left the river for more than a few days. He has no attachment to any particular church, "but I am sure the religious teachings of my boyhood laid a profound impression on my mind and have affected my life, knowingly or unknowingly, for which I shall always be thankful," he said sincerely.

The closed world of the river has kept Captain Nyhammer somewhat isolated from the broader political and social developments in the changing America of the last three decades. Week after week, year after year, he has travelled up and down middle America, but the problems of farmer, factory worker, and southern Negro do not touch him too deeply when Iowa, Illinois, Missouri, and Tennessee silently float past his cabin window. He voted once, in 1932 for Hoover, and would have liked to have had a chance to vote for Stassen in 1948. But lack of permanent residence deprived him of this privilege. When I asked him about the role of Negroes on the river, he said that aside from a few boats that have all Negro crews—and they are among the best-manned boats on the river—Negroes have little opportunity. Jim Crow apparently prevails on the river, for when very infrequently Captain Nyhammer has had mixed crews, the Negroes always have separate quarters. "They should stay on their side, we on ours," he said, expressing not so much a personal conviction as a thoughtless prejudice of the river.

There have been no labor problems on the river so far as Captain Nyhammer is concerned. The crews are unionized and his company has always anticipated the needs of its employees before any demands from them are necessary. So he is somewhat distrustful of the American labor leaders. "Too many are out to get as much as they can for themselves," he observed. "But there has been one exception, and that was Andrew Furuseth, who was loved by all 'seafarring' people," said this stanch American with Norway in his accent.

25

A Great Emancipator

THE SCENE IS the United States Senate chamber on an October afternoon, 1913. Senator Robert M. La Follette has the floor and is trying to get his colleagues to consider a bill dealing with safety at sea, a part of the legislation for seamen that has engaged his attention for several years. But the Senators dilly-dally, wasting precious minutes talking about quorums, absenteeism, postponement of business, pro and con. Up in the gallery a gaunt, carelessly clad figure sits, patient, his beak-nosed face intense, the lines melancholic as his sharp gaze examines the familiar faces of the Senators—Borah, Smoot, Burton, Cummins, and others on the floor below. At long last the bill is read, every sentence of which the man in the gallery knows. La Follette begins to speak again. Senators interrupt with question after question. Replying to one the Senator from Wisconsin glances up at the figure in the gallery and says: "Mr. President, of course I am a landlubber and have to take my tutelage from those men who have been at sea. I shall never be able to express my great obligation to Andrew Furuseth, who for the last four years has called on me almost every Sunday morning to talk with me about this legislation. Andrew Furuseth is a sailor. He is a Norwegian Americanized, one of the most intelligent men it has been my good fortune to meet. For nineteen years he has been sitting up there in that corner of the gallery waiting to be made free."

Andrew Furuseth was close to sixty then. For three decades he had been working for the betterment of seamen's conditions. Before that he had sailed the high seas on Norwegian, Swedish, and other nations' vessels. The known details of his personal life are meagre. Aside from a short statement he made in 1931 in a letter to Victor Olander, a fellow labor leader, he consistently refused to talk about himself. When a reporter once asked him where in Norway he was born, Furuseth snapped, "What has that got to do with it?"

He was born in Romedal, in the inland district of Hedemarken in 1854, shortly after Norway's first labor organizer, Marcus Thrane, had been imprisoned for trying to better the lot of families like the Furuseths, so poor that Andrew, the fourth of eight children, was at the age of eight "fostered away" from his parents. Until he was confirmed he lived with a family from whom he received board in return for work on the farm. Six years of common school was his education. Then followed a few years of clerking in a grocery and service in the *Norske jaegercorps* (police) during which time he studied English, French, and German. When he was about nineteen he went to sea, and inhuman as conditions were, he stuck to it, for he had no other trade. Once stricken with fever in the Indian Ocean, he was forced by a mate to continue working almost to the point of collapse. Later in his bunk in the filthy, crowded fo'c'sle, he clasped a knife in his hand ready to strike the mate should he order him back on deck. Recovering after days of delirium, Furuseth remembered with shock and shame this impulse to kill. Pondering his plight during long wheel watches, he saw clearly that seamen must band together in order to end the intolerable bondage under which they worked and lived.

He saw men abused, beaten into insensibility. He saw sailors try to escape from unseaworthy vessels upon which they had been lured to serve, saw them hunted down and put into the ship's hold in chains; he saw overinsured and undermanned ships go down at sea with an appalling loss of life, all because greedy owners would not provide skilled seamen to sail them or enough lifeboats for passengers and crews. He ate insufficient, badly prepared food; lived in the unsanitary, crowded fo'c'sle. On shore he saw the runners, crimps, and boardinghouse masters fleece the seamen, get them into debt and sell them aboard ship to the highest bidder. He saw sailors drugged and shanghaied. He saw that the ships were being manned by the riffraff of all nations. Decent men stayed away from this calling. Slowly a feeling of responsibility grew within him. Sailors not only of Norway but the world over must be freed. But where should the fight be carried on? He chose the United States, because, he told a friend, it was the first country that dared to declare in a political document "that all men are created equal; that they are endowed by their Creator with certain unalienable rights; that among these are life, liberty, and the pursuit of happiness."

In August, 1880, Andrew Furuseth landed in San Francisco, and, instead of shipping out again, went to the Columbia River to fish salmon.

Already, seamen in San Francisco were banding together to protect their rights; Furuseth, fishing and sailing along the coast, learned to know these men, thought of means to increase the effectiveness of their attempts. With a handful of comrades in a dingy room on the waterfront in 1885 he started the Coast Seamen's Union, later to become the Seamen's Union of the Pacific. In a few months membership grew to three thousand; a shipping office was opened; a co-operative union boardinghouse was established. In June, 1886, the union called its first strike. Working closely with Furuseth were three other Norwegians— John P. Hansen, P. H. Olsen, Peter B. Gill; a Swede, Oscar Baldwin; and a German, Alfred Fohrmen.

In 1887 Furuseth was elected secretary of the union. His work, he saw clearly, had to be done in two steps: first build up the unions, then start the fight for proper legislation. And for that he knew he would need not only all his wits but more knowledge than he possessed; so he set about educating himself. Old-timers on the San Francisco waterfront recall the light that burned far into the night in his little room on East Street. He studied maritime history from the days of Greece to the days of steam, learning the laws of each country. He saw how nations rose and declined in power as their sea-borne commerce waxed and waned. He felt keenly how the ruling classes had kept in bondage those who produced the food, clothing, and shelter. He saw how the people of the land had risen up and thrown off the yoke that oppressed them. And he exhorted his fellows of the sea, still bound to the vessel as the serf to the estate, as the slave to the master, to do the same.

Seamen on the Great Lakes and the Atlantic as well as the Pacific were organizing. In 1890 Furuseth was a delegate to an international seamen's convention in Glasgow. Returning from Scotland he met for the first time Samuel Gompers, the Jewish cigar-maker from London who was already a power in American labor. In his autobiography *Seventy Years of Life and Labor,* Gompers records his meeting with the 36-year-old seaman:

Then, as ever, he was tall, gaunt, and on fire with zeal to free the seamen. . . . We had a long talk and I felt drawn to the man as I have to few persons, by his intensity, his clearness of thinking, and his stalwart character. Furuseth was a genius with extraordinary dramatic power. He had come ashore to fulfill a mission—to make the world understand the wrongs of the seamen and to secure redress for them. He went about that mission with the spirit of a crusader. He accepted no more pay than the wages of a common seaman. On the sea he traveled in steerage. He had no ties of the flesh, either family or kindred, to interfere with the absolute dedication of his time to the seamen's cause. He was then beginning the study of history and maritime law that made him a world authority on questions relating to seamen.

A year later Furuseth represented the Sailors' Union of the Pacific at a convention of the American Federation of Labor where he presented plans for a world-wide organization of seamen. The next year, 1892, saw the birth of the National Seamen's Union of America; three years later, 1895, the name was changed to the International Seamen's Union of America, and in 1899 three districts were established: the Pacific, the Great Lakes, the Atlantic, each of which was to have its own autonomous unions of seamen employed on deck, in the engine room, and in the cooks' and stewards' departments. The international organization, still affiliated with the American Federation of Labor, is now known as the Seafarers' International Union of North America. From 1908 to 1938 Andrew Furuseth was president of the International Seamen's Union. Working closely with him through all these years was Victor Olander, a Great Lakes sailor of Norwegian Swedish background, who held several high offices in the union, took an active part in Illinois labor circles, particularly as secretary-treasurer of the Illinois State Federation of Labor, and has served on numerous local, state, and national boards.

Meanwhile the second phase of Andrew Furuseth's work had begun. The International Seamen's Union preferred reform through legislative action rather than through strikes, and it is in this work that Furuseth rendered his greatest service. In 1894 he was sent to Washington, which, except for short periods in San Francisco, was to be his home for many years. His first task was to lobby for the Maguire Bill, introduced by James G. Maguire, who sat for a waterfront district in San Francisco. This bill, forbidding imprisonment for desertion from vessels running in the coastwise trade and denying crimps the right to keep wages or attach clothing of sailors in this trade, was passed by Congress in 1895. The next Furuseth victory was the passage of the White Act in 1898, containing provisions for better food and larger sleeping quarters. Also, flogging was made unlawful; a majority of the crew could compel the survey of a ship deemed unseaworthy; imprisonment for desertion, except from a vessel in a foreign port, was abolished; further restrictions were placed on the allotment of sailors' wages.

Although these laws brought improvements, Furuseth was by no means satisfied. He continued to talk to Congressmen, to appear before committees, to write, to attend conventions. "What did I come to Washington for?" he said many years later. "To lobby, and lobbying is what I have done all these years. Speak before committees of the Senate and the House—get a hearing when new bills were presented, and thereafter to discuss the matter with the individual members and convince them." But he needed someone *in* Congress to do battle for him. His friend, attorney Olaf Ray, whom he visited one day in Chicago and who himself had been a sailor before settling in America, suggested La Follette. From a letter Ray wrote to the secretary of the Norwegian-American Historical Association over thirty years later, in 1943, we get an interesting glimpse of what happened.

> Having been an admirer of the La Follette movement in Wisconsin politics I strongly advised Furuseth to tie up with "Old Bob" and get him going for the sailors. Furuseth knew La Follette, but thought he might be a little too radical to take the lead for the sailors. I urged upon Furuseth that the sailors' cause was a radical step and that a radical man could best and most sincerely fight for the sailors. I wrote "Old Bob" strongly to put on his mittens for the sailors. . . . Well, La Follette was persuaded by Furuseth, who camped on his trail, to take on the fight for the sailors.

La Follette himself told the story in an editorial in *La Follette's Magazine* in 1915:

> One morning in December 1909 there came into my office in the Capitol building a tall, bony, slightly stooped man, with a face bespeaking superior intelligence and lofty character. It was Andrew Furuseth. He wanted to interest me in the cause of the American sailor, he said, and he wanted to "be free." I did not know what he meant. I questioned him. Surely there were no slaves under the American flag. Bondsmen there were—but Lincoln changed all that. And it had been written in the amended Constitution.
>
> "Yes," he said, "but not for the sailor. All other men are free. But when the amendments were framed, they passed us by. The sailor was forgotten."

I asked him to tell me all about it. Sitting on the edge of the chair, his body thrust forward, a great soul speaking through his face, the set purpose of his life shining in his eyes, he told me the story of the sailor's wrongs. He said little of himself, excepting as I drew him on to speak of the long, long struggle of which he was the beginning, and is now finally the end. He spoke with a strong Scandinavian accent, but with remarkable facility of expression, force, and discrimination. He knew the maritime law of every country; the social condition, the wage level, the economic life of every seafaring nation. He was master of his subject. His mind worked with the precision of a Corliss engine. He was logical, rugged, terse, quaint, and fervid with conviction.

From that day forward the two men worked together. The first bill they prepared failed to pass Congress in 1910. In 1912 Congress passed the bill but it failed to become law because of a pocket veto by President Taft. The bitter opposition of the shipowners was too strong. But once more Furuseth and La Follette set to work, fighting the tide of protest that flooded Congress from chambers of commerce the country over, and from shipping and financial interests not only in the United States but in foreign countries. Furuseth worked tirelessly sending letters to newspapers explaining the important provisions of the bill; newspapermen like Carl Lynch of the *Bayonne Times,* Bayonne, New Jersey, wrote and lectured on Furuseth and his mission. In San Francisco, Portland, and New York, lawyers like Silas B. Axtell, who became president of Friends of Andrew Furuseth Legislative Association, threw aside promises of lucrative careers to devote their legal talent to this almost penniless cause. Test after test was carried to the United States Supreme Court. La Follette held conferences with newly elected President Wilson. Furuseth, too, presented the case to Wilson and received a note from him in June, 1913: "I think I appreciate fully the deep significance of the seamen's cause, and you may be sure that I will espouse it in every way that is possible."

The bill finally passed Congress toward the end of the session in 1915 and was sent once more to the White House. Anxiously awaiting Wilson's signature, Furuseth, accompanied by Samuel Gompers, called on the President for a final appeal. "When he sat there before the President," wrote Gompers in his autobiography, "and told his story in his characteristic incisive Anglo-Saxon vocabulary with vivid directness, he held the President's attention so completely that Mr. Wilson was leaning forward, eager to get the story in its entirety." It is said that after the interview President Wilson telephoned Tumulty, his secretary, "I have just experienced a great half hour, the tensest since I came to the White House." A few days later, according to Gompers, in the closing hours of the session on March 4, President Wilson signed the bill. In 1947 the Honorable William Denman, United States Circuit Court Judge, 9th Circuit, San Francisco, writing to Silas B. Axtell, recalled those days: "Andy sought my advice on one of the legal questions involved in this Seamen's Bill. When it finally reached the White House, President Wilson sent for me to aid him in analyzing some of its provisions. . . . When the signed bill was returned to Congress, he gave the Press my name as one of his advisers. Nothing in my somewhat extended experience in legislative campaigns has given me greater satisfaction than this minor participancy in the crowning accomplishment of my friend's career."

This charter of freedom, sometimes called the La Follette Act, sometimes the Furuseth Seamen's Act, made it unlawful to imprison sailors who deserted ships, gave seamen the right to demand half the wages due them when their vessels entered a port to receive or discharge cargo, increased the safety of sailing by requiring that sixty-five per cent of the crew should be certified able seamen, that seventy-five per cent in all departments be able to speak the language of the officers,* that more lifeboats and pontoons be provided, that the crew be divided into three watches.

Shortly after the act was passed statistics showed that wages on European vessels followed the American "as a cart follows a horse," said Furuseth. But his work was not over. He had to defend the act against the continued protest of the vested interests at home and abroad. He had to elucidate its various provisions and, as a member of the navigation laws committee appointed by the United States Shipping Board, had to investigate, study, and recommend any necessary revision. Foreign governments not only denounced the Furuseth Act, known to shipowners everywhere as "the iniquitous seamen's law"; they even sought to contest its legality in American courts on the ground that by passing it Congress had, internationally, exceeded its powers.

---

* This language requirement was particularly offensive to American shipowners who hired cheap labor from foreign ports. Many disasters at sea had occurred because the crew were unable to understand orders of their officers in an emergency.

After the first World War Furuseth went to the Peace Conference in France because he feared that some international agreement might either wholly or partially nullify the effects of his act. He first visited England where he met opposition not only in government and financial circles but even among the British seamen. In France he found lack of understanding and indifference. He also made a trip to Norway, interviewed the premier and the minister of the merchant marine, and campaigned for legislation to abolish the law which in Norway still punished desertion of seamen by imprisonment. In succeeding years Furuseth was active at the International Labor Conferences held under the auspices of the League of Nations, even though as a United States delegate he was there only as an observer.

While Furuseth was working on international problems in Geneva, Genoa, London, and Washington, trouble was brewing in the West Coast seamen's unions. The I.W.W., trying to get control of the Seamen's Union of the Pacific, succeeded in electing one of their men editor of the *Seamen's Journal,* published by that union but also organ of the International Seamen's Union of America. Furuseth advised that the *Seamen's Journal* no longer be considered the official organ of the latter union in order to protect it from legal action that might result from statements by an editor "of whose discretion we have no definite knowledge." Eventually the editor was dismissed for advocating revolutionary doctrines, but behind the scenes the fight raged on. Rumors spread through labor circles that the Sailors' Union of the Pacific had repudiated Furuseth. False though these rumors were, Furuseth had to go to San Francisco to again urge upon his men the old A.F. of L. principle of craft unionism as opposed to industrial unions. Many felt that Furuseth was too conservative, but he stood pat even though, as George West, a labor journalist, wrote in 1923, "The I.W.W. comes at him from the rear, fighting him with ribald tomahawk-and-war-whoop tactics. On his flank press the organized longshoremen of the A.F. of L., demanding amalgamation. . . . And on his front . . . the organized shipowners, a remorseless phalanx carrying the banner of the open shop, victorious at last after a campaign planned and executed by the United States government through its shipping board."

This was the figure who during his early years in Washington was regarded as a dangerous radical. Wherever he went detectives dogged the footsteps of this carelessly dressed man with the long mane and the sharp face, who shuttled in and out of the halls of Congress, back and forth between his office in the American Federation of Labor building and his bare room, where, when he did not study, he passed his lone evenings reading the world's great literature. During his whole life he would accept no more than an ordinary sailor's wage. When Senator La Follette asked Furuseth, after he had spent close to a quarter of a century in the service of his union, what provision he had made for his own old age, Furuseth's "keen eye mellowed," said the Senator, "and a placid contemplative expression smoothed out the seams of his weatherbeaten face, as he answered, 'When my work is finished, I hope to be finished. I have no provision against old age, and I shall borrow no fears from time.'"

He died in 1938 at the age of eighty-four. His body lay in state in the auditorium of the Department of Labor building, where hundreds came to honor the memory of a man who through his long life had been one of the loneliest of men. Threatened once with imprisonment for dis- obeying a court order in a strike in San Francisco, he said: "You can put me in jail, but you cannot put me in a smaller room than I have always had; you cannot give me plainer food than I have always eaten; you cannot make me any lonelier than I have always been." These words have been inscribed on a monument erected in his memory in San Francisco. But seamen's clubs have been named after him; a Liberty Ship was called *Andrew Furuseth;* his birthday is observed by groups and associations the country over.

26

Who Belongs?

WHEN ONE SETS out to account for the Norwegians in the professions a flock of questions rise up like a covey of birds from a thicket. To decide what contributions have come into American culture via the hyphen is not easy. At what point does the hyphen drop off in the subtle process of assimilation? In some cases it is a matter of a few years, in others of two or even three generations. If a Norwegian-trained engineer discovers, while working for a steel company in Pittsburgh, a new process for smelting ore, is that a Norwegian American contribution? If the son of immigrants becomes a great American newspaper publisher, is he still a Norwegian American? If the grandson of a pioneer Lutheran pastor becomes a teacher of Scandinavian literature at St. Olaf or Luther College is he not, in a sense, more Norwegian than his contemporary, the Norwegian-born engineer? Since, in what follows, I attach a "Norwegian American" tag, as it were, to all these types of Americans, perhaps it would be wise to distinguish them at least theoretically in some fashion. Roughly speaking, they might fall into three groups.

In one group I would place those, no matter what generation, who have consciously felt themselves to be guardians of an Old World culture in the New and who have made their contributions as representatives of that kind of Norwegian American life, whose matrix has been largely, though not entirely, the agricultural Middle West. In this group are the pioneer as well as the later clergymen and educators, men like Laur. Larsen and Lars W. Boe; the editors of the Norwegian-language newspapers; O. E. Rölvaag among the literary figures; Rasmus B. Anderson among the scholars, and F. Melius Christiansen among the musicians.

In another group I would put those who came, most of them after the 1880's, well-equipped from the Norwegian institutions and ready to give immediate service to industrial, social, and educational life. Among these would be many engineers, professors like Hjalmar H. Boyesen and Agnes M. Wergeland, and the mathematician Øystein Ore, people who have made contributions, not necessarily as Norwegians or as Norwegian Americans but as specialists that America had need of. Their ties are to their professional circles in urban America, and by and large they have had little if any contact with so-called Norwegian American life.

In a third group, the largest, I would place all those, coming from both the older prairie and the newer urban society, who have distinguished themselves in certain fields as Americans, who think of themselves only as Americans, but who, because they happen to have come from Norwegian stock, can be brought into a study of this sort. In this group are people like Alfred Owre, Ernest Lawrence, and Lauris Norstad. It will be simpler to group the figures by their professions. But I shall as often as possible try to make clear where they belong in this triad.

The Norwegian Americans were slow to enter the professions, slower, for example, than their Swedish and Danish cousins who also came from agricultural countries but whose migration began later in the nineteenth century. The special circumstances in Norway had something to do with this. The country was poorer, industrialization came later, as did, likewise, the development of an independent professional and intellectual class. The uneducated rural masses that made up the bulk of the immigrants up to 1875 brought with them no intellectual aspirations. To own land was their chief desire, and, as long as the supply of good free land lasted, this goal crowned all others. Also the fact that they tended to settle in closely knit units to a greater degree than did the other Scandinavians delayed the growth of new interests among them.

What intellectual needs they had, found outlet in scriptural study and theological debate. If a gifted son wanted to leave the farm to pursue a higher education, his parents and his mentor, the pastor, urged him to study for the ministry. Quite a number, undoubtedly, went into this profession because they knew of no other way to satisfy their yearning for an intellectual life. Thus for a fairly long period in the history of the Norwegian Americans the professional structure of the group was top-heavy with clergymen. The *Dictionary of American Biography,* which only includes Americans who died before the end of 1935, has biographies of thirty-four Norwegian Americans, about half of whom were Lutheran clergymen.* Because I do not choose to repeat here the oft-reviewed accomplishments of the great church leaders like Laur. Larsen, U. V. Koren, Gjermund Hoyme, the Preuses, the Stubs, the Ylvisakers, and others, does not mean they are without significance. We may deplore, on the one hand, the tribalism they fostered, but on another score their presence in the Middle West had a salutary effect. Like the Swedish and German Lutherans, they established and preserved a form of Protestantism which, anchored in theological system and formal ritual, provided a valuable antidote to the emotional, anti-intellectual strain that came into midwestern Protestantism through the atmosphere of the evangelical camp meeting.

Not infrequently we find men who, after a brief sojourn in the church, worked their way out of the ministry into other professions like journalism, law, and politics. Peer Strømme was such a one. Born in a pioneer Wisconsin settlement, Peer Strømme was undeniably a gifted son. He was sent to Luther College in Decorah, Iowa, from there to Concordia Seminary in St. Louis. For a few years he stayed in the ministry; but his restless, brilliant mind was too searching for the orthodox paths. He was, as the historian Laurence M. Larson wrote of him, "obviously on the wrong shelf." During the rest of a career that included teaching mathematics at St. Olaf College for a brief period and sporadic activity in the Democratic Party he was mainly occupied as a writer and as an editor of various Norwegian-language newspapers in the Middle West. His novels and short stories, highly appreciated by the Norwegian Americans, were crisp with a humor reminiscent of Mark Twain. In 1911 he made a world tour under the auspices of a North Dakota Norwegian paper, which, because of his articles written from all parts of the globe, promptly became the most widely read newspaper in the Norwegian American field. Had he lived in a richer and more stimulating intellectual environment a larger America might have come to know the writings of the unquenchable Peer Strømme.

However that may be, in the closing decades of the nineteenth century the state universities of the Middle West and elsewhere began to draw men of Norwegian birth and ancestry to their faculties. The field in

---

* One regrets the absence of such figures as Rear Admiral Peter C. Asserson, Colonel Hans Christian Heg, Paul Hjelm Hansen, Marcus Thrane, A. M. Holter, Olaf Hoff, whose contributions to American life were of more far-reaching significance than those of the minor church figures who are included.

which they first made their mark in the world of scholarship was, naturally, Scandinavian studies. Throughout the 'eighties and 'nineties Scandinavian departments were introduced in most of the major universities of the country and in part staffed with men of Norwegian origin.

27

Scholars and Scientists

RASMUS B. ANDERSON WAS instrumental in the establishment of the first Scandinavian department in the country at the University of Wisconsin in 1869. This loquacious, pugnacious editor, professor, writer, was the American-born son of early Fox River pioneers who later moved to Wisconsin. His father, an agitator and dissenter from the state church in Norway, came from the peasant class, his mother from an aristocratic military family. America was the answer to this mesalliance. Like his father, Rasmus Anderson was a rebel. In 1865 he led a students' strike at the newly founded Luther College in Decorah, Iowa, and was expelled. He began to work for the appointment of Norwegian teachers in American schools; received an instructorship at the University of Wisconsin in 1869; led opposition to the clergy in the parochial *vs.* public school controversy; and, in general, was an ever-present source of irritation to the clergy in the 'seventies and early 'eighties, during which time he was also an ardent defender of Bjørnson and managed the poet's lecture tour in the Middle West. Later Anderson's opposition to the clergy lessened and he moved back into the orbit of Lutheran orthodoxy; simultaneously he became critical of Bjørnson's agnosticism and his growing literary realism.

But through all this Anderson always believed that his main task in life was to introduce Norse culture to America and to preserve it among the immigrants and their children. To that end he momentarily arrested the attention of the general public by an emphatically titled book, *America Not Discovered by Columbus* (1874), in which he defended the hypothesis that Vinland lay in Massachusetts and that Columbus knew of the Norse discoveries. In 1875 under the auspices of Henry W. Longfellow and an array of other prominent writers and scholars he published a volume, *Norse Mythology*. In his own estimation Anderson's greatest service to American letters was his editorship of the sixteen-volume *Norroena Library,* a collection of books dealing with Scandinavian antiquities, reprints of Anderson's translations of Norse sagas and eddas, a history of Scandinavian literature, his translation of Bjørnson's romantic novels and Georg Brandes' critical essays. Theodore Roosevelt told Anderson that his set was among the books he valued most. Although later scholars questioned some of Anderson's work, they have agreed that his translations first introduced Scandinavian literature to America. Certainly he was the first Norwegian American in the Middle West nationally recognized as a scholar.

The University of Wisconsin's Scandinavian department, afterward under the direction of Julius Olson and now under Einar Haugen, has continued the fine tradition established by Anderson. Today the University of Wisconsin and the University of Minnesota are the nation's leading centers for Scandinavian studies. Through a grant of $200,000 from the Carnegie Corporation a five-year program of research is now being carried on at the two universities under the direction of Einar Haugen. Although he is American-born, Haugen's ties to Norway and its culture are close. His Norwegian-born mother, Kristine Haugen, has for a generation been prominent in Norwegian American circles, her articles on Norwegian culture appearing extensively in the Norwegian American press. For a year after the second World War Einar Haugen was cultural attaché for the United States government in Oslo.

The year Rasmus Anderson published his book on the Vinland voyages, a novel, *Gunnar,* by an unknown writer, Hjalmar Hjorth Boyesen, was being discussed in Boston literary circles. Boyesen is a clear-cut representative of that group of Norwegians who came to America equipped to take their place in professional life and who made their contributions as specialists rather than as Norwegian Americans. Quite early in his youth he decided to become a writer, somewhat to the discomfort of his upper middle class family. After receiving a degree from the University of Oslo, he, with his younger brother Ingolf, was sent to America for a year's travel. They arrived in New York on April first, 1869. Neither of them returned to Norway except to visit. Furthermore, a third brother, Alf, joined them in 1870. The two younger Boyesens became lawyers, Ingolf in Chicago and Alf in St. Paul.

After a few months of travel in New England, the Boyesen brothers came west, Hjalmar accepting a position on the editorial staff of *Fremad,* a Dano-Norwegian weekly newspaper in Chicago. "With his arrival in the West in 1869," writes Larson, "we date the beginning of a new chapter in the intellectual history of the Norwegian people in the United States." But Boyesen realized that if he was to make his career as a writer in America he must master the English language, and that he could do only by abandoning "all Scandinavian contacts," as he wrote many years later. For the next few years he was a tutor of Latin and Greek in a small Swedenborgian institution called Urbana University in the drab little town of Urbana, Ohio. But it chanced that he went to Boston during the summer of 1871 with the manuscript of a novel he had just completed. His own experiences there read like a novel.

On a visit to the Harvard library he was asked to sign the visitors' register by Professor Ezra Abbott, assistant librarian, who, when he saw the young man's name, asked him his nationality. Upon hearing that he was a Norseman, he requested Boyesen's permission to introduce him to Professor Francis J. Child, the distinguished student of balladry, who needed a translator of Norwegian ballads. The two spent the afternoon together. Boyesen told Child of his manuscript and the professor promptly arranged a dinner to which he invited, among others, William Dean Howells, then on the staff of the *Atlantic Monthly* and soon to become its editor. Howells was impressed by the chapters Boyesen read to the guests; invited him to spend a few days in his home; eventually accepted the novel for publication. Two years later *Gunnar* appeared serially in Howells' magazine. Boyesen was the first writer of Norwegian birth to publish in the English language in a journal of standing in the American literary world. In 1874 *Gunnar* appeared in book form.

Meanwhile Boyesen's connections with the Boston Brahmins had changed his career. He was offered a teaching position at Cornell University in the department of German. In 1874, after a year of study and travel in Germany and France he assumed his duties at Cornell. In Paris he had become acquainted with Turgenev and for the rest of his life was his devoted admirer. In 1881 he accepted a position at Columbia University where he successively held the Gebhard professorship of German and the chair of Germanic languages and literature. Brilliant though not profound, he yet infected many generations of students with his enthusiasm for German literature. A prolific writer, he published novels, short stories, poetry, essays, and reviews by the score in all the leading journals of the day. For many years his books and essays were widely read, the most important of them appearing in German, Norwegian, Italian, and Russian translations. His interpretation of *Faust* in his volume on Goethe and Schiller was long considered the best in the English language. But today Boyesen is read only by historians of late nineteenth century American literature and literary criticism.

American though Boyesen was in his attitudes, in his professional associations, and in his personal life, as a writer he drew abundantly from his Old World background. He married Elizabeth Morris Keen of New York. The family were members of the Episcopal Church, although Boyesen, after shedding the Swedenborgianism in which he had been reared, was more or less independent in his religious thinking.

His first novel, *Gunnar,* with a Norwegian setting and written in the romantic style of Bjørnson's early work, was followed by an autobiographical novel, *A Norseman's Pilgrimage.* Then, moving into realism like his literary idols, Howells, Bjørnson, and Turgenev, he wrote in the late 'seventies *Falconberg,* a novel portraying life in a Norwegian immigrant community in Minnesota. The book won him few friends among his countrymen in the Middle West, for through his main character, an arrogant, bigoted, and domineering Norwegian-educated clergyman, Boyesen hit directly at the leadership in the Norwegian Synod, which, he felt, was retarding the development of normal American life among the immigrants. Boyesen was accused of viciously caricaturing the clergy and of painting a false picture because he, as an easterner, knew nothing of conditions in the pioneer Middle West. But one remembers that at least two of Boyesen's contemporaries, Marcus Thrane and Kristofer Janson, intellectuals of high calibre, who did live in the Middle West, shared his opinions.

While *Falconberg* was being read and reviewed in the Middle West with sympathy from few quarters, the audacious Bjørnson arrived to try ministerial tempers further. In the light of the unfavorable reception of *Falconberg* one can understand Boyesen's burst of anger as he defended Bjørnson in a letter to the *Critic* in March, 1881: "The clergy, as usual the representatives of obscurantism and bigotry, began a fierce and determined warfare upon him the moment his arrival was announced." Boyesen's views had not changed a decade later when he wrote an article on the Scandinavians in America for the *North American Review* (1892). Under the leadership of the clergy all "the old customs are . . . preserved . . . the parson knowing that his influence will endure only so long as he can exclude American ideas." But Boyesen believed that though they might resist the influence of national life for a whole generation and make the process of assimilation extremely difficult for their children, neither the Norwegians nor any other nationality "are strong enough to remain permanently alien in our midst."

Boyesen died in 1895, three years after this article appeared, at the early age of forty-seven. President Seth Low of Columbia University, Nicholas Murray Butler, Carl Schurz, and such literary lights as William Dean Howells, Richard Watson Gilder, and Brander Matthews were among his pallbearers. This proud list is not without significance. Boyesen was the first of his group who had been received into the inner circle of America's intellectual elite.

While Boyesen was at the height of his career, a young Norwegian woman arrived in America, like him already trained to render service to the intellectual life of the country. Agnes Mathilde Wergeland was the first Norwegian woman in the world to earn a Ph.D. degree. The Wergeland name was already famous in Norway when Agnes Mathilde was born in 1857. Her cousin, Henrik Wergeland, who died in 1845, was one of the great figures in the early period of national romanticism and Norway's finest lyric poet; his sister, Camilla Wergeland Collett, Norway's greatest woman writer of the nineteenth century, published her first novel in 1855. The most universally known picture in Norway, the "Eidsvold Constitutional Assembly," which hangs in the assembly hall of the Storting, was painted by Oscar Wergeland, an older brother of Agnes. She herself had musical, artistic, and literary talents. Grieg, with whom she studied piano, had the highest regard for her musicianship; her attempts in painting and drawing, though untutored, revealed considerable natural ability; her two volumes of Norwegian poems show sensitivity. But it was as a scholar and teacher that she made her most lasting contribution.

Her family was poor and she lived in a period before Norway believed in educating its women for professional and intellectual careers. In vain she applied for stipends to go abroad after she had completed her work at Nissen's School for Governesses, the highest educational institution for women in Norway at that time, the late 'seventies. Finally in 1883, aided by friends, she was able to go to Munich to study old Norse and Icelandic law with the famous legal historian, Konrad Maurer. Back in Norway she was again refused a stipend. Friends once more enabled her to continue her studies, this time at Zurich, where she received her Ph.D. in 1890. Then, winning a scholarship to Bryn Mawr, she came to America to take up life as a lecturer on the history of art. She encountered resentment and jealousy and after two years this quiet, unassuming "foreigner," for so she was treated, resigned her position.

During the following decade she continued to study both in America—at the University of Chicago—and abroad, to write, and to lecture. In 1896 she was appointed a lecturer in history at the University of Chicago; but professional and financial security did not come to her until 1902, when she accepted the headship of the history department at the University of Wyoming. The friendliness of the westerners, their appreciation of her as a teacher and a scholar, her enthusiasm for the mountainous West and for the institution she was helping to build up brought her the peace and happiness she had long been denied. It brought, too, renewed energy for scholarly production, and although no large single book came from her pen, her shorter works, particularly the monograph *Slavery in Germanic Society during the Middle Ages,* brought her recognition in the historical field. But her long years of semi-starvation as a student had undermined her health, and in 1914, at the age of fifty-seven, she died. An Agnes Mathilde Wergeland History Scholarship at the University of Wyoming and a five thousand dollar endowment fund at the University of Oslo to enable Norwegian women students to study history and economics in the United States were established by her close friend, Dr. Grace Hebard, librarian and professor of economics at the University of Wyoming.

Later historians might regret, as Laurence Larson did, that Agnes Wergeland "wasted her splendid talents on the desert airs of Wyoming," but it is not strange that a European-educated woman of that period had to go to a young western institution, free from prejudices and unfettered by traditions, in order to fulfill her ambitions. The American West gave Agnes Wergeland the opportunity to achieve a place in the *Dictionary of American Biography,* a distinction granted to but few women.

Broadly speaking, the humanistic disciplines—the traditional paths for the scholarly—have until recently been ruled over by old-stock Americans. The Norwegians, like other early nineteenth century groups, were too young, too inexperienced intellectually to make great headway in this domain. But among the sons and daughters of the pioneers who did find their way into these professions a few have become recognized historians, philologists, and archeologists. After preliminary training in midwestern colleges and universities, many of them went to eastern institutions and to European centers for further study, afterward often returning to the Middle West, particularly to the universities of Illinois, Wisconsin, and Minnesota. Some achieved real eminence in their fields and can be said to have had significant influence; many certainly were highly competent and have served their professions and their institutions beyond the call of duty. It is impossible in a book of this sort to select more than a few representatives from this large group.

Among historians Laurence M. Larson's career is noteworthy. Born in Norway, he came to America in 1870 at the age of two, grew up on a farm in Iowa, attended Drake University in Des Moines, and after five years as the principal of a Scandinavian academy in Wisconsin, studied for his Ph.D. at the University of Wisconsin during the golden era of Frederick Jackson Turner and Charles Homer Haskins. In 1907 he accepted a position in the department of history at the University of Illinois and remained there until his death in 1938. His eminent scholarship in early English and Norse history brought him, at the close of his life, one of the highest distinctions that can come to an American historian, the presidency of the American Historical Association. To the student of Norwegian American history his volume of essays, *The Changing West,* and his autobiographical *The Log Book of a Young Immigrant* are of particular interest.

In 1938 the University of Illinois and the American historical profession lost another outstanding scholar when Marcus Hansen died at the age of forty-seven. His two volumes, *The Atlantic Migration 1607–1860* and *The Immigrant in American History* had already marked him as a brilliant social historian. Among present-day historians Theodore C. Blegen, dean of the graduate college at the University of Minnesota, is the country's leading authority in Norwegian American history. Through two major volumes, *Norwegian Migration to America, 1825–1860* and *Norwegian Migration to America: The American Transition,* several monographs, countless articles and as managing editor of the publications of the Norwegian-American Historical Association since its founding in 1925 he has made lasting contributions to American social history. Although he is now primarily an educator and administrator, Bryn Hovde, until recently head of the New School for Social Research, New York City, made his mark in the realm of scholarship with his impressive two-volume work, *The Scandinavian Countries, 1720–1865: The Rise of the Middle Classes*. Norwegian-born Paul Knaplund, for several years chairman of the department of history at the University of Wisconsin, has done special work on the period of Gladstone.

In the area of classical history and archeology two Norwegian Americans, both of them sons of early Lutheran educators, are prominent. Jakob A. O. Larsen * of the University of Chicago has published extensively on various aspects of Greek and Roman politico-economic life. Carl W. Blegen,† professor of archeology at the University of Cincinnati, has been director of the American School of Classical Studies in Athens, field director of the University of Cincinnati Archeological Expedition in Turkey and Greece, and has published numerous works on Greek archeology. In 1945–1946 he was cultural attaché at the American embassy in Athens.

Although the major scholarly work has been done on university campuses, the Norwegian Lutheran colleges, particularly in the last two decades, have sheltered a few competent scholars. One of the first was Knut Gjerset of Luther College with his *History of the Norwegian People* and a *History of Iceland*. At St. Olaf College notable contributions have been made by Karen Larsen in her recent *A History of Norway;* by Theodore Jorgenson with his *Norway's Relation to Scandinavian Unionism, 1815–1871,* and other volumes; by Kenneth Bjork with his *Saga in Steel and Concrete,* and by Agnes Larson in her *History of the White Pine Industry in Minnesota.*

The outstanding philologist among Norwegian Americans has been George T. Flom of the University of Illinois. Born in Wisconsin in 1871, Flom, after studying in American and European institutions, received his Ph.D. at Columbia in 1900. For three and a half decades he taught Scandinavian languages and English philology at the University of Illinois and published many notable linguistic and antiquarian studies. His interests, like Laurence M. Larson's, extended to Norwegian American history, particularly to the early period of Norwegian immigration. In many English departments of the midwestern universities there are second generation Norwegian Americans whose

---

* He is the son of Laur. Larsen, founder of Luther College, and the brother of Karen Larsen, historian at St. Olaf College, and of Henning Larsen, philologist and dean of the college of liberal arts at the University of Illinois.

† He is the son of John W. Blegen, for many years a professor at Augsburg College, Minneapolis, and the brother of Theodore C. Blegen.

reputations in philology and literature are well established. Teaching at the University of California for a number of years, Sigurd B. Hustvedt, brother of Vice-Admiral Olaf M. Hustvedt, has specialized in English and Norse balladry.

As a group the Norwegian Americans came of age, intellectually, as the nation began to turn to the scientists and the technically trained for leadership, when America began to call experts into the laboratories not only of educational institutions, but hospitals, industrial plants, and government agencies. It is in these areas that the immigrant stock has had its greatest opportunities and made a larger share of its contributions.

By the turn of the century a few Norwegian-born men like Magnus C. Ihlseng and Storm Bull, brother of the violinist Ole Bull, had led the way into academic laboratories. Ihlseng, who received his Ph.D. degree from Columbia University, taught physics at that institution, continued his career in the next decades as professor of mining engineering at the Colorado State School of Mines, as dean of the school of mines at Pennsylvania State College, and professor at Brooklyn Polytechnic Institute. In addition to these and extensive duties as a consulting engineer, he was the author of numerous articles and a standard *Manual of Mining*. He died in 1930. Storm Bull graduated from the Polytechnic Institute at Zurich, became an instructor in mechanical engineering at the University of Wisconsin in 1879 and in 1886 professor of steam engineering. He, too, wrote a number of scientific papers and was prominent in national engineering affairs. He also found time to serve as mayor of Madison for a time.

The new century witnessed a steadily increasing number of Norwegian American scientists taking posts in American institutions. Oswald Veblen, now seventy years old and one of the most distinguished living mathematicians, began teaching at Princeton University in 1905. From 1907 to 1938 John A. Eiesland, who came to the United States from Norway in 1888 and received his Ph.D. from Johns Hopkins in 1898, was head of the department of mathematics at the University of West Virginia. One of America's leading mathematicians today is the algebraist Øystein Ore of Yale University. Born in Oslo in 1899, he received his Ph.D. in Norway and studied on the Continent before coming to Yale in 1927. Since 1931 he has been Sterling professor of mathematics and from 1936 to 1945 served as chairman of the department. During the war Professor Ore was a member of the board of directors of American Relief for Norway and in 1945 visited Norway as chairman of the Relief Mission to Norway.

In the related sciences of astronomy and physics some of the nation's most eminent figures are men of Norwegian birth or ancestry. Early in the century John August Anderson taught astronomy at Johns Hopkins and, since 1916, has achieved recognition as a spectroscopist on the staff of the Mt. Wilson Observatory in Pasadena. At Northwestern University, Oliver Justin Lee, who has been head of the department of astronomy and director of Dearborn Observatory, has done notable work in astrophysics. Wisconsin-born Henry A. Erikson, head of the department of physics at the University of Minnesota from 1915 to 1938 and now emeritus professor, is starred in *American Men of Science,* as is Norwegian-born F. W. H. Zachariasen, head of the department of physics at the University of Chicago. After receiving his Ph.D. at the University of Oslo in 1928 and spending a year in England as a Rockefeller Fellow, Zachariasen came to the University of Chicago in 1930.

Probably the most widely known physicist of Norwegian background is Nobel Prize winner Ernest O. Lawrence, now director of one of the world's greatest research units, the radiation laboratory at the University of California. Born in the small Norwegian American town of Canton, South Dakota, Lawrence was educated in Norwegian Lutheran and state institutions in the Middle West before receiving his Ph.D. at Yale. In 1928 he went to the University of California where his invention and development of the cyclotron brought him the 1939 Nobel award.

A boyhood friend of his, who had lived across the street in Canton, was Merle Tuve, another second generation Norwegian destined to play a leading role in American science. Closely associated with Tuve in much of his work has been still another American of Norwegian descent, Lawrence Hafstad, who was born in Minneapolis and, like Tuve, received his Ph.D. at Johns Hopkins. They have worked together at the Johns Hopkins Applied Physics Laboratory on an experimental demonstration of uranium fission and, at the Carnegie Institution's laboratory for terrestrial magnetism, on the development of the proximity fuse and on guided missile research. Dr. Tuve, who received the John Scott award in December, 1948, for his outstanding contribution in the latter development, is director of the department of terrestrial magnetism at the Carnegie Institution in Washington, D.C.

At the end of the second World War Dr. Hafstad was made director of the Johns Hopkins Applied Physics Laboratory at Silver Springs, Maryland. In December, 1948, he was named director of the atomic energy commission's program for development of atomic power and larger supplies of explosives.

Another physicist of Norwegian descent is Tacoma-born Philip H. Abelson, who was listed as one of the ten outstanding young nuclear physicists in *Chemical and Engineering News* in December, 1947.

The list of chemists of Norwegian extraction who have achieved success in both academic and industrial laboratories is long. Perhaps the practical turn of mind, patience, and attentiveness to detail that so frequently belong to people of Norwegian stock is partially responsible for this success. An early figure of some eminence in the area of agricultural chemistry was F. Wilhelm Woll, who came to the United States after getting his B.S. and did graduate work at Wisconsin in the 'eighties. During his teaching career at that institution and later at the University of California he published many studies on animal nutrition. He died in 1922. John A. Widtsoe's work in agricultural chemistry at the University of Utah has already been mentioned. For a number of years Gerhard Rollefson, who was born in Grand Forks, North Dakota, in 1900, has done significant research in physical chemistry at the University of California, Berkeley. Norwegian-born and educated Lars Onsager has been professor of theoretical chemistry at Yale since 1934. Recognized for his studies in electrochemistry and thermodynamics, he was, in 1947, made one of the twenty-eight "immortals" of the National Academy of Science. Conrad A. Elvehjem, dean of the graduate school and chairman of the department of biochemistry at the University of Wisconsin, is noted for his discoveries that led to the use of nicotinic acid in the treatment of pellagra and for his nutritional investigations that have contributed to the knowledge of vitamin B. He was born in a Norwegian rural community in Wisconsin in 1901.

In the biological sciences the name of Leonhard Stejneger has long been internationally known. He was born in Bergen in 1851, came to the United States in 1881 and until his death in 1943 was connected with the Smithsonian Institution. For several decades he was head curator of the department of biology at the United States National Museum. Serving almost as long as curator of the Brooklyn Botanic Garden has been another Norwegian-born American, Alfred Gundersen, who came to America in the 'nineties, and studied at Stanford

University, the University of Minnesota, and at Harvard. Important research in plant pathology, particularly on virus diseases of plants and on soil sterilization, has been done by James Johnson at the University of Wisconsin. At Iowa State College Irving E. Melhus has for a number of years done significant work in plant parasitology. Chief biologist for the National Park Service for several years was H. P. K. Agersborg, who received his early training in Norway and his Ph.D. in zoology at the University of Illinois in 1923. He published extensively during his varied career in teaching and applied zoology. Recognized contributions in the field of paleontology have been made by Frederick William Sardeson, who taught at the University of Minnesota before the first World War and for many years afterward served as the geological expert of the State Securities Commission of Minnesota.

The work done by Norwegian Americans in the field of psychology has been more pedestrian. The only figure of any prominence is Martin L. Reymert, director of the Moosehart Laboratory for Child Research, at Mooseheart, Illinois. A city of some six hundred children ranging in age from nursery through high school, Mooseheart is maintained by the Loyal Order of Moose for dependent children of members. In this scientifically planned and directed community about fifty per cent of the work of the laboratory consists of research on every conceivable problem relating to child development, projects being carried on in cooperation with leading universities. Before coming to Mooseheart as director in 1930, Oslo-born Martin Reymert taught psychology at the University of Oslo and in America held fellowships and taught at Clark University, the University of Iowa, and Wittenberg College, Springfield, Ohio.

28

Medical Men

THE "NORWEGIAN DOCTOR" is not, like the "Norwegian pastor," a frequent figure in the reminiscences of pioneer settlers. For the ills of the body the immigrants depended for the most part on local blood cuppers and patent medicine venders. But a few honestly trained medical men were on the frontier as early as the 1840's. Hans Christian Brandt, after taking his medical examination at the University of Oslo, came to Illinois in 1840 to practice among his countrymen. Another graduate of the medical course at Oslo, Theodor A. Schytte, worked in the Koshkonong settlement in Wisconsin during the middle 'forties. Later the settlement was served by Johan C. Dundas (Dass was the family name), who had studied medicine not only in Oslo but in Sweden, Finland, Germany, and Switzerland. He seems to have been an unusual person, tough-minded and so gruff with the settlers that they called him only when the situation seemed critical. A man of literary inclinations, he was a friend of Ole Bull; Bjørnson, who became acquainted with him during his visit in America, regarded him as one of the most remarkable persons he had ever met. In 1856 the Koshkonong settlement welcomed the arrival of another well-educated Norwegian physician, Søren J. Hanssen, who was also something of a poet. Though he was considered the ablest doctor in the region, his outspoken contempt for orthodox religion led some settlers to believe that their souls could not be saved if their bodies were treated by Dr. Hanssen. In 1865 he published a work called *Orthodoxy and Christianity*. These country doctors gallantly fought the frequent epidemics of malaria and typhus, vaccinated the immigrants against fresh outbreaks, and preached sanitation to them. They served in the Union Army during the Civil War; afterward settled in the growing towns and cities of the Middle West. Toward the end of the century the more ambitious sons of the immigrants began to enter medical schools, later setting up practices in Norwegian centers like Minneapolis, or following the westward-moving population to the newer cities of Fargo and Grand Forks, North Dakota, and to Washington and Oregon.

Among the Norwegians there have been several families of doctors, like the Gundersens in La Crosse, Wisconsin, who have given immeasurable service to thousands of Norwegian Americans. After receiving his medical degree at the University of Oslo in 1890, Dr. Adolph Gundersen came to America and became an assistant and then a partner of a well-known Norwegian American surgeon, Dr. Christian Christensen, in La Crosse. They built a Lutheran hospital and in connection with it Dr. Gundersen later established his own clinic, which became the medical center of a large area. Six of his seven sons became physicians, three of them associated with their father in the clinic, which under their direction is continuing to expand its services. Before his death in 1938 Dr. Gundersen's reputation as a surgeon was well established on both sides of the Atlantic. As a member of the board of regents of the University of Wisconsin, he took an active part in planning its medical school and hospital. He was an honorary member of the Olso Surgical Society and the Norwegian Medical Society, received the Order of St. Olav, and at his death left a legacy of 100,000 kroner for young Norwegian surgeons to study in English-speaking countries. The Gundersen home in La Crosse was a center of Norwegian art and culture; Mrs. Gundersen founded an Ibsen club; the family frequently spent their summers in Norway.

The scholarly contributions of Norwegian Americans to the medical sciences are neither greater nor less than those of any other comparable group. Probably one of the most distinguished figures, recognized particularly for his cancer research, has been Dr. Ludvig Hektoen of Chicago. Born of immigrant parents in Westby, Wisconsin, during the Civil War, Hektoen studied at Luther College, Rush Medical College in Chicago, at Upsala, Prague, and Berlin. He has held numerous posts in hospitals and medical institutes some of which are affiliated with the University of Chicago where he was head of the department of pathology from the turn of the century until 1933. In 1920 he was made director of the John McCormick Institute of Infectious Diseases, holding that position until 1939 when the institute was taken over by the University of Chicago. In 1938 he became president of the Chicago Tumor Institute, one of the leading cancer research centers in the country. For a number of years he was the chairman of the medical section of the

National Research Council. The culmination of a career filled with honors came on his eightieth birthday in 1943 when the Hektoen Institute of Medical Research at Cook County Hospital, Chicago, was dedicated. He has been the editor of several medical journals and his own research is embodied in some three hundred or more publications. It has been said that he stimulated among Chicago medical students a spirit of pure research and that one heard everywhere of "Hektoen's laboratory, Hektoen's school, Hektoen's men."

Cancer research, too, was the dominating interest of Albert Soiland, who was born in Stavanger, Norway, received his education in America and settled in Los Angeles where his work in radiology brought him wide recognition. He founded the American College of Radiology and the Los Angeles Tumor Institute. Returning to Norway for a visit in the spring of 1946, he died in his birthplace at the age of seventy-three. A large part of his fortune of close to a million dollars was left for cancer research.

At the University of Minnesota, Owen H. Wangensteen, trained both in America and abroad, is one of the country's leading chest specialists and has published numerous articles on thoracic surgery. He is director of surgery and chief surgeon of the University of Minnesota Hospital.

The great figure in the field of dentistry, not as a scientist but as an educator, was Dr. Alfred Owre, who fought passionately throughout his life to elevate dentistry from its position as the neglected stepchild of medicine to one of equality with its parent discipline; who worked doggedly for a system of socialized dentistry.

Alfred Owre's parents came from Norway. His father, Lars Owre, was a Quaker, and, wishing to escape the restrictions, economic and social that were placed upon this religious group in Norway in the middle of the nineteenth century, he sought freedom in America. With a knowledge of German, French, Finnish, and Russian and with training in accounting and public administration, he was better equipped than most immigrants to make his way in the New World. In 1870 Lars and Laura Owre and their American-born daughter, Anna, returned to Norway for a visit that lasted fourteen years. Two weeks after their return to their homeland, Alfred was born in the northern city of Hammerfest. In 1884 Lars Owre, homesick for America, took his family to Minneapolis.

Alfred began working at the age of fifteen, first for a wholesale hardware firm and later as a bill collector for a Quaker doctor. At the same time he prepared himself for college, and, though his formal education had been irregular, he successfully passed the entrance examinations and was accepted as a student in the college of dentistry at the University of Minnesota in 1891. Following his graduation in 1894, he studied medicine and surgery, receiving his M.D. degree in 1895. He entered private practice, and in addition taught half-time as an instructor in the dental school. In 1902 he was made a full professor, and in 1905 at the age of thirty-four he was appointed dean of the college of dentistry. His goal was to build so fine a school that it would become a model for a higher type of institution for dental education.

With determination he began a battle that lasted all his life: the elimination of the commercial dental schools, which at the beginning of his career dominated the profession. Nearly every fair-sized city had its "diploma mill," which required little beyond the payment of a fee in return for a certificate that enabled "Dr. So-and-So, Dentist" to advertise, in the weekly gazette of a boom town, that he had arrived to cure the toothaches of its citizenry. In those days the woods were still close enough to the frontier to be full of quack doctors, pettifogging lawyers, as well as charlatan dentists. And Owre fought them tooth and drill. He believed that dental education should be controlled by the scientific schools, namely, the universities; and until dental education was freed from the influence of commercial interests, he was willing to lead the crusade against them. One of Dean Owre's greatest contributions to his profession during his Minnesota years was his work on a commission set up by the Carnegie Foundation to make a survey of dental education in the United States and Canada. The recommendations made by the report did more to achieve a unified standard and type of training for the dental profession than any other measure in the preceding half century.

One of Owre's convictions was that dentistry should be closely integrated with medicine, and, when he accepted the deanship of the Columbia University dental college in 1927, he hoped this ideal could be realized at America's largest university. A teaching clinic, large enough to care for people whose incomes did not permit them to go to the higher priced private dentists, was established in the Medical Center. Threatened by the success of the clinic, dentists and dental associations in the New York City area began an attack on Owre that soon spread to the profession at large. Editors of dental journals refused to print his articles on dental education. His school was repeatedly given a B rating by the Dental Educational Council of America. During the depression his own faculty turned against him, recommending to President Butler that Dean Owre be asked to terminate his connection with the school on the grounds that he had advocated educational plans deemed unsound by his faculty, that he had been unwise and inefficient in the administration of the school, et cetera. Owre thereupon sent in his resignation. The administration, postponing decision, suggested a year's leave of absence, which Owre spent in Europe inspecting dental schools and clinics in Austria, Hungary, Russia, Germany, and Italy. What he learned from the European systems made him more certain than ever that to fight for state control of dentistry and medicine was his mission.

Back in America he made plans to present his ideas of health insurance and public clinics to mothers' clubs, legislatures, and any civic organization that would listen. It took courage for a man of sixty-three to plan a campaign, in the face of powerful organized hostility from the dental and medical professions, to awaken an inert public to the need for an entirely new medico-dental system, socially planned and executed. Furthermore, he no longer had the prestige and backing of an institution from which to carry on his operations, for in the spring of 1934 his resignation was accepted by the university. Once again Nicholas Murray Butler's willing hand had moved to safeguard the status quo.

But the thread had broken. Owre's plans to educate the public were still in the correspondence stage when he was stricken by an illness from which he did not recover. A few months later, on January 2, 1935, Alfred Owre died.

29

Social Scientists

THE VARIOUS BRANCHES of education have had a goodly number of Norwegian Americans, scores of them with prominent positions in teachers' colleges and departments of education throughout the country. The first Norwegian to become the head of an American university was Edward Olsen, a professor of Greek, who was called to be president of the University of South Dakota in 1887. In 1912 Aven Nelson, chairman of the botany department at the University of Wyoming, was made president of that institution. During the same time in Utah John A. Widtsoe was serving as president of the university.

A present-day educational leader is Ernest O. Melby, who after serving as dean of the school of education at Northwestern University, became president of the University of Montana; in 1945 he became dean of the school of education at New York University. His services in the interest of the public are wide. In the summer of 1948 he was named temporary chairman of the National Citizens Council on Civil Rights, organized by forty-eight religious, educational, civic and business leaders to promote a governmental commission on civil rights. Both Ernest Melby and Bryn Hovde, former head of the New School for Social Research, have been vigorous in defense of freedom of speech and press in activities occasioned by the banning of the liberal weekly, *The Nation,* from the New York City schools by the board of superintendents of the city.

Prominent in the public life of the nation, Bryn Hovde is a fine example of a person whose interest in his national background remains alive but who makes his contribution as an American. Of third generation Norwegian stock, he graduated from Luther College, the alma mater of his father and grandfather, both of whom were clergymen in the Norwegian Lutheran Church. He taught at Luther College early in his career, received his Ph.D. from the University of Iowa in 1924, taught at Allegheny College, Meadville, Pennsylvania, and at the University of Pittsburgh. Fellowships abroad enabled him to collect material for his volumes on the Scandinavian countries cited earlier. During the depression he worked on the problem of relief for the unemployed in the Pittsburgh area. In 1938 he was appointed director of the department of public welfare for the city of Pittsburgh; later he was chief of the State Department's division of cultural co-operation. He served as technical expert on the staff of the American delegation to the United Nations Conference in San Francisco and in the same capacity at the London Conference, which established the United Nations Scientific and Cultural Organization. From 1945 to 1950 he was head of the New School for Social Research in New York.

Also of Norwegian stock, Frederick Hovde became president of Purdue University in 1946 after an administrative career at the universities of Minnesota and Rochester and in the government during the second World War. At the University of Kansas City, Robert Mortvedt has been dean of education, dean of the college of liberal arts, and at present is vice-president of the university in charge of the educational program of the institution.

The famous "Springfield Plan," a program of education for citizenship carried on in the schools of Springfield, Massachusetts, was started by Dr. John E. Granrud, superintendent of the schools from 1933 to 1945. This program emphasizes through all the grades racial and religious tolerance and mutual appreciation of ethnic groups. The plan stimulated a Warner Brothers motion picture, *It Happened in Springfield*. Continuing his crusade against prejudice, after retiring from his superintendency, Dr. Granrud is now western field director of the commission on educational organizations for the National Conference of Christians and Jews.

From time to time I have drawn on the records of the Berdahl family who pioneered in the Dakota Territory. A son of one of these pioneers, Clarence Berdahl, has for a number of years been chairman of the political science department at the University of Illinois. He has contributed scholarship to his profession; he has served his government. As a consultant for the Department of State during the last war, he was sent to the San Francisco Conference as assistant executive officer on one of the constitutional commissions. At the University of Minnesota William Anderson has been head of the political science department for several years. Peter Odegaard, formerly president of Reed College, Portland, Oregon, is now head of the department of political science at the University of California in Berkeley. In 1947 Henry J. Peterson retired after twenty-seven years as head of the political science department at the University of Wyoming.

In the field of agricultural economics, particularly in the marketing aspects of farming, Oscar Jesness, chief of the division of agricultural economics at the University of Minnesota, is well known. He has served on several government boards, councils, and committees. Recognized work in the theory of marketing has been done by Harry S. Tosdal, who for a number of years has played a prominent role in the Harvard University Graduate School of Business Administration. An associate professor in the same school, Henrietta M. Larson, the first and for many years the only woman professor at Harvard, has published extensively. One of her most recent works is a *Guide to Business History;* at present she is directing the research and writing the history of the Standard Oil Company (New Jersey). She is a sister of Agnes Larson, chairman of the history department at St. Olaf College. Another sister, Nora Larson, is a research associate in the department of chemistry at Columbia University, New York City. There is drama in the thought that three granddaughters of Ole Østerud, who had three days of formal schooling and came to America in the 'fifties to pioneer in southern Minnesota, have earned Ph.D. degrees and have achieved eminent positions in their professions.

30

The Veblens

On September 16, 1847, Thomas and Kari Veblen arrived in Milwaukee, Wisconsin, four and a half months after leaving their home in the district of Valders, Norway. They had three dollars in cash, and Thomas, having had typhoid fever during the voyage across the Atlantic, was none too strong. But he found work for the winter with a friend some distance from Milwaukee and the next summer built a home on the shore of Lake Michigan in the village of Port Ulao. The second son, Andrew—their first-born had died in Norway—was born there in September, 1848. The next year the family moved to a homestead in Sheboygan County in a community settled heavily by Dutch people. The 1850 census lists only three Norwegian families in the county, and it was probably the desire to live among their own people that prompted Thomas in 1854 to move northward to Manitowoc County, in a township where Norwegians had already begun to settle in significant numbers. There in the sturdy frame house Thomas Veblen built, Thorstein, the sixth of their twelve children, was born in the summer of 1857. In this pioneer Norwegian environment, in a home where *Skandinaven* and the Norse sagas were read, where the children went to school in the living room and were taught by a strict old Norwegian schoolmaster in a frock coat, where Christmas festivities lasted two weeks as they did in Norway, Thorstein spent the first eight years of his life.

Successful though he was in Wisconsin, Thomas Veblen in 1865 moved his family to southeastern Minnesota on a tract of prairie land that would free him from the drudgery of stump clearing. Their new home was twelve miles from the village of Northfield, where a group of New England men established Carleton College in 1866 and a Norwegian Lutheran pastor founded St. Olaf College in 1874. When in 1871 Andrew Veblen, the oldest of the children, was ready for college his father sent him to Carleton, where after three years of preparatory training and three years of college work, he received his A.B. in 1877. For the next four years Andrew Veblen taught at Luther College in Decorah, Iowa. From 1881 to 1883 he studied mathematics at Johns Hopkins, then accepted a position at the State University of Iowa as an instructor in mathematics. Three years later he was put in charge of the physics department, remaining its head until his resignation in 1905. For the rest of his life he was occupied largely in Norwegian American affairs, particularly the collection of Norwegian pioneer historical material in connection with the *bygdelag* movement, which he initiated.

Meanwhile as Thomas Veblen's other children grew up they were sent, like Andrew, to Carleton College, the girls as well as the boys. It is said that Emily Veblen was the first Norwegian American girl to graduate from college in America. The fact that Thomas Veblen continued to send his children to an American college after a Norwegian Lutheran institution was established in the same community speaks for a greater independence of mind and behavior on the part of the elder Veblens than the majority of the Norwegian settlers thereabouts had. They were indeed accused of "putting on airs," but Thomas was determined that his children should have as broad an education as it was possible for him to give them. To cut down on expenses he built in a week's time—able carpenter that he was—a small house for his children close to the campus.

Thorstein entered the Carleton College preparatory department in 1874. Throughout his six years there he was the "queer" campus figure, regarded by students and most of the faculty as supercilious, sardonic, lazy, and sometimes brilliant. One member of the faculty, John Bates Clark, professor of political economy and history, appreciated him. Among the students the president's niece, Ellen Rolfe, an intelligent, gifted girl, brought him the only companionship he knew. They were married in 1888. At the graduation exercises in the Congregational church in 1880, Thomas and Kari Veblen listened admiringly to their son's oration on "Mill's Examination of Hamilton's Philosophy of the Conditioned." For a year thereafter Veblen taught at a small Lutheran academy in Madison, Wisconsin, witnessing Bjørnson's entrance into the Middle West and the squall of anger that swirled through the Norwegian settlements in his wake.

In the fall of 1881 Thorstein went east with Andrew to study philosophy at Johns Hopkins. Financial and intellectual circumstances prompted him to leave the institution before the year was over and to enter Yale University to pursue his philosophical studies with Noah Porter, president of the university, and social theory with William Graham Sumner. In 1884 he received his Ph.D. degree after two and a half years of struggle with debt and loneliness. Although he left the institution with a high recommendation from its president and others, he was not able to find a teaching position. For the next seven years he lived on his father's farm, read widely, married Ellen Rolfe and settled with her on her father's farm in Iowa, translated the Laxdaela Saga from the Icelandic, and tried ineffectively to secure a teaching position. Finally deciding that the only path to academic work lay in returning to an institution as a graduate student, he enrolled in 1891 at the age of thirty-four at Cornell University, Ithaca, New York. Attired in a coonskin cap and corduroy trousers, he presented himself to the head of the economics department, J. Laurence Laughlin, who was so impressed with the quality of the man's mind that he secured for him a special grant. When Laughlin became head professor of economics at the newly founded University of Chicago the following year, he arranged a $520 teaching fellowship for Veblen there. For the next two decades Veblen pursued a troubled academic career and an uneasy personal life. He left the University of Chicago in 1904, taught at Leland Stanford Junior University from 1906 to 1909, at the University of Missouri from 1911 to 1918, and at the New School for Social Research in New York from 1919 to 1922. During these years he and Ellen Rolfe were divorced and he later married Anne Fessenden Bradley, mother of two children. His final years were spent in isolation in California with his stepdaughter Becky, his second wife having died in 1920. Thorstein Veblen died on August 3, 1929.

The appearance of *The Theory of the Leisure Class* in 1899 catapulted Veblen into prominence and made him one of the most controversial figures on the contemporary intellectual scene in America. In a letter to his brother Andrew on October 18, 1899, Thorstein comments, "Opinion seems to be divided as to whether I am a knave or a fool, though there are some who make out that the book is a work of genius—I don't know just how." His books and articles in succeeding years further increased the number of his admirers as well as that of his detractors. Laying aside all question of the originality or commonplaceness of his social and economic ideas, of their popularity or unpopularity, Veblen's thought, understood or not, has become part of the intellectual fabric of this century. It would be fatuous and futile to try to say any more in a work like this.

Yet another Veblen has made his place among the honored of the intellectual world, Oswald Veblen, the mathematician, son of Andrew. He was born in Decorah, 1880, while his father was teaching at Luther College; grew up in Iowa City and graduated from the University of Iowa in 1898; received another A.B. at Harvard University in 1900, then went to the University of Chicago, where his uncle Thorstein was then teaching, and studied for his Ph.D., receiving it in 1903. For two years he stayed on at the University of Chicago to teach mathematics and in 1905 went to Princeton University, teaching there until 1932 and since then at the Institute for Advanced Study in Princeton, New Jersey. He received honorary degrees from the University of Oslo in 1929, from Hamburg in 1933, and from the University of Chicago in 1941. His research and publications on the foundations of geometry and in the field of topology have made him one of America's front-line mathematicians.

31

Wars and Expeditions

RUMORS OF WAR grew louder after Lincoln's election in November, 1860; and when the elderly folks in a Norwegian community in Black-hammer Township, Minnesota, saw that the northern lights, visible almost every night that fall and early winter, were brilliantly crimson they took it as a portent of bloodshed. They were not surprised when news finally reached their frontier settlement that there had been an outbreak at Fort Sumter. More than a dozen young men from this farm community of scarcely more families hurried to the nearest recruiting station to enlist. So it was in Norwegian communities all over the upper Middle West; eight hundred from Minnesota, four hundred from Iowa, three thousand from Wisconsin, and many from the older settlements in Illinois. Solidly opposed to slavery they were eager to carry arms in defense of the Union. For the most part they served in the ranks, but a few rose to high command, notable among them Colonel Hans Christian Heg, who fell at the battle of Chickamauga and became the symbol of the Norwegian Americans' contribution to the great war.

Colonel Heg, talented and forceful, was the son of the well-known Muskego settlement leader, Even Heg. In his youth he had joined the rush to the California gold fields. When the Civil War broke out he was the state prison commissioner of Wisconsin. Like many other national groups, particularly the Germans and the Irish, the Scandinavians felt they could best express their patriotism by forming regiments of their own people. Thus the Fifteenth Wisconsin regiment was organized, the governor of Wisconsin consenting to commission Heg as its colonel. Nine hundred Scandinavians, most of them Norwegians, and a few native Americans were recruited. C. L. Clausen, the pioneer minister, was chaplain, and a Norwegian physician from Kansas, Dr. S. O. Himoe, was surgeon. Before the war was over the regiment had seen action in Missouri, Kentucky, Mississippi, Tennessee, Alabama, and Georgia, and had participated in Sherman's march to the sea, to be mustered out at Chattanooga in 1865. A third of the regiment had been killed in battle or died from wounds, including their first leader, who was fatally wounded in 1863.

Heg's letters to his wife during the early part of the war reveal a person of warm humanity with a zest for living. "You know," he wrote, "I am generally lucky in making friends where ever I go, and I shall succeed here just as well as I have done before." And in a later one: "I tell you my Dear—I would not have missed taking the course I did for all I am worth. I have done more for the government than any man that has gone from Wisconsin. . . . You know I can afford to brag to you." He tells her that if he should "go and see some of the *fine, handsome* Grass Widdows" she must not wonder at it, giving her permission to do the same. "I am not very handsome for I have got to be quite careless about my dress, and I do not know but I ought to get me one of these women to take care of me if I can not get you down here." Frequently he asks her to send him delicacies like butter, lump sugar, preserves, cheese, a keg of currant wine, and another time a box of Catawba wine. Cheerful and optimistic himself, he was annoyed to see his Company K never "do anything except read their Norwegian prayer books and hang out a long face." At the time of his death he was the leader of a brigade, and, according to his commanding general, would soon have received the rank of brigadier general had he lived. In his last letter to his wife he wrote: "The 'Gen.' will call and see you the first thing you know—probably surprise you."

While the soldiers cemented their allegiance to their new land on the battlefield, in prisons, and in hospitals, the immigrant women ran the farms; organized soldiers' aid societies and sent bandages and supplies to the wounded and sick, poring over the reports in *Emigranten* written by its editor, C. F. Solberg, who went with the regiment as a war correspondent. In the midst of all this the immigrants on the northern Iowa and southern Minnesota frontier lived through the horrors of the Sioux uprising—that is, those who were fortunate enough to live through it. For the Sioux massacres were as bloody as any.

In both World Wars the thousands of Norwegian Americans who served were, with few exceptions, strictly American doughboys and G.I.'s, indistinguishable from any other group. However, in the second World War a Norse battalion was formed as part of the Ninth Infantry Regiment stationed at Fort Snelling. Trained for winter warfare to help in liberating Norway, the soldiers in this battalion were required to speak Norwegian reasonably well.

Among the many military figures brought into the spotlight during the last war there were a few of Norwegian descent. Evans Carlson, leader of the Marine battalion known as Carlson's Raiders, was on his paternal side of Norwegian stock. His grandfather was one of the small band of 'forty-niners who left Norway for the California gold fields. But Evans Carlson grew up in a New England environment, his father settling there as a Congregational minister and marrying into a New England family. Nevertheless, there was something of the viking about this New England boy. He began his military career in 1912 when, at the illegal age of sixteen, he ran away from home to join the Army. Except for a few years, he spent his life in the Army and the Marine Corps, saw service in different parts of the world. His experiences in China as an observer of the Eighth Route Army's guerrilla warfare against the Japanese profoundly influenced both his military and political thinking. He used similar techniques as leader of the raider battalion that made the surprise attack on Makin Island and fought so gallantly on Guadalcanal. The exploits of this battalion became the basis for the movie *Gung Ho,* a phrase, adopted by Carlson from the Chinese soldiers, which epitomized for many a Marine the democratic ideals that Carlson constantly fought for. Carlson died in 1947 at the age of fifty-one.

Another prominent military figure is Lieutenant General Lauris Norstad, son of a Chicago Lutheran pastor. He served on General Arnold's advisory council helping plan the North African campaign, became director of operations of the Mediterranean Allied Air Forces at the age of thirty-six, and as chief of staff of the Twentieth Air Force implemented the strategy that culminated in the dropping of the atomic bombs on Japan. Since the war he has taken a major part in the negotiations that led to the unification of the armed forces. It has been said that he "master-minded" the Army's role in the pre-unification debate and was its principal exponent before congressional committees. With the setting up of the Air Force as a self-contained arm and with the reorganization of its staff Norstad has been appointed deputy chief of staff operations, serving directly under Air Force chief of staff, General Hoyt S. Vandenberg. In this position he would in time of war be responsible for translating into action our over-all plan for aerial defense and attack.

General Douglas MacArthur's personal physician all through the war was Colonel Roger O. Egeberg, whose father, a civil engineer, was born in Norway. Another officer close to MacArthur was Major General Leif Sverdrup of the Army's Engineering Corps, who was born in Norway in 1898, came to the United States in 1914, studied engineering, and achieved a high reputation in his profession. He is the senior partner in the firm of Sverdrup and Parcel in St. Louis, Missouri. In an interview for the *Nordisk Tidende*, Colonel Egeberg, referring to General Sverdrup, said: "Between us we made MacArthur definitely conscious of Norway and Norwegians and introduced the Norwegian anthem to many an officers' gathering."

The recall, at his own request, of Colonel Bernt Balchen to active duty with the United States Air Force in 1948 brought back into the service of his adopted country a man who was once described as "the greatest pilot in the world, bar none." Bernt Balchen was born in Kristiansand in 1899 and received his training at the Royal Naval Aviation Flying school at Horten. Rescues and mercy flights have made him one of the most publicized flyers in the world. He was the "hero of the hour" when he flew Byrd, whom he has accompanied on several polar expeditions, across the Atlantic in 1927. Fogbound over Paris for three hours with the gas tank menacingly low, he brought the plane back to the coast and landed safely on the surf. He became an American citizen in 1931 while he was working for the Fokker Aircraft Corporation but later returned to Norway to become manager of the Norwegian Airlines in Europe. When the Nazis invaded Norway he was in the United States inspecting aircraft. Immediately he joined the British Royal Air Force, shuttled bombers from Bermuda to England and evacuated some two thousand Norwegians to Britain in a daring ferry service. Transferred to the United States Air Corps, he was detailed to head a secret expedition to Greenland to establish the northernmost American airbase in the world. After the war he returned to Norway to become manager and director of the Royal Norwegian Airlines. Now in the United States Air Force again, Balchen is with the Alaskan Air Command studying problems of arctic defense, a fitting assignment for one who is credited with more logged hours over ice and snow than any other airman.

Polar exploration has been an area in which Norwegians have played a conspicuous role. In 1947 a Norwegian-born explorer and engineer, Finn Ronne, led under the auspices of the American Geographical Society an expedition to the Antarctic where he mapped the last uncharted coastline in the world. Upon his return in 1948 he announced that he had definitely established that Antarctica was *one* continent. As an explorer Finn Ronne followed in the footsteps of his father who was with Roald Amundsen when he discovered the South Pole and with Byrd in his first Antarctic expedition. He himself accompanied Byrd on two later polar expeditions. The Norwegian oceanographer, Harald Ulrick Sverdrup, was called to the United States in 1936 to become director of the University of California's Scripps İnstitute of Oceanography. In 1948 he returned to Norway to head the Norwegian Institute for Polar Research and to lead a Swedish-Norwegian-British expedition to Queen Maud Land in the Antarctic.

32

Politics and Government Service

SOON AFTER HIS arrival in the Midwest the Norwegian immigrant began to take part in the political life of his adopted country. He came with some political training, for ever since 1814 his responsibilities in the affairs of the parish had been increasing. Thus in America he was ready to assume the public duties his new environment thrust upon him. His first experience was on the local level as a township or county officer. Much of the official business in these townships, which not infrequently bore names like Numedal, Throndhjem, Norway, Arendahl, Ibsen, and Tordenskold, was carried on in Norwegian. Election notices, sometimes even ordinances and laws were printed in that language. The first Norwegian to serve as a delegate to a constitutional convention was James D. Reymert, also, as we remember, the editor of the first Norwegian newspaper in the Middle West. In 1847, the year *Nordlyset* was founded, Reymert was a member of the Wisconsin constitutional convention, and in succeeding years served in the house and in the senate of the state legislature. Another early editor, Knud Langeland, was a member of the same body in 1860.

But the Norwegians exercised no significant influence in state politics until after the Civil War. Those who had served in the war returned home with prestige which not infrequently gave them a start in politics. Suspicion of the foreign-born was greatly reduced by his patriotism during the war. The rapid growth of the Norwegian population in the Middle West and their increasing prosperity brought greater political opportunities, so that after 1870 the number of Norwegians who served in the state legislatures steadily increased. They soon found their way into the executive and administrative departments of the states; some of the offices, such as the secretary of state in Minnesota and the lieutenant governorship in North Dakota eventually came virtually to belong to either a Norwegian or a Swede.

The first and one of the most distinguished Norwegian Americans to serve in Congress was Knute Nelson. He came to America as a youngster with his widowed mother at the halfway mark of the century, studied law and entered politics in Wisconsin after the Civil War, moved to Minnesota in the 'seventies, and within a few years was serving in the state legislature. In 1883 he was elected to Congress, serving three terms. In 1892 he became governor of Minnesota, the first Norwegian American governor in America. His election to the United States Senate in 1895 took him back to Washington where for almost three decades he served the nation. A conservative Republican, as the majority of the Norwegian Americans in Congress have been, the Senator from Minnesota expressed his unhappiness under the Democratic regime in a letter to his Norwegian American friend, Nicolay Grevstad, then Minister to Uruguay and Paraguay:

[December 22, 1913] We have now been in continuous session for over a year, one session running into the other. So far the President seems to control his Party absolutely and has made it do just as he has desired. . . . It has been the worst and most disagreeable session I have attended for years. Wilson has turned out to be a worse tyrant than Roosevelt was. Wilson's conduct has reconciled me to Roosevelt so that I would be willing to support him. Anything to get rid of Wilson. . . . The South is now in the saddle and practically control the Government. . . . I sometimes wish I had not stood for another election as it is so disagreeable to serve under Democratic caucus rule, as it practically makes us Republicans, so far as important matters are concerned helpless.

But Senator Nelson's services as chairman of the commerce committee, the judiciary committee, and as a member of the banking and currency committee, to mention a few of his duties, were appreciated even by the opposition, President Wilson supporting him in the elections of 1918. Senator Nelson died in office shortly after his eightieth birthday in 1923.

Since 1883, when Knute Nelson first entered Congress, about three dozen Americans of Norwegian descent have served in the House of Representatives, about a dozen in the Senate.

A *Nordisk Tidende* reporter's account of the Seventeenth of May celebration in the nation's capital in 1948 reveals that invitations were issued to the three United States Senators and seven Congressmen with "more or less Norwegian blood in their veins." They were Senators

Warren Magnuson (Washington), Edward J. Thye (Minnesota), Alexander Wiley (Wisconsin); Congressmen Henry Jackson and Thor C. Tollefson (Washington), August Andresen, Harold C. Hagen, and Harold Knutson (Minnesota), Henry O. Talle (Iowa), and Leroy Johnson (California).

One of the best known members of the House was Gilbert N. Haugen, a Republican from Iowa, who served from 1899 to 1933. His activities centered on the agricultural program, the McNary-Haugen bill receiving most public notice. Second generation Andrew Volstead, Republican from Minnesota, wrote the law that brought America the speakeasy, bootleggers, bad gin, and *The Great Gatsby*. The bulk of the Norwegian American Congressmen have allied themselves with the conservative wing of the Republican Party; a few of them, like Harold Knutson, have been notorious isolationists. But the rise of the Farmer-Labor Party in Minnesota brought a more liberal element into Congress. In the 1948 elections the Democratic, New Deal mayor of Minneapolis, Hubert H. Humphrey, whose mother was born on a farm near Kristiansand, Norway, was elected to the United States Senate. He has been one of the leaders in the fight for civil rights legislation. A progressive note, too, is being heard from the Far West in the able second generation Norwegian, Henry Jackson from Washington, whom *The Nation* referred to as "a scholarly and sincere" New Deal Democrat whose career might well lead him to the United States Senate.

Among the almost two dozen men of Norwegian extraction who have sat in governors' chairs, one of the ablest, most liberal, and most colorful was Minnesota's Floyd Bjørnstjerne Olson, whose death in 1936 at the age of forty-four halted a career that was leading him to the United States Senate, and, many predicted, could have culminated in the presidency of the United States. He had all the attributes for a political career in Minnesota. His mother was Swedish, his father Norwegian, he was born in a Jewish working class neighborhood in Minneapolis, and married a Czechoslovakian woman. He could speak Norwegian, Swedish, or Yiddish as the occasion demanded. At his funeral a Lutheran minister, a Catholic priest, and a Jewish rabbi participated. A sensational career as county attorney in the 'twenties, during which he successfully fought moneyed interests, endeared him to the working classes, and he was elected the first Farmer-Labor governor in 1930. His great personal charm won him blind devotion from high-minded reformers, unreformed union racketeers, honest working people, desirables and undesirables.

Lawyers, bankers, and manufacturers were in his intimate circle; and he still held their allegiance when, standing on the steps of the Minnesota Capitol in 1934, he shouted to the crowd of unemployed, "You bet your life I'm a radical," as he told them he would declare martial law and take steps to provide relief if the legislature failed to do so, adding that if capitalism could do nothing to prevent the recurrence of present conditions, "I hope the present system of government goes right down to hell."

Although Olson was succeeded by a Farmer-Labor governor, Elmer Benson, also of Norwegian background, the strength of his party waned as it split into right- and left-wing groups. But his principles lingered on beneath the surface of the official Republicanism that again came into power in Minnesota with Harold Stassen and the even more orthodox Republican administrations of Edward Thye, now United States Senator, and Luther Youngdahl. In recent elections Farmer-Labor-Democrats (the revived form of the original Farmer-Labor Party) like Theodore Jorgenson, professor of Norwegian at St. Olaf College, and Karl Rölvaag, son of the great novelist, have made unsuccessful attempts to enter the political picture in Minnesota.

Among hundreds of mayors of Norwegian descent is Henry O. Jaastad, known until his retirement in 1947 as the Perpetual Mayor of Tucson, Arizona. During eighteen years of conservative but constructive administration he made Tucson one of the model cities of the country.

Quite a few Norwegian Americans have been in the diplomatic and consular service, most of them occupying minor consular offices in various parts of the world. The first of ministerial rank was Rasmus B. Anderson, who from 1885 to 1889 was Minister in Denmark. Laurits S. Swenson began his thirty-seven years of diplomatic service in 1897 as Minister to Denmark, continuing his career as Minister to Switzerland, Norway, and The Netherlands. He died in 1947. From 1911 to 1917 Nicolay A. Grevstad, editor of *Skandinaven,* was Minister to Paraguay and Uruguay. The late John A. Gade served the military and state departments in many capacities during a long career that took him to several European legations. His autobiography, *All My Born Days,* is a full-flavored account of childhood years in an upper class Norwegian family, his education at Harvard, his life as an eminent architect, Wall Street banker, and naval intelligence officer.

In the nation's capital many Norwegian Americans have carried on their careers as civil servants. They have been numerous in the Department of Agriculture, both in major and minor positions. During most of the 1920's Carl W. Larson was chief of the bureau of dairying. For several years Alfred Stefferud, a St. Olaf College graduate of 1925, has been editor of the important *Yearbook* of the Department of Agriculture. Jesse E. Saugstad, born in the Norwegian American community of Westby, Wisconsin, has been head of the shipping division of the Office of Transport and Communications Policy in the State Department since the middle 'forties. Dr. Everett E. Hagen is chief economist for the Bureau of the Budget. Distinguished work in the cataloging division of the Library of Congress has been done by at least three Norwegian Americans. J. C. M. Hanson founded the Library of Congress cataloging system, reorganized that of the University of Chicago Library, and was sent by the Carnegie Corporation to Rome to catalog the Vatican Library. Juul Dieserud, who came to the United States in 1892 after his graduation from the University of Oslo, was head of the catalog division for several decades. He died in 1947. Thorstein Jahr was a cataloger, reviser, and an expert on Scandinavian materials for many years. Thorvald Solberg gave many years of service as Register of Copyrights in the Library of Congress.

If one scans volumes of the *Official Register of the United States* one constantly comes across obviously Norwegian names like Alf Oftedal and Sigurd B. Qvale, to say nothing of the many Larsons, Nelsons, and Petersons who might be Norwegian, serving in a variety of capacities; so that one is definitely left with the impression that the Norwegian American group has in good measure, through administration after administration, helped keep the intricate machinery of the national government in motion.

33

Newspapermen

OUT OF THE Norwegian American group came a man who was a dominant force in the American newspaper world, Victor F. Lawson, publisher of the *Chicago Daily News*. At the time of his death in 1925 the publishers of the *New York Times* called him "the dean of American newspaper publishers." Lawson ran his paper on sane conservative lines with occasional bursts of progressive spirit that grew weaker as the years advanced. He kept the paper independent politically, but his personal political sentiments, like those of many prominent Norwegian Americans, were clearly expressed in his dislike of President Wilson and his administration. In the history of journalism he will be remembered as the founder, with Melville Stone, of the Associated Press, becoming its first president from 1894–1900, and later a director. He has been called, too, "the father of the Postal Savings Bank." His newspaper framed a proposed bill for Congress and through several years of discussion helped swing public opinion in favor of it. When in 1910 the bill passed Congress, President Taft sent the Chicago publisher the pen used by him in affixing his signature to the bill.

Partly responsible for Lawson's conservatism in many matters was his invalid wife, a rigid New Englander, who, for example, disapproved of any secularization of the Sabbath, a day on which the Lawsons engaged in no social activities. Lawson would not back a plan for free weekly band concerts on Sunday afternoons, suggested by one of his staff as a public enterprise for his newspaper. And when the Chicago Orchestra Association made plans to inaugurate "workingmen's concerts" on Sunday afternoons, he threatened to withdraw his usual $25,000 support. After his death in 1925 several large bequests were received by religious organizations, including the Chicago Y.M.C.A. and Y.W.C.A. and the Chicago Theological Seminary, which received over a million dollars. There was general disappointment and much public comment when control of the *Daily News,* valued at fourteen millions, was left in the hands of a trust company instead of to associates who had worked with Lawson to build up the newspaper. Frank Knox later became the publisher.

Well known in midwestern newspaper circles is the veteran Wisconsin Progressive, William Evjue, editor of the *Madison Capital-Times,* a modern muckraker, a blunt, outspoken critic of corruption in government, who belongs to the small group of independent and influential editors in the Middle West who have become a tradition in this region of otherwise conservative newspapers.

Among reporters who have a Norwegian background perhaps Eric Sevareid is the best known. Grandson of an immigrant, he was born in North Dakota, educated in Minneapolis and got his first newspaper experience on the *Minneapolis Journal.* He went to Paris, worked on the *Paris Herald,* and when the second World War broke out reported news on the Columbia Broadcasting System from Paris and later from London. His autobiographical *Not So Wild a Dream* is a fine expression of some of the best qualities in American life, the devotion to democratic ideals tempered by an objective and critical spirit.

34

Business and Finance

THE MARKET PLACE and the counting house have held a limited attraction for Norwegian Americans. On the level of individual and local exchange of goods and money they have produced their quota of able managers, but big enterprises involving millions in investment and mass production they have left to other groups whose history of urban dwelling, whose training in the world of commerce, is older. The Norwegian's past on a small farm in a secluded valley, counting kernels of corn in the palm of his hand, numbering livestock on his fingers, has shaped his personality, his talents, and determined his course. When he acquired a little money in America he did not gamble with it, but put it into land or a small store. His empire was his farm, his workshop, his general store. He had no dreams of power and grandeur. Consequently, his name appears infrequently on the roster of eminent figures in the history of American business.

There were some, however, who prospered into middle class comfort through their business enterprises. Closely connected with agriculture as they were, it is not strange that a few of them with some inventive skill made improvements or designed new tools for the farmers' use. We have already mentioned T. G. Mandt, maker of the Stoughton wagon. Another Wisconsin Norwegian farm implement manufacturer was J. A. Johnson (Gisholt), founder of the Gisholt Manufacturing Company in Madison, one of the most influential Norwegians of his time. He had come to Wisconsin as a boy in 1844, and while he was preparing for confirmation, lived in the parsonage of Pastor Dietrichson, the first of the University-trained clergymen to come from Norway. Later in life he became a Unitarian and was sharply critical of the Norwegian Americans who clung to their old culture. For several years Johnson was connected with a concern that handled the Walter A. Wood reapers and mowers in the Northwest, but later started out on his own, organizing in 1899, with the aid of four sons who were trained machinists, the Gisholt Machine Company. This company made a special kind of turret lathe invented by Johnson, which was sold all over the world. But generally speaking, there has been no John Deere or Cyrus McCormick among the Norwegians in America. Among present-day manufacturers with a Norwegian background is Walter Geist, president of the Allis-Chalmers machine and farm implement company in Milwaukee.

While a few modest fortunes were accumulated by Norwegian American manufacturers of the upper Middle West during the 'eighties and 'nineties, one of considerable magnitude was developing under the shrewd stewardship of a St. Louis plumbing manufacturer, Nelson Olson Nelson. Although his activities and interest kept him outside the stream of Norwegian American life, his contributions, hitherto neglected by historians of the Norwegian people in America, are well worth recording in some detail. Except for his name, Nelson Olson Nelson deviated sharply from what is usually thought of as the Norwegian American "type." He was small and wiry, weighing only 130 pounds; he became a millionaire, a social experimenter, a Unitarian.

Born in Lillesand, Norway, in 1844, he was two years old when his parents, in a party of over seventy, sailed from the Norwegian port of Grimstad. The year before Nelson was born, this group had sent the liberal newspaper editor, Johan R. Reiersen, to America to investigate conditions and possible locations for settlement. In Reiersen's book, *Pathfinder for Norwegian Emigrants to the United North American States and Texas,* which was published in Norway in 1844, he advised the prospective emigrants to come to the West by way of New Orleans and the Mississippi River. Thus they reached the New World in January, 1847, proceeding to Missouri, where they bought "improved" land from Yankee squatters. There on the frontier among Kentuckians, Virginians, and his own kinsmen, Nelson spent his youth, remembering it in later years as a happy and romantic time. With Carlyle he believed in "the blessed glow of Labor" and scorned those who wailed about the grinding toil and bleakness of farm life. Throughout his life this pleasure in work remained with him, and, incidentally, paid off well.

When the Civil War broke out, he, like the other men and youths among the Norwegian settlers in Missouri, left his Secessionist friends and neighbors, to serve in the Union Army. War over, he drifted into the wholesale grocery business in St. Louis, sold when business became dull, ran a retail store for five years in Kansas, and finally in 1872 took a position as a bookkeeper in a St. Louis wholesale hardware and plumbing goods house. From a set of books, a helpful bookkeeper, and days of work that ended at eleven P. M., he learned his trade, earned not only a raise but partnership in the firm at the end of a year. That was in 1872. In 1873 the house of Jay Cooke fell and brought down with it business concerns the country over. Under Nelson's managership the hardware and plumbing company pulled through.

Four years later Nelson had acquired enough confidence to do business alone, whereupon, at the age of thirty-three, he organized the N. O. Nelson Manufacturing Company, which, in spite of periodic business slumps, became one of the largest building and plumbing supply companies in the world. The white enamel tub came on the market shortly after he had built a large copper tub factory, necessitating a conversion to other kinds of manufacture. When marble washstands went out of fashion, Nelson turned to the larger operations of marbelizing the big hotels, skyscrapers, and public buildings.

The success that came from his enterprise did not convince Nelson that the industrial system in which he operated was the best of all possible systems. He was not a keen economic thinker, but he was practical, fair, honest; he knew that the capitalistic system would outlive him; but he knew, too, that the war between labor and capital would not abate until labor had its just share of the dollar harvest being reaped by Big Business. By 1886 he could afford to experiment, which he did by following the example of several large European manufacturers who had introduced profit-sharing. His employees each year received dividends in the form of stock, thus becoming part owners of the company. In 1905 he began to share profits with the customers. His objective was to have his employees and customers eventually become the complete owners of the business, thus making it a genuinely co-operative enterprise. When he began sharing profits with customers, he stopped taking any profit or interest for himself, being satisfied with a living wage for his work as manager of his many factories and plants.

Always concerned with the living conditions of the working classes, Nelson very early in his career began to promote enterprises that would make life less bleak for them. In 1879 he organized a fresh-air mission providing free excursions on the Mississippi to tenement mothers and children. Believing firmly that better houses, schools, and more pleasant

surroundings were essential for the happiness of his workers, he bought
125 acres of rolling upland twenty miles east of St. Louis, moved his
principal factories there, erected comfortable houses for his employees,
and planned what he hoped would be an ideal village community.

Named after the French social worker LeClaire, the village had no
government, no mayor or council, no policemen. No churches were
built, but everyone was free to worship as he pleased. At the auditorium
and recreation center the villagers held dancing classes and club meetings; lectures by eminent speakers were featured during the winter
months. A library was built up; kindergarten, grammar and high schools
were started, staffed by well-trained teachers. An industrial school for
non-residents over sixteen years of age was established, pupils coming
from Colorado, Kentucky, Arkansas, Missouri, and Illinois. Students
spent the mornings in classwork, the afternoons in the factory, on the
farm run by the community, or in helping to build new houses. They
were paid for their work, their only expenses at the school being the
cost of co-operative board. Nelson planned student trips to the St. Louis
Art Museum, to the Columbian Exposition in Chicago, to large newspaper plants, and other places that he felt would increase their knowledge of the world as well as help in their own vocational training.

Wherever Nelson went he found an outlet for his humanitarian and
social impulses. In Bessemer, Alabama, where he owned a soil-pipe factory, he established a co-operative community for Negroes similar to but
smaller than his LeClaire colony. While wintering in California in 1902,
he saw that many consumptives, who had come there for their health,
were stranded in the winter fogs of the coastal area. Without thought of
returns, he bought 125 acres of desert valley rimmed by brown and blue
mountain ranges; there he built a tent city, irrigated, planted alfalfa,
cantaloupes; pepper, umbrella, poplar, and almond trees; bought cows
and chickens, and publicly invited consumptives to come to the camp.
They could remain as long as they wanted to, with a slight charge for
tent and board, and if they were able, help with the garden work. During
the first two winters of the camp some fifty consumptives enjoyed the
warmth and dryness of the desert and the pleasant surroundings of the
camp.

Visiting in New Orleans in 1910, Nelson organized a group of dairy
farmers into a co-operative association. A creamery was erected, a store
was established, and soon several neighborhood stores were in operation.
Commodities were sold for cash and at the lowest possible margin of

profit. The association built its own bakery and sold a five-cent loaf of bread for three and one-half cents. Nelson stores became famous in New Orleans for the correct weight of their flour sacks, and it was largely through the persistent honesty of the "Nelson weight" that the Louisiana legislature passed one of the strictest weight and measure laws on the books of any state. In 1915 Nelson turned over to his three hundred workers his fifty grocery stores, three meat markets, condiment factory, the the large dairy plant, and truck farm. He was sure that the co-operative venture was firmly established, but a succession of losses brought failure in three years and Nelson filed a personal petition for bankruptcy on the New Orleans undertaking. But this devoted disciple of the co-operative movement, who as one of its American leaders attended international meetings, never lost faith in his ideal.

Nelson was active in political as well as in social movements. In 1887 he was elected to the St. Louis city council, fighting for reform measures without great success during his four years of tenure. In 1894 he ran for Congress on the Single-Tax Ticket, but in spite of good newspaper support and public enthusiasm for Henry George, who came to St. Louis to speak during the campaign, the candidate received but a small vote. Leaders of the reform movement often gathered at the Nelson dinner table: the genial Henry George and his wife; Charlotte Perkins Stetson (Gilman) with her caustic witticisms; Sam Jones, the "Golden Rule" Socialist mayor of Toledo; big honest John Fiske, propounding his evolutionary theories. Every time Fiske came to St. Louis Nelson called together a dozen or so of the town's intellectuals after the lecture, and with Fiske as the center they repaired to the cheerful gloom of the old vaulted Ratskeller under the Equitable Building to lunch on caviar, Swiss cheese and beer. For several years Nelson was host to these little intellectual feasts honoring Fiske.

Nelson's life is a success story of the Horatio Alger type. He was good, honest, unselfish, but shrewd enough to turn a dollar over on its best side; and with his money he brought happiness and a better life to scores of people. He practised his own philosophy of sharing with the underdog, but perhaps he did not realize that it was his own personality, brains, and energy that made his theories work out successfully.

Another type of business leader is the late Arthur Andersen, who made his contributions as a professor of accounting at Northwestern University and as the head of a large accounting firm in Chicago. His parents emigrated from Norway and settled in Illinois, where in 1885

Arthur Andersen was born. Orphaned in early youth, he struggled to get an education; in 1908 he received a C.P.A. from the University of Illinois and in 1917 a B.B.A. from Northwestern University. In 1909, a year after the organization of Northwestern University's school of commerce, Andersen was appointed a lecturer in the accounting department. In addition he worked as a public accountant. In 1912 he was promoted to an assistant professorship, a few months later to the headship, and in 1915 he was made a full professor. During his administration the accounting department was reorganized; new courses and a very able staff were developed. Meanwhile, in 1913 he and Clarence M. DeLany had formed a partnership, buying out an old but small accounting firm. The new firm prospered; in 1915 an office was opened in Milwaukee. After DeLany's retirement in 1918 the firm, though now including Paul Knight, Abraham Silvertrust, and later additional partners, took its present name of Arthur Andersen and Company. Andersen had begun to specialize in Federal taxation and organized a series of lectures at Northwestern which were attended by business leaders from every part of the nation. The consequent expansion of the firm to handle tax business eventually made it necessary for Andersen to resign his academic duties. Offices were opened in Washington, D.C., and in New York in 1921. By the middle 'forties the firm employed several hundred people, had offices in fourteen large American cities from coast to coast and foreign representatives in Canada, England, Gibraltar, Malta, the Dutch East Indies, Spain, and Sweden.

Until his death early in 1947 Andersen continued to take an active interest in education. In 1927 he was elected a member of the board of trustees of Northwestern University, and in 1930 became the first of Northwestern's graduates to serve as president of the Board of Trustees. After his resignation from the teaching staff, he turned over to the University all royalties from his book *Complete Accounting Course,* which by the early 'forties had amounted to some $100,000. His interest extended beyond his alma mater, however, to the Norwegian American colleges, particularly to St. Olaf and to Luther, and to the Norwegian-American Museum in Decorah, which received gifts of money as well as rare art pieces. For several years he was president of the Norwegian-American Historical Association, and during the last war he was national treasurer of American Relief for Norway. In 1939 he received the commander's cross of the royal Order of St. Olav from King Haakon of Norway. Honorary degrees were conferred on him by

Northwestern University, Luther College, St. Olaf College, and Grinnell College in Grinnell, Iowa. His publications include several books and articles in the fields of accounting and economics.

The new owner of the Waldorf-Astoria, Conrad Hilton, "collects hotels as other people collect stamps," reads a headline in Brooklyn's *Nordisk Tidende* of November 10, 1949. Hilton's father, August, at the age of eight in 1861, left his farm home near Oslo and came to Fort Dodge, Iowa, where an older brother was living. Some years later, seeking a dryer climate for his health, he went to the southwest, eventually settling in San Antonio, New Mexico, where he operated a hotel, bank, and other business establishments. There Conrad Hilton grew up. He bought his first hotel just after the first World War. By the time he was thirty-six he owned five hotels valued at a quarter of a million dollars. Today Hilton owns thirteen hotels, among which are the Waldorf-Astoria, the Hotel Plaza, and the Roosevelt Hotel in New York City; the Stevens and the Palmer House in Chicago; and the Mayflower in Washington, D.C.

Another "hotel king" of Norwegian descent is Arnold Sigurd Kirkeby, who was born in Chicago. Among his ten hotels are the Gotham, Hampshire House, and Warwick in New York City and the Blackstone in Chicago.

35

Engineers

AMERICAN INDUSTRIAL LIFE owes an immense debt to the European technical schools. At a time when American institutions were still quite inadequate for the training of the army of experts that was needed to build America, Europe supplied the demand. In this migration of skills, to use Kenneth Bjork's phrase, as in the recent case of the intellectual refugees from Hitler, Europe lost, America gained invisible capital of strategic value, quite out of proportion to the numbers involved. Norway alone gave to America about a thousand well-trained engineers and architects in the sixty-year period between 1870 and 1930, almost half of this number coming between 1900 and 1914, in some years almost fifty per cent of the graduating classes. Their work, admirably recorded by Kenneth Bjork in his *Saga in Steel and Concrete,* is an impressive chapter in the history of immigrant contributions. Theirs was a roving occupation. Wherever tunnels, bridges, skyscrapers, factories, and subway systems were being built, they went. They tended to concentrate, however, in New York, Philadelphia, Detroit, Chicago, Minneapolis, San Francisco, and Seattle. Most were successful; some even amassed fortunes. By and large their transition from middle class homes in Norway to middle class life in America was comparatively easy. Their work brought them into close and immediate contact with Americans, and in a relatively short time the Norwegian engineer's family and business life was indistinguishable from that of an American urbanite. There were, of course, Old World touches in his home—Norwegian books and journals, special foods for holiday seasons, occasional use of his native tongue. Moderately conservative politically and socially, he felt most comfortable in the Republican Party.

In the history of underground transportation in America three Norwegian Americans are of conspicuous prominence—Olaf Hoff, Ole Singstad, and Sverre Dahm. Hoff came in 1879 after graduating from Oslo's Technical College with the highest honors ever granted by that institution. A few years before this, an attempt to build a tunnel under the Detroit River between Windsor, Canada, and Detroit had failed. The difficulties encountered were so formidable that the project was not revived until after the turn of the century. At this point Olaf Hoff, by this time an established engineer, came into the picture. His firm, Butler Brothers–Hoff Company, submitted plans and a bid and received the contract. The construction between 1906 and 1910 of the unique tunnel with its many innovations was followed with great interest by engineers the country over. After completing this project, Hoff was made consulting engineer for the building of the Harlem River tunnel in New York, again using the sunken-tube method of tunnelling that perpetuates his name.

Ole Singstad, often called the dean of tunnelling engineers, pioneered when he planned and constructed the Holland Tunnel between Manhattan and New Jersey, the first one large enough for modern motor traffic. Born in Norway in 1882, coming to this country immediately after he graduated from Trondheim's Technical College in 1905, Singstad for a few years designed railroad structures, eventually got into tunnel and rapid-transit subway work in New York. Thus, when in 1919 New York and New Jersey decided to build a tunnel under the Hudson River, Singstad already had an established reputation in the field. The chief engineer of the project, Clifford M. Holland, who had worked with him on previous projects, asked Singstad to become chief designer. Singstad planned the tunnel, worked out an original ventilation system, after Holland's death in 1924 became chief engineer, completed the tunnel and operated it for two and a half years afterward. When the Posey Tunnel was built between Oakland and Alameda, California, in 1925–1928, Singstad acted as a consultant. Between 1930 and 1933 he contributed several distinctive features as consulting engineer for the construction of two tunnels under the Scheldt River at Antwerp, Belgium. In the later 'thirties he was again building tunnels in New York, the Lincoln Tunnel and the Queens Midtown Tunnel, completed in 1940 under Singstad's supervision as chief engineer for the New York Tunnel Authority, a body created by the state legislature. When Singstad retired from public service in 1945 to engage in private practice, he was recognized as the greatest tunnel authority in the world. He has written extensively for technical journals, lectured at Harvard and New York universities, and has received honorary doctoral degrees from several institutions.

Another Norwegian American closely linked with New York's transportation system was Sverre Dahm, who came to America in 1883 and became one of the leading engineers associated with the construction of the subway network in Greater New York from 1900 to his death in 1932.

Two of Dahm's close friends in the Norwegian American engineering circle were Gunvald Aus and Kort Berle, partners in the Gunvald Aus Company, famous for their construction of the Woolworth Building, an engineering feat that aroused the admiration of the entire world. They built federal, state, and municipal government buildings all over America and in many foreign countries—the Supreme Court building in Washington, D.C., the American embassy in Paris, the Capitol at San Juan, Puerto Rico; large hotels and apartment houses by the score and many buildings on university campuses—the Harkness Memorial Quadrangle at Yale University, the Columbia University library, the Union Building at the University of Wisconsin, to mention only a few. Several other Norwegian engineers played a vital role in the early history of the skyscraper, the first one—a ten-story building—making its appearance in Chicago in 1886. The Columbian Exposition brought many engineers to Chicago, one of them Joachim G. Giaver, son of a prominent Norwegian merchant and landowner, who became assistant chief engineer for the Exposition. His greatest contribution came after 1898 when he joined the firm of D. H. Burnham, described by a British architect as "the architect who grasped the significance of American industrialism." Giaver has been credited with several innovations in the construction of early skyscrapers and is largely responsible for the engineering designs of the Flat Iron, the Gimbel, Maiden Lane, and Equitable buildings in New York, the Field Museum, Continental and Commercial National Bank in Chicago, as well as many others.

The Columbian Exposition also brought to America a young Norwegian chemical engineer, E. A. Cappelen Smith, one of the most distinguished figures in the field of metallurgy. His first dozen years were marked by restlessness; we find him in Chicago as a chemist with Armour and Company, with the Chicago Copper Refining Company, in Montana as superintendent of the electrolytic refinery of the Anaconda Copper Mining Company, and in a little town in Washington organizing a company for the extraction of gold from local ores, visiting Norway, returning to America to become assistant to the engineer in charge of metallurgical operations at the Baltimore Copper Smelting and

Rolling Company. Guggenheim Brothers bought the firm in 1907 and in 1912 Smith became their general consulting metallurgical engineer, in succeeding decades rising to high executive positions in the far-flung Guggenheim empire.

Cappelen Smith's contributions to metallurgy have been many and significant. Early in his career he helped put into general use an improved method of furnace refining that made possible the use of giant furnaces for copper smelting; revolutionized smelting practices by a new method of basic copper converting; contributed to the development of a basic-lined converter known as the Pierce-Smith converter. In 1912 the Guggenheims sent him to Chile, where, for want of a satisfactory extracting process, the Chuquicamata mine lay fallow in the mountainous desert region. By 1929 it was the largest developed copper deposit in the world, producing four hundred million pounds of copper annually. For his hydrometallurgical pioneer work at Chuquicamata, Smith was awarded the gold medal of the Mining and Metallurgical Society of America in 1920. While in Chile, Smith also studied the nitrate industry and there, too, developed a new process. The Guggenheims, who realized its possibilities, bought up nitrate-bearing desert areas in northern Chile and put Smith in charge of the construction of a plant that became the nucleus of their nitrate empire. Smith eventually became a member of the firm of Guggenheim Brothers and took a leading part in several international conferences relating to the nitrate industry.

Tinius Olsen, of Philadelphia, founder of the Olsen Testing Machine Company, now under the managership of his son Thorsten Y. Olsen, is identified with the development of many kinds of machines now widely used for the testing of industrial materials. In the development and introduction of scientific management, Carl G. Barth collaborated with Frederick W. Taylor, the father of the movement, and after the latter's death became the leading exponent of the Taylor system. Magnus Swenson, a prominent Norwegian American in the Middle West, inventor and chemical engineer, designed and built machinery for the sugar and other industries; became an executive in several big corporations; served after the first World War under Herbert Hoover as chief of mission of the American Relief Administration for Northern Europe; during the early 'thirties, in the closing years of his life, as president of the Norwegian-American Historical Association. Ole Evinrude, who was born in Norway and grew up on a farm in Wisconsin, was the inventor of the first practical outboard motor.

36

Literature and the Arts

THE OUTSTANDING MAN of letters among Norwegian Americans is, without the shadow of a doubt, Ole Edvart Rölvaag. Also, he is the rare case of an "American" writer of first rank who did not write in English. As we had reason to mention before, he was and considered himself an apostle and preserver of the old culture within the new. And he became, in translation, an American author only because of the artistic excellence of his novels and because of the "American" subject with which they dealt. Before his time American Norwegian writers like Tellef Grundysen, H. A. Foss, Kristofer Janson, Peer Strømme, and Waldemar Ager had written fiction that brought them status within the group. Boyesen's novels with a Norwegian American setting, written in English, had reached a wider public. But it was left to Rölvaag to create, in *Giants in the Earth,* a masterpiece that commanded national as well as international attention.

Giants in the Earth was first published in 1924 by the leading publishing house in Norway where it became almost immediately a literary sensation. The American version, translated by Lincoln Colcord in cooperation with the author, was published by Harper and Brothers in 1927. It was selected by the Book-of-the-Month Club for June of that year and not long afterward sales reached the two hundred thousand mark. *Giants in the Earth* was eventually translated into Swedish, Finnish, German, Dutch, Hungarian, and Spanish. There is also a Braille edition. This novel and its sequels, *Peder Victorious* and *Their Fathers' God,* place Rölvaag beside Hamlin Garland and Willa Cather as one of the foremost interpreters of the Middle West in its pioneer period. Twenty years after its publication an American steamship company, desiring to establish a memorial library on each of its ships running between this country and South America, asked two thousand of the nation's educators, authors, critics, and editors to nominate one hundred volumes for inclusion. Those receiving the most votes in the fiction classification were: Rölvaag's *Giants in the Earth*, Mark Twain's *Huckleberry Finn*, Sinclair Lewis' *Arrowsmith*, Thomas Wolfe's *Look Homeward, Angel*, Willa Cather's *My Antonia*, and Edna Ferber's *So Big*.

Rölvaag's personal life was little affected by his growing literary fame. But for the last years, when his health began to fail him, he travelled little and devoted himself faithfully to his teaching duties at his beloved St. Olaf in Northfield, Minnesota, where he died in 1931. Three years before, he had seen Norway for the last time as one of the four Americans the government had invited to participate in the celebration of the Ibsen centennial.

There are competent American writers of Norwegian background, but none of Rölvaag's stature. Martha Ostenso's novels have been widely read. She was born in Hardanger, Norway, in 1900, and two years later came to this country with her parents who later settled in Canada. In 1925 her novel *Wild Geese* won a $15,000 competition and brought her immediate literary recognition. Two of her novels have been translated into Norwegian by C. J. Hambro, for many years president of the Norwegian Storting. Wallace Stegner has drawn on his Norwegian family background and childhood memories in his novel *The Big Rock Candy Mountain*, the story of Elsa Nordgaard, a Norwegian American girl from a rural community in Minnesota who marries outside her group. In recent years a Norwegian American family in San Francisco has charmed America through Kathryn Forbes' autobiographical book, *Mamma's Bank Account*, which later reached the stage, screen and recently television as *I Remember Mamma*. Less well known are Borghild Dahl, a South Dakota writer whose novel *Karen* is a story of pioneer days on the Dakota prairies, and Joran Birkeland, the author of *Birchland: A Journey Home to Norway*. Norwegian-born Ingri Parin d'Aulaire has achieved success as a writer of children's books. Since coming to America in 1929, she and her Swiss-born husband, Edgar Parin d'Aulaire, whose father was French and mother American, have collaborated on both the text and illustrations of numerous books depicting life in Norway and elsewhere. Very popular are their books about Ola, the golden-haired, blue-eyed Norwegian boy.

During the last years phonograph records have brought some of the treasures of old Norse literature into the American nursery. Responsible for this is a Norwegian-born grandmother of over seventy-five, Mrs.

Gudrun Thorne-Thomsen, of Los Angeles, who since her school-teaching days back in the earlier part of the century has told children the fairy tales of Norway. In 1911 she wrote them down in book form, *East o' the Sun and West o' the Moon*. She has lectured on the use of folk tales as literature before schoolteachers and educators, travelled the length and breadth of the country telling the Norse fairy tales to school children. With the years the charm of her storytelling spread so far that in 1944 the Library of Congress asked her to record her stories for the documentary department's archives. She has since been recording Norwegian folk tales for RCA Victor and has become one of their most popular narrators for children's records.

Carrying a fiddle under his arm, F. Melius Christiansen came to America in 1888, at the age of seventeen, determined to become a great violinist. He became a great choirmaster instead. In 1903 he went to St. Olaf College to become head of the music department. Circumstances there, study in Leipzig under Gustav Schreck, director of the St. Thomas-schule choir, propelled his interest toward choral work; the barrenness and dearth of good church music, particularly in the primitive musical environment of a midwestern village, compelled him to compose for the church choir he directed, most of his pieces being at first arrangements of old Lutheran hymns.

Realizing that the Norwegian Americans had forgotten the rich heritage that was theirs in the sturdy old chorales, he sought to revive this musical tradition, first through a student octet that travelled through the Norwegian American settlements in Dakota, Iowa, and Minnesota; later through a student choir. In 1913 this choir toured Norway; finally in 1920 the time seemed ripe for the St. Olaf Lutheran Choir to sing to America at large. On an April night New Yorkers at Carnegie Hall heard a group of college students from an unknown school sing a program of Bach, Mendelssohn, Gretchaninoff, Lutheran chorales, and Norwegian folk melodies arranged by Christiansen. It wasn't just another college chorus; it was a cathedral choir from the Old World, singing with unbelievable beauty and perfection. Year after year the fame of the group and its conductor spread. In 1930 the choir made a European tour.

At the college in Northfield visiting musicians studied Christiansen's technique; his students went out to train others in the art of a cappella singing. The movement gained momentum and by the 'thirties the change from glee clubs to a cappella choirs in the colleges and high schools of the nation was well under way. In the summer of 1935 the Christiansen Choral School was started, a short summer course for choral teachers which continues year after year with great success. Now almost eighty, Christiansen watches his sons carry on his work. Olaf Christiansen has taken his father's place as director of the St. Olaf Choir; Paul Christiansen is director of the Concordia Choir at Moorhead, Minnesota, and the Paul Christiansen Choral School.

Christiansen's contribution to American music is by now a matter of record. A prolific composer, Christiansen's best known works are "Fiftieth Psalm," an arrangement of the twelfth century Crusaders' hymn known as "Beautiful Savior"; and the delicate "Lullaby on Christmas Eve," his arrangement of an old Norwegian folk melody. Choirs all over America, many of them directed by his students, are singing these songs. And they were sung in Europe during the second World War by the Soldier Chorus under the direction of one of Christiansen's students, Luther Onerheim, who first organized it as the Fifth Infantry Chorus at Fort Benning, Georgia, in 1944.

This a cappella choir, which specialized in religious and classical secular numbers, though it included some popular classics in its repertoire, came to be recognized as the finest soldier ensemble in the European theater. They sang for General George Patton, broke an ancient precedent by appearing in the Salzburg Festival, and at General Eisenhower's request toured the Frankfurt area, singing throughout Bavaria. Paul Robeson, Clifton Fadiman, and Raymond Massey were lavish in their praise of Onerheim and the chorus. German civilians were amazed to hear American boys singing Bach, Palestrina, Antonio Caldara, Pergolesi from the choir lofts of their cathedrals. Onerheim was killed in an auto accident while still in Germany early in 1946, but the chorus continued under the baton of his assistant director.

In the East, Ole Windingstad has dominated the musical life of the Norwegian Americans since he arrived in America in 1907, after receiving his musical training in Oslo and in Leipzig with the famous conductor Arthur Nikisch. He has been particularly noteworthy in introducing Scandinavian composers to American audiences. For many years in Brooklyn he was the conductor of the Norwegian Singing Society and the Scandinavian Symphony Orchestra; from 1939 to 1944 he was the conductor of the New Orleans Symphony; in later years he has been the director of the Dutchess County (New York) Philharmonic

Society and the Albany Symphony Orchestra. Another popular Norwegian American musician in the East is the violinist, Carl H. Tollefsen, director of the Brooklyn Chamber Music Society. For many years he and his wife, the eminent pianist, Augusta Schnabel Tollefsen, have had a studio in Brooklyn.

During her career in America Bertha Feiring Tapper won high recognition as a pianist and teacher. After receiving her training in her native land and in Germany, she came to America, played principally with chamber groups, taught at the New England Conservatory of Music and later at the Institute of Musical Art in New York City. Among her students were Leo Ornstein, Newton Swift, and Abram Chasins. Her husband, Thomas Tapper, was a well-known musician, editor, and author.

In the group of Norwegian American singers Olive Fremstad and Kaja Eide Norena, Metropolitan stars, have been outstanding. Among the younger Americans of Norwegian extraction who give evidence of promising careers is Camilla Wicks of California, who at the age of seventeen in 1947 was a soloist with the Philharmonic Orchestra in New York.

Among the successful painters in the Norwegian American group the most noteworthy has been Jonas Lie, nephew of the famous Norwegian novelist of the same name. In his early youth he studied art in Oslo; at the age of twelve he spent a year in Paris with his novelist uncle and there met Ibsen, Bjørnson, Grieg, Sinding, Georg Brandes and other leading figures in the world of art and letters. After his father's death his American mother brought her family to America in 1893; although his early influences were Norwegian, he identified himself completely with his adopted country. From 1935 until shortly before his death in 1940 he was president of the National Academy. As one may infer from this honor, his own painting was conservative, but he was hospitable to and appreciative of the younger generation of modern painters. He was also a trustee of the Metropolitan Museum of Art, a member of the New York Art Commission, and a member of the board of control of the American Federation of Arts in Washington. His pictures hang in the Metropolitan Museum of Art in New York, the Luxembourg Museum in Paris, the Corcoran Gallery in Washington, D.C., the Carnegie Institute in Pittsburgh, and other galleries. Franklin D. Roosevelt owned his picture of *"Amberjack II,"* a yacht on which the President cruised; another of his pictures hangs in the home of Crown Prince Olav and

Crown Princess Martha of Norway. Ten of his twelve well-known paintings of the building of the Panama Canal, painted while the canal was under construction in 1913, hang in the Military Academy at West Point.

When Johan Bull came to this country in 1925 he was already a recognized pen-and-ink artist. At the time of his death in 1945 he had a well-established reputation as an able illustrator, cartoonist, portrait and landscape painter, and etcher. His work appeared in *The New Yorker, Woman's Home Companion, The New York Times,* and *The New York Herald Tribune.*

Perhaps no family is more dear to the hearts of Norwegian American art lovers of the Middle West than the Fjeldes. Jacob Fjelde, after winning a reputation as a promising sculptor in Norway, followed his father, a woodcarver and carpenter, to the New World in 1887 and settled in Minneapolis. Before his premature death in 1896 he had finished a group of figures over the entrance to the Library building at the University of Minnesota, a monument to the First Minnesota Regiment erected on the Gettysburg battlefield, a bust of Henrik Ibsen in St. Paul, a figure of Hiawatha and Minnehaha in Minnehaha Park in Minneapolis, and, his last work, a statue of Ole Bull in Loring Park, Minneapolis.

Jacob Fjelde's widow took her four children and, with the courage of pioneer women, settled on a homestead in North Dakota. There one of Jacob's sons, Paul, growing up under conditions that were hardly rich in artistic influences, early showed promise of having inherited his father's talent. He was sent to Minneapolis to live with relatives and attend art school. When he was twenty he became a pupil of Lorado Taft in Chicago, remaining with him for several years. He later made his home in New York where in recent years he has been an instructor in modelling and sculpture at Pratt Institute in Brooklyn. Many of his works commemorating pioneer days and figures are to be found in the Middle West.

Although not an artist himself, but a physician in North Dakota, Dr. Herman Fjelde, a brother of Jacob, was known throughout the Middle West as a patron of the arts, trying to keep alive the literary and artistic traditions of Norway among the hard-working farmers and businessmen in North Dakota, organizing art committees and raising funds for art projects. Through his zeal statues of Ibsen, Bjørnson, Ivar Aasen, Hans Nielsen Hauge, and Wergeland were erected in various North Dakota towns. Another member of the family, Pauline Fjelde of Minneapolis, a sister of Herman and Jacob, was a specialist in Norwegian art weaving, one of her tapestries winning the Rosenwald Prize at the Chicago Art Institute.

Yet another family of artists should be mentioned—the Hammers. Trygve Hammer, a sculptor and designer, came to America in 1904 and settled in New York where his work soon became well known. He died in 1946. His brother Rolf Hammer was a singer who, after touring America with a Norwegian chorus, settled here in 1910. He and his wife, Borgny Hammer, the actress, lived for a time in Chicago where they organized a group of players known as "The Norwegian Theatre," introducing the works of modern Norwegian playwrights to the Middle West. Later they lived in Seattle before going to New York, where again Borgny Hammer organized a Norwegian theater. Meanwhile her group of players toured America giving performances of Bjørnson and Ibsen. Borgny Hammer, perhaps America's greatest interpreter of Ibsen, made her last appearance in 1945 on the fiftieth anniversary of her theatrical debut. She died in 1946.

Not too many performers of Norwegian background have found their way into motion pictures. The best known, of course, is Sonja Henie, whose numerous pictures have kept her popularity in America at a high pitch. The dancer Vera Zorina, whose Norwegian name is Brigitta Hartwig, has achieved considerable success in American films. Sigrid Gurie, born in Brooklyn of Norwegian parents, has played in several films. Few people know that James Cagney's mother was Norwegian. Blonde-haired Celeste Holm, who has had several successes in Hollywood after first starring in the musical comedies *Oklahoma* and *Bloomer Girl,* is the daughter of Norwegian-born Theodor Holm and a Scotch-Irish mother, Jean Parke Holm, an artist and author. It is amusing to note that when a Norwegian men's chorus touring America recently called on her in Hollywood, several of the members turned out to be her cousins. The Andrews sisters, popular singing trio now in Hollywood, started their career in Minneapolis in the 'thirties where their Norwegian-born mother and Greek father had settled in the restaurant business.

37

Sports

IN THE SPORTS world one of the most prominent figures of the 1920's was
the tennis star, Molla Bjurstedt Mallory. She was trained in her native
Oslo as a teacher of gymnastics, and after coming to America won the
Women's National Outdoor Tennis Championship seven times.

But the greatest Norwegian American figure of that period, and still
unsurpassed as a football coach, was Knute Rockne. He came from the
district of Voss in Norway, where his father's people had been carriage
and wagon builders; his mother, Martha Gjermo, came from a family of
educators, clergymen, and physicians. Attracted by the Columbian Exposition, where he exhibited and won a prize for his carriage, Rockne's
father came to Chicago, long one of the centers of Vossing settlement in
America. From early childhood Knute Rockne was devoted to sports
and when in 1910 two of his friends decided to go to Notre Dame University they persuaded Knute to enroll as well. There his outstanding
record as a football player brought him a position as coach in 1914,
which he held until his death in an airplane accident in 1931. The
tributes paid to the memory of Knute Rockne exceeded anything known
in the history of athletics. King Haakon of Norway, who had previously
bestowed on Rockne the Order of St. Olav, ordered the Norwegian
consul at Chicago to attend the funeral at South Bend with a delegation
of Norwegians. The lustre of his name as a symbol of good sportsman-
ship has hardly dimmed by the passing of time.

In the 1930's Ralph Guldahl, whose father was born in Norway,
won champion honors in golf. All Norwegian Americans point with
pride to the incomparable skater Sonja Henie whose American career
began in 1930 at Madison Square Garden before an audience of fourteen thousand in an ice-skating carnival entitled "In the Land of the
Midnight Sun." Her many and successful movies, and her well-
established Hollywood Ice Revue have made her one of America's
wealthiest women.

But it is in skiing that Norwegians have had their greatest influence in American sport. "It is a known fact," wrote Frank Elkins, ski editor of *The New York Times,* in 1947, "that skiing . . . was introduced in this country by Scandinavian sailors who had deserted their ships in San Francisco Bay to join the rush to the 'gold diggin's' in 1849." The story of Snowshoe Thompson, who carried mail over the Sierra Mountains for twenty years, has already been told. The first ski clubs founded in the country were organized in the 1880's by Norwegians in Berlin, New Hampshire, Red Wing and Minneapolis, Minnesota, and Ishpeming, Michigan, which later, in 1904, was the birthplace of the National Ski Association of America, an organization which then and later has been led by Norwegian Americans. Since those early days when enthusiasm for skiing was confined largely to areas where descendants of mountain-dwelling Norwegians were numerous, love of skiing has infected out-door people all over snow-covered America. But American skiers of Norwegian birth and extraction are still taking top honors in national, international, and Olympic meets. To single out one figure is an injustice to many, but outstanding among them was the late Torger Tokle, a Brooklyn Norwegian who came to America in 1939. He "was to the American ski sport what Babe Ruth was to baseball and Jack Dempsey to boxing," wrote Elkins. His phenomenal ski jumps held the sport world breathless with wonder. When during the second World War Tokle joined the Mountain Division, which fought back the Germans in their final drive in the Po Valley, he said, "I will do everything for my adopted country to help it remain the champion of the small and downtrodden nations of Europe." He was killed while leading an attack in the Apennines.

AFTER THREE GENERATIONS

THREE GENERATIONS OF Norwegians have lived on American soil. What has happened to them and what is becoming of them? Time has, I think, even given us the right to put the question in the past tense— what did they become?—for they are no longer Norwegians. For the first generation American life was primarily a physical struggle. They were among the millions who were, as Emerson wrote in 1860, "ferried over the Atlantic and carted over America, to ditch and to drudge, to make corn cheap and then to lie down prematurely to make a spot of green grass on the prairie." But through all the drudgery they ob-stinately and optimistically clutched a dream they had brought with them from the barren slopes of Norway: to bequeath land to their children, to give them economic security. This they did, but they also bequeathed to the second generation a new dream and a new struggle.

This was an inward struggle, caught as the second generation found itself between the Norwegianism of home and church and the Ameri-canism of school and profession. But one can make too much of that "inward struggle." It wasn't the same for all national groups, and it must be remembered that the Norwegians were among the "preferred stock" in the Anglo-American order of things. So for the Norwegians, or any of the Scandinavians for that matter, the immigrant psychosis and the adjustment problems of the second generation, though they cannot be dismissed, were not as acute as for the children of, say, Polish, Russian, Lithuanian, Italian, or Greek immigrants. The son of a father who can't speak English but who owns land, a decent frame house, livestock and machinery is not as hard hit by prejudice as the youth whose foreign-speaking father has earned a bare living in a sweatshop, slaugh-ter house, or mine and reared his children in the crowded tenement of a city. And then, too, the Norwegians, settling in closely knit groups, *created* the culture of many rural communities. A child who grows up a member of the locally dominant culture, even if he later discovers it to be a subculture, does not carry the burden of early insecurity into the more American environment of his later life. What inferiority he may feel he can gradually overcome when he finds it rather easy to get a higher education, to enter business or a profession.

Nevertheless, the sting of struggle was not entirely absent; thus it became the dream of the second generation to bequeath to their children a secure place in the American scheme of things. And by the time this third generation reached manhood the "Norskie" background had, indeed, become a legend, an entirely acceptable background to middle class respectability. So once again we have the story of a group whose frail hold on economic security and whose depressed social status in the Old World brought them to the New, where without too much pain they made themselves at home within the span of two generations.

Though part of an epic, this story is not itself cast in the grand style. It is a sober record, the story mainly of people who plowed the earth, seined fish, felled trees, sailed boats, built houses and barns, repaired machinery. Few were those who preached, taught, and wrote. Yet they, too, were important because through them we have come to know how the rest lived and thought. Nor were these men only articulators and recorders of the group's thought; they were also the guardians of its values and thus, at least in part, responsible for the quality of the Norwegian contribution. The great center of all this preaching, teaching, and writing was, not unnaturally, the Lutheran Church, the institution which, more than any other, kept the Norwegian people together.

Just as the Norwegians remained more faithful to the Lutheran Church than, say, the Swedes or the Danes, so they also stayed longer on the land. At the turn of the century the Norwegians had, among all nationalities, the highest percentage of first and second generation farmers. Half of the first generation and over sixty per cent of the second tilled the soil, while in the German group, for example, only slightly more than a quarter of the first two generations were farmers in 1900. These two great attachments, to soil and church, it seems to me go very well together. And, no doubt, they are the twin causes of that Old World touch one still finds in many Norwegian homes, particularly in the Middle West, even in the unself-consciously American third generation. So, "acceptable" as they were, the Norwegians of their own accord moved rather slowly into American life.

The tempo of assimilation varied from region to region, slower in the Middle West, faster in the coastal areas. Also, it is not the same kind of Norwegian culture that is preserved in these regions. The middle-westerners, even though they are third generation—or, rather, *because* they are third generation—retain the folkways of the mid-nineteenth century Norway which their grandparents brought with them. The Norway of today with its socialism, its modern architecture, and its "New Norwegian" language is not the Norway they know and appreciate. Sigrid Undset, who met these people on her tour of the Middle West in 1940, described their customs as "something reminiscent of pressed flowers in an album." The workers, artisans, and professional men who, since the turn of the century, have come from the cities of Norway to settle in ours already knew a more industrialized, somewhat more liberal Norway. So they did not long remain strangers to our labor movement and to the latitudinarianism of our churches. Small wonder, then, that these later immigrants stepped into American life either almost immediately or within one generation.

Today there are probably about two and a half million Americans whose family roots are in Norway. The bulk of them are farmers, artisans, tradespeople, government clerks, and small businessmen. Not numerous in the higher ranks of capital and management, they are very well represented in that huge army of highly trained specialists who make the world go round in this day and age. Though some of these are brilliant scientists and scholars, the majority prefers the applied fields to theoretical pioneering, the teachers college to the graduate seminar. Norwegian representation in politics, particularly in the Middle West, is rather heavy. Their contribution to literature, the theater, the arts in general is far from conspicuous. On the whole, then, I think it is fair to say that my people are a sure-handed and clear-headed people, sane and sound, perhaps less brilliant than some yet steadier than many, and, all in all, not unworthy of the opportunities they found in these United States.

General Sources

Anderson, Rasmus B.: *The First Chapter of Norwegian Immigration, 1821–1840, Its Causes and Results* (Madison, Wis., 1896).

Babcock, Kendric C.: *The Scandinavian Element in the United States* (Urbana, Ill., 1914).

Blegen, Theodore C.: *Norwegian Migration to America, 1825–1860* (Northfield, Minn., Nor.-Amer. Historical Assoc., 1931).

———: *Norwegian Migration to America: The American Transition* (Northfield, Minn., Nor.-Amer. Historical Assoc., 1940).

Flom, George T.: *A History of Norwegian Immigration to the United States* (Iowa City, 1909).

Gjerset, Knut: *History of the Norwegian People* (New York, 1915, 2 vols.).

Hovde, B. J.: *The Scandinavian Countries, 1720–1865: The Rise of the Middle Classes* (Boston, 1943, 2 vols.).

Langeland, Knud: *Nordmaendene i Amerika* (Chicago, 1888).

Larsen, Karen: *A History of Norway* (New York, 1948).

Nelson, O. N.: *History of the Scandinavians and Successful Scandinavians in the United States* (Minneapolis, 1893).

Norlie, Olaf M.: *History of the Norwegian People in America* (Minneapolis, 1925).

Qualey, Carlton S.: *Norwegian Settlement in the United States* (Northfield, Minn., Nor.-Amer. Historical Assoc., 1938).

Other basic sources of information were the files of the following periodicals: The Norwegian-American Historical Association *Studies and Records,* 15 volumes (volumes 5–15 of this series contain excellent bibliographies relating to Norwegian American history compiled by Jacob Hodnefield); *The American-Scandinavian Review; Sons of Norway;* the journals of the midwestern state historical societies; *Nordmanns Forbundet;* numerous Norwegian American newspapers, particularly *Nordisk Tidende* and *Decorahposten.* United States Census Reports were the source of all statistics concerning population.

Notes

The Background

I: These Came Early

For the section on Vinland voyages and viking settlement and exploration in America I depended most heavily on G. M. Gathorne-Hardy, *The Norse Discoveries of America: The Wineland Sagas* (Oxford, 1921); Einar Haugen, *Voyages to Vinland* (New York, 1942); William Hovgaard, *Voyages of the Northmen to America* (New York, 1914); Hjalmar R. Holand, *Westward from Vinland: An Account of Norse Discoveries and Explorations in America 982–1362* (New York, 1940); Rasmus B. Anderson, *America Not Discovered by Columbus* (Chicago, 1874). See also two articles in *The American-Scandinavian Review:* A. W. Brögger, "The Vinland Voyages," XXIV, 197–215; Guttorm Gjessing, "Viking Ships in a New Home," XXII, 218–226. My main sources for material on the Kensington Rune Stone and other viking relics in America were: Hjalmar R. Holand's two books, *Westward from Vinland* and *America 1355–1364* (New York, 1946); Milo M. Quaife, "The Myth of the Kensington Rune Stone," *The New England Quarterly,* VII, 613–645; Laurence M. Larson, "The Kensington Rune Stone," *Minnesota History,* XVII, 20–37. For material on Columbus I consulted Samuel Eliot Morison, *Admiral of the Ocean Sea: A Life of Christopher Columbus* (Boston, 1942); Charles Duff, *The Truth About Columbus and the Discovery of America* (New York, 1936); Salvador De Madariaga, *Christopher Columbus: Being the Life of the Very Magnificent Lord Don Cristobal Colón* (New York, 1940). For an account of modern viking voyages see Knut Gjerset, *Norwegian Sailors in American Waters: A Study in the History of Maritime Activity on the Eastern Seaboard* (Northfield, Minn., 1933).

The most comprehensive treatment of Norwegians in the Dutch colonial settlement is John O. Evjen, *Scandinavian Immigrants in New York, 1630–1674* (Minneapolis, 1916). Articles on Anneke Jans by Torstein Jahr are to be found in *The American-Scandinavian Review,* IV, 336–341, and in *Scandinavia,* February, 1924. Further accounts of seventeenth and eighteenth century Norwegian settlement in America are found in: Halvdan Koht, "First Scandinavian Settlers in America," *The American-Scandinavian Review,* XXXII, 136–142; George T. Flom, *A History of Norwegian Immigration to the United States.*

II: Norway—The Land and the People

My main sources for this chapter were: Knut Gjerset, *History of the Norwegian People* (New York, 1915, 2 vols.); Karen Larsen, *A History of Norway* (New York, 1948); B. J. Hovde, *The Scandinavian Countries, 1720–1865: The Rise of the Middle Classes* (Boston, 1943, 2 vols.); Halvdan Koht and Sigmund Skard, *The Voice of Norway* (New York, 1944); Oscar Falnes, *National Romanticism in Norway* (New York, 1933); Theodore Jorgenson, *History of Norwegian Literature* (New York, 1933). The quotation from Sigrid Undset's *Kristin Lavransdatter* (New York, Alfred A. Knopf, Inc., 1935) is from p. 227.

III: "And Out You Sweep to Sea"

The title for this chapter is taken from a poem written by the Norwegian hymn writer, Magnus B. Landstad, and first published in a newspaper in Norway in 1842. I have used Martin Ruud's translation entitled "To Our Brothers Emigrating to America" found in his article, "Norwegian Emigrant Songs," *Studies and Records,* I, 7. Other ballad quotations are from this same source. See also Theodore C. Blegen and Martin Ruud (ed. and trans.), *Norwegian Emigrant Songs and Ballads* (Minneapolis, 1936). From the Norwegian-American Historical Association I received permission to reprint Theodore C. Blegen's verse translation of the ballad "Oleana," published in *Studies and Records,* XIV, 117–121.

The most complete treatment of the background of and causes for emigration from Norway is to be found in Blegen's *Norwegian Migration to America, 1825–1860* (hereafter cited as Blegen (I)); see also Ingrid Gaustad Semmingsen, "Norwegian Emigration to America During the Nineteenth Century," *Studies and Records,* XI, 66–81. Thorstein Veblen has an interesting essay on Scandinavians entitled "An Experiment in Eugenics," found in *Essays in Our Changing Order* (New York, 1934), a collection of his essays edited by Leon Ardzrooni. I have quoted from p. 239. For a concise treatment of religious conditions in Norway see J. Magnus Rohne, *Norwegian American Lutheranism up to 1872* (New York, 1926). A translation of Bishop Jacob Neumann's "Word of Admonition to the Peasants" by Gunnar J. Malmin is found in *Studies and Records,* I, 95–109. My example of the attitude of the *bønder* toward emigration came from Andreas Ueland, *Recollections of an Immigrant* (New York, 1929), pp. 21 ff.

Material on "America" books and letters, and quotations from them were taken from: Blegen (I), 172, 102–104, 197–200, 204; Theodore C. Blegen (trans. and ed.), *Ole Rynning's True Account of America* (Minneapolis, 1926); Arne Odd Johnsen (ed.), "Johannes Nordboe and Norwegian Im-

migration: An 'America Letter' of 1837," *Studies and Records,* VIII, 35, 36;
Lyder L. Unstad (trans. and ed.), "The First Norwegian Migration into
Texas: Four 'America Letters,'" *Studies and Records,* VIII, 68–69; D. G.
Ristad, "A Doctrinaire Idealist: Hans Barlien," *Studies and Records,* III, 17,
20; Richard B. Eide (comp.), *Norse Immigrant Letters: Glimpses of Norse
Immigrant Life in the Northwest in the Fifties* (Minneapolis, 1925).

The Spread

IV: FROM STAVANGER TO "ELLENAAIS"

My main sources for the story of the "Sloopers" were Blegen (I), chap. II;
Henry J. Cadbury, "The Norwegian Quakers of 1825," *Studies and Records,*
I, 60–94; see also William W. Comfort, *Stephen Grellet, 1773–1855* (New
York, 1942), p. 107. Gunnar Malmin has translated a few letters of Martha
Larsen which are published in *The American-Scandinavian Review,* XIII,
361–364. Material on Cleng Peerson is plentiful, but perhaps the most comprehensive is Theodore C. Blegen, "Cleng Peerson and Norwegian Immigration," *Mississippi Valley Historical Review,* VII, 303–331. For migration to
and settlement in Illinois I used Carlton Qualey, *Norwegian Settlement in
the United States,* chap. II; Rasmus B. Anderson, *The First Chapter of Norwegian Immigration, 1821–1840, Its Causes and Results;* George T. Flom,
A History of Norwegian Immigration to the United States. See also Laurence
M. Larson's essays, "The Changing West" and "The Norwegian Element in
the Northwest," in *The Changing West* (Northfield, Minn., 1937).

V: WISCONSIN

For settlement in Wisconsin see Qualey, *Norwegian Settlement,* chap. III;
Guy-Harold Smith, "Notes on the Distribution of the Foreign-born Scandinavians in Wisconsin in 1905," *Wisconsin Magazine of History,* XIV, 419–
436; Louise Phelps Kellogg, "The Story of Wisconsin, 1634–1848," *Wisconsin Magazine of History,* III, 314–326; John G. Gregory, "Foreign Immigration to Wisconsin," *Proceedings* of the Wisconsin Historical Society, 1902,
pp. 137–143. For a popular treatment of Old World settlements in Wisconsin
see Fred L. Holmes, *Old World Wisconsin* (Eau Claire, Wis., 1944), chap. V,
"Festive Vikings Devour Lutefisk." Quotations from the letters of the
Stortroen brothers and from the diary of Charles Tuttle were taken from
Wisconsin Magazine of History, XV, 363–364, 70. Joseph Schafer's *A History
of Agriculture in Wisconsin* (Madison, 1922) has good material on the part
played by immigrant groups in the development of agriculture in the state. I

used examples of pioneer life from Oluf Erickson's "Olaf Erickson, Scandinavian Frontiersman," *Wisconsin Magazine of History,* XXXI, 7–28, 186–207, 326–338, and from Nils P. Haugen's *Pioneer and Political Reminiscenses* (Evansville, Wis., 1930). The main sources for material on tobacco growing were *Wisconsin Industrial Review,* June, 1906, an issue devoted to Edgerton, the tobacco center, and *The Wisconsin Tobacco Reporter,* October 16, 23, 1947; January 22, 29, 1948. Erling Ylvisaker's *Eminent Pioneers: Norwegian-American Pioneer Sketches* (Minneapolis, 1934) has a good sketch of T. G. Mandt, pp. 93–104.

On a collection of items and photographs in an album on Nissedahle in the archives of the Norwegian-American Historical Association at St. Olaf College I based my story of this Norwegian center; see also Phil Drotning, "Valley of the Elves," *Saturday Evening Post,* May 12, 1945, pp. 27, 90–91. For material on Norwegian Moravians and Nils Otto Tank I used Joseph Schafer, "Scandinavian Moravians in Wisconsin," *Wisconsin Magazine of History,* XXIV, 25–38; W. A. Titus, "Nils Otto Tank: Norwegian Aristocrat and Philanthropist," *Wisconsin Magazine of History,* XXII, 385–395; Hjalmar R. Holand, "Nils Otto Tank," *Proceedings* of the Wisconsin Historical Society, 1908, pp. 146–154.

My story of the Anderson family grew out of conversations with them during a visit at Little Sister Bay in 1947. For historical accounts of Door County peninsula see Hjalmar Holand's two books: *History of Door County, Wisconsin* (Chicago, 1917, 2 vols.) and *Old Peninsula Days* (Ephraim, Wis., 1925). Herman Hogenson of Ephraim furnished me with names of schooners and their owners.

VI: Crossing the Mississippi: Iowa

For details on the settlement of Norwegians in Iowa I used Qualey, *Norwegian Settlement,* chap. IV; H. Fred Swansen, "The Norse in Iowa to 1870," doctor's thesis, University of Iowa, 1936; H. Fred Swansen, "The Sugar Creek Settlement in Iowa," *Studies and Records,* IX, 38–44; H. F. Swansen, "The Norwegian Quakers of Marshall County, Iowa," *Studies and Records,* X, 127–134. See also Louis T. Jones, *The Quakers of Iowa* (Iowa City, 1914). The quotation from Hans Barlien is from D. G. Ristad, "A Doctrinaire Idealist: Hans Barlien," *Studies and Records,* III, 19. The item about Martha Larson I found in *Utah Genealogical and Historical Magazine,* XXX, 127. I used material from a study made by Christine Owen, "A History of Private Recreation in the Norwegian Community of Decorah, Iowa," master's thesis, University of Iowa, 1939. The *Des Moines Register* frequently has items and stories on Norwegian Americans in the state; see issues of December 29, 1946, for story on Chris Loseth; March 2, 1947, for article on Mrs. Sigurd Reque; June 6, 1948, for article on the Tjernagel family. Further material on this family is to be found in O. M. Norlie, *History of the Norwegian People,* p. 533. For information on the Norwegian-American Historical Museum see Knut Gjerset, "The Norwegian-American Historical Museum," *Studies and Records,* VI, 153–161; see also item in the *Des Moines Register,* May 9, 1948.

VII: A Considerable Norwegian Settlement: Minnesota

The title of this chapter is taken from C. L. Clausen's letter to Alexander Ramsey, first territorial governor of Minnesota. This letter, from which I have quoted, and other Clausen documents have been translated and edited by Carlton C. Qualey, "Claus L. Clausen: Pioneer Pastor and Settlement Promoter," *Studies and Records,* VI, 12–29. Quotations from Fredrika Bremer's account of her visit to St. Paul are taken from her book *The Homes of the New World: Impressions of America* (New York, 1853), II, 24–26, 57–58. A good treatment of the official attitude of states toward the settlement of immigrants within their borders is found in Livia Appel and T. C. Blegen, "Official Encouragement of Immigration to Minnesota during the Territorial Period," *Minnesota History Bulletin,* V, 167–203. My references to Knute Steenerson and his family came from "Knute Steenerson's Recollections: The Story of a Pioneer," *Minnesota History Bulletin,* IV, 130–151. His brother, Halvor Steenerson, studied law, served in the Minnesota legislature, and from 1903 to 1921 was a representative in Congress. Material on Sacred Heart and the Vorkin brothers came from a scrapbook of newspaper clippings and articles dealing with the town's pioneer days sent to me by O. O. Enestvedt, one of the town's pioneers and historians. Information about Bjørgulv Bjørnaraa came from material which Louis Adamic turned over to me, including a letter of Jarle Leirfallom to Adamic (Sept. 5, 1939), from which I have quoted. A portion of my material on the social structure of St. Paul and Minneapolis came from Carey McWilliams, "Minneapolis: The Curious Twin," *Common Ground,* Autumn, 1946, pp. 61–65. O. M. Norlie's *History of the Norwegian People* was written for the Norse centennial held in Minneapolis in 1925.

VIII: The Red River Valley and the Dakotas

Quotations of American consuls in Norway were taken from Halvdan Koht, "When America Called for Immigrants," *Studies and Records,* XIV, 171, 173. See also Theodore C. Blegen, "The Competition of the Northwestern States for Immigrants," *Wisconsin Magazine of History,* III, 3–29. The quotation on p. 101 is from William Marin, "Sod Houses and Prairie Schooners," *Minnesota History,* XII, 154–156. Source material on pioneer life in the Dakotas is abundant. I am particularly grateful to have had at my disposal a typescript of the Berdahl family records and manuscripts which were sent to me by James Berdahl of Sioux Falls, South Dakota. They include two lengthy accounts written by Erick Berdahl and Andrew Berdahl, father-in-law of O. E. Rölvaag. Other sources were: John T. Blegen, "A Missionary Journey on the Dakota Prairies in 1886," *North Dakota Historical Quarterly*, I, 16–29; Mrs. H. E. Crofford, "Pioneer Days in North Dakota," *North Dakota Historical Quarterly*, II, 129–137; Alex Tollefson, "Historical Notes on the Norwegians in the Red River Valley," *Collections* of the State Historical Society of North Dakota, VII, 133–191; G. Bie Ravndal, "The Scandinavian Pioneers in South Dakota," South Dakota Historical *Collections*, XII, 297–330; Omon B. Herigstad, "Norwegian Immigration," *Collections* of the State Historical Society of North Dakota, II, 186–201. For material on Knut Hamsun I used John T. Flanagan, "Knut Hamsun's Early Years in the Northwest," *Minnesota History*, XX, 397–412 and Kristofer Janson, *Hvad Jeg Har Oplevet* (Oslo, 1913), pp. 222–224.

The following publications were especially useful in the writing of this chapter: Harold E. Briggs, "Early Bonanza Farming in the Red River Valley of the North," *Agricultural History*, VI, 26–37; Harold E. Briggs, "The Settlement and Economic Development of the Territory of Dakota," 2 vols., doctor's thesis, University of Iowa, 1929; John Lee Coulter, "Industrial History of the Valley of the Red River of the North," *Collections* of the State Historical Society of North Dakota, III, 529–672; J. M. Gillette, *Social Economics of North Dakota* (Minneapolis, 1942); James B. Hedges, "The Colonization Work of the Northern Pacific Railroad," *Mississippi Valley Historical Review*, XIII, 311–342; Matthew Josephson, *The Robber Barons: The Great American Capitalists, 1861–1901* (New York, 1934), chap. XI, "Giants of the Northwest"; Sigvart L. Rugland, "The Norwegian Press of the Northwest, 1885–1900," master's thesis, University of Iowa, 1929; Anton Hillesland, "The Norwegian Lutheran Church in the Red River Valley," *Collections* of the State Historical Society of North Dakota, VII, 195–283. For an article on John O. Engesather see *Sons of Norway*, January, 1948, p. 5.

IX: MONTANA

Joseph Kinsey Howard's *Montana High, Wide, and Handsome* (New Haven, 1943) is a spirited account of some of the problems, economic and otherwise, that have troubled the state during its history. Most of the material on A. M. Holter came from his article, "Pioneer Lumbering in Montana," *Contributions* of the Historical Society of Montana, VIII, 251–281. Further information on Holter was furnished me by Lucinda B. Scott, librarian of the Historical Society of Montana at Helena. The source for my material on the Gyppo contract system was O. M. Grimsby, "The Contribution of the Scandinavian and Germanic People to the Development of Montana," master's thesis, University of Montana, 1926. The story about Martin Grande came from Arne Kildal, *De Gjorde Norge Større* (Oslo, 1945), pp. 32 ff. In addition to the United States Census Reports I consulted *Reports* of the Bureau of Agriculture, Labor, and Industry of the State of Montana, particularly the Eighth (1902), and Eleventh (1908).

X: THE FAR WEST

Kenneth Bjork pointed out the parallel between the early Norwegian migration to America and the later migration from the Middle West to the Far West in "Norwegians in the Golden West," *Nordisk Tidende,* December 9, 1948, pp. 13, 23. At present material on the Norwegians in the West is scattered and not easily available, but Mr. Bjork is preparing for the Norwegian-American Historical Association a comprehensive history of this group, which will greatly add to the story of Americans from Norway. My story on Benedikte Steffensen is based on family records published in *Utah Genealogical and Historical Magazine,* XXIV, 10–12. Kenneth Bjork, *Saga in Steel and Concrete: Norwegian Engineers in America* (Northfield, Minn., Nor.-Amer. Historical Assoc., 1947) has material on Martinius Strand and other engineers mentioned in this chapter. Tosten Kittelson Stabaek's "An Account of a Journey to California in 1852" has been translated by Einar I. Haugen, *Studies and Records, IV, 99–124. See Ylvisaker's *Eminent Pioneers,* pp. 67–78, for a sketch of Snowshoe Thompson. For an account of the Olson shipping company see Jack McNairn and Jerry MacMullen, *Ships of the Redwood Coast* (Stanford University, 1945), pp. 60–65.

XI: THE PACIFIC NORTHWEST

The quotation at the beginning of this chapter is from "Chance Days In Oregon" by H. H., *Atlantic Monthly,* January, 1883, p. 119. My main sources for this chapter were: James B. Hedges, "Immigration to the Pacific Northwest," *Mississippi Valley Historical Review,* XV, 183–203; Sverre Nord, *A Logger's Odyssey* (Caldwell, Idaho, 1943); John Storseth, "Pioneering on the Pacific Coast," *Studies and Records,* XIII, 162 (for quotation on p. 122); Thos. Ostenson Stine, *Scandinavians on the Pacific, Puget Sound* (Seattle, 1900); Sverre Arestad, "The Norwegians in the Pacific Coast Fisheries," *Pacific Northwest Quarterly,* XXXIV, 3–17. Arne Kildal, *De Gjorde Norge Større* has material on Norwegians in Alaska mentioned in this chapter (pp. 25–27, 37–39, 42–44); see also John G. Holme, "The Reindeer Industry in Alaska," *American-Scandinavian Review,* X, 356–361; Arthur S. Peterson, "The Introduction of Domesticated Reindeer into Alaska," *Studies and Records,* XI, 98–113.

XII & XIII: The Atlantic Coast and The Century Mark

The main source for material on the Norwegians on the eastern coast is A. N. Rygg, *Norwegians in New York: 1825–1925* (Brooklyn, 1941); from various issues of *Nordisk Tidende* I used items. President Calvin Coolidge's address at the Norse-American Centennial, June 8, 1925, is printed in *American-Scandinavian Review*, XII, 483–490. Laurence M. Larson has an excellent article, "A Century of Achievement, 1825–1925, The New Norway in the New World," *American-Scandinavian Review*, XIII, 333–347.

Prairie Society

XIV: Taking Roots

For the title of the section I am indebted to J. Useem and R. H. Useem, "Minority Group Pattern in Prairie Society," *American Journal of Sociology*, L, 377–385, which is a comparative study of two Norwegian groups, one in a city in western Iowa, the other in a near-by South Dakota farm community. Material on O. E. Rölvaag and quotations are from Theodore Jorgenson and Nora O. Solum, *Ole Edvart Rölvaag* (New York, Harper & Bros. 1939). The incident related by U. V. Koren is from his *"Nogle Erindringer fra min Ungdom og min første Tid i Amerika,"* Symra, 1905, p. 30. For an excellent study of mental diseases among Norwegian immigrants see Örnulv Ödegaard, "Emigration and Insanity: A Study of Mental Diseases among the Norwegian-born Population of Minnesota," *Acta Psychiatrica et Neurologica, Supplementum IV* (Copenhagen, 1932). The quotation on p. 134 is from Fredrika Bremer, *Homes of the New World,* I, 631 ff. The quotation on p. 135 is from Olaus Fredrik Duus, *Frontier Parsonage: The Letters of Olaus Fredrik Duus, Norwegian Pastor in Wisconsin, 1855–1858* (Northfield, Minn., Nor.-Amer. Historical Assoc., 1947), p. 74. The Berdahl family records in my possession are the source of several quotations. See N. O. Nelson, "My Business Life," *World's Work,* XIX, 12388, for quotation on pp. 137, 139; see Nils P. Haugen, *Pioneer and Political Reminiscences,* p. 13, for quotation on p. 137; see Henry H. Bakken (ed.), "Pioneers in Dakota Territory, 1879–89," *Studies and Records,* XIII, 30–31, for quotation on pp. 137–38. My material on the language problems of the immigrants is based on the excellent study by Einar Haugen, "Language and Immigration," *Studies and Records,* X, 1–43. Other material came from K. Neutson, *Memoirs of a Pioneer* (privately printed, 1938), p. 3. On name-changing among immigrants see Marjorie M. Kimmerle, "Norwegian-American Surnames," *Studies and Records,* XII, 1–32. Among the A. A. Veblen Papers at the Minnesota State Historical Society there is a 9-page manuscript criticism of Joseph Dorfman's *Thorstein Veblen and His America.* In the course of the criticism the author, one Mr. Haga, discusses name-changing among Norwegian immigrants, takes Rölvaag to task, and tells the story of the scandalized mother whose son changed his name. The quotation at the end of the chapter is from Eric Sevareid, *Not So Wild a Dream* (New York, Alfred A. Knopf, Inc., 1946), p. 11.

XV: THE CHURCH

Out of the voluminous literature on the history of the Norwegian Lutheran Church in America I am referring to but a few standard and readily accessible accounts, the best of which is J. Magnus Rohne's *Norwegian American Lutheranism up to 1872;* see also T. Eggen, *"Oversigt over den Norsk-Lutherske Kirkes Historie i Amerika,"* in *Norsk-Amerikanernes Festskrift 1914,* pp. 204–244; Blegen, *Norwegian Migration . . . The American Transition* (hereafter referred to as Blegen (II)); Babcock, *The Scandinavian Element in the United States;* Alfred O. Fonkalsrud, *The American-Scandinavian* (Minneapolis, 1915). Fredrika Bremer's observations are from *Homes of the New World,* I, 612. The quotation on p. 151 is from U. V. Koren, *"Nogle Erindringer . . . ,"* p. 36. For the experiences of a pioneer pastor's wife see Elisabeth Koren, *Fra Pioneertid* (Decorah, Iowa, 1914). These reminiscences are among the most charmingly written and valuable accounts of pioneer life in the immigrant literature of the Middle West. For further material on pioneer clergymen and their families see Karen Larsen, *Laur. Larsen: Pioneer College President* (Northfield, Minn., Nor.-Amer. Historical Assoc., 1936); quotations are from pp. 46–47, 52. See also Duus, *Frontier Parsonage.*

The common school issue is well presented in Laurence M. Larson, " 'Skandinaven, Professor Anderson, and the Yankee School' " in *The Changing West,* pp. 116–146. See also Arthur S. Paulson and Kenneth Bjork (trans. and ed.), "A School and Language Controversy in 1858: A Documentary Study," *Studies and Records,* X, 76–106. The quotation on p. 154 is from Hjalmar Hjorth Boyesen, "The Scandinavian Element in the United States," *North American Review,* CLV, 535. The quotation on pp. 154–55 is from the Berdahl family records. I have quoted from Anton Hillesland, "The Norwegian Lutheran Church in the Red River Valley," p. 258. Portions of the diary of P. J. Reinertson, from which I have quoted, are in O. M. Grimsby, "The Contribution of the Scandinavian and Germanic People to the Development of Montana," pp. 91–102. I have used the annual reports of the Evangelical (Norwegian) Lutheran Church, particularly *Annual Report, 1948* (Minneapolis, Minn.). The quotation on p. 159 is from B. J. Hovde, "Norwegian Americans" in *One America,* ed. by F. J. Brown and J. S. Roucek (New York,

Prentice-Hall, 1946), p. 55. Attitudes that ran counter to the prevailing Lutheran point of view are found in Janson, *Hvad Jeg Har Oplevet*, pp. 252–257; Steenerson, "Recollections . . . ," p. 147. The letter from which the quotation on p. 161 is taken is in the Kristian Prestgard Correspondence in the Norwegian-American Historical Association archives at St. Olaf College. The Olaf Ray letter, quoted on p. 162, is in the Olaf Ray Correspondence in these archives.

XVI: Two Colleges

My sources for material on Luther College were Karen Larsen, *Laur. Larsen* (quotation from p. 164); Andrew Veblen, "At Luther College, 1877–1881," unpublished manuscript in the Veblen Papers at the Minnesota State Historical Society, St. Paul; Harcourt H. Horn, *An English Colony in Iowa* (Boston, Christopher Publishing House, 1931), pp. 66, 53. The most recent and detailed history of St. Olaf College is William C. Benson, *High on Manitou, A History of St. Olaf College 1874–1949* (Northfield, Minn., 1949). For further details on F. Melius Christiansen see Leola Nelson Bergmann, *Music Master of the Middle West: The Story of F. Melius Christiansen and the St. Olaf Choir* (Minneapolis, 1944). See also Erik Hetle, *Lars Wilhelm Boe: A Biography* (Minneapolis, 1949).

XVII: The Press

The best account of the Norwegian press from its beginnings up to 1914 is found in *Norsk-Amerikanernes Festskrift 1914:* Carl Hansen, *"Pressen til borgerkrigens slutning"* and Johannes B. Wist, *"Pressen efter borgerkrigen."* See also Theodore C. Blegen, "The Early Norwegian Press in America," *Minnesota History Bulletin,* III, 506–518; Albert O. Barton, "The Beginnings of the Norwegian Press in America," *Proceedings* of the Wisconsin Historical Society, 1916, pp. 186–212. The following publications were especially useful in the writing of this chapter: O. M. Norlie, *Norwegian-Americana Papers 1847–1946* (Northfield, Minn., 1946). This is a valuable compilation of more than five hundred newspaper and periodical titles, giving their date of publication, place, and editor. Carl Fredrik Solberg, "Reminiscences of a Pioneer Editor" (ed. by Albert O. Barton), *Studies and Records,* I, 134–144; Harold M. Tolo, "The Political Position of *Emigranten* in the Election of 1852: A Documentary Article," *Studies and Records,* VIII, 92–111; Agnes M. Larson, "The Editorial Policy of *Skandinaven,* 1900–1903," *Studies and Records,* VIII, 112–135; Sigvart Luther Rugland, "The Norwegian Press of the Northwest, 1885–1900," master's thesis, University of Iowa, 1929. Quotations on p. 174 are from J. P. Hertsgaard, *Early Community History: Kindred, North Dakota, 1870–1900* (Northfield, Minn., c. 1949), pp. 31–32; Blegen (II), 549. The quotations from Birger Osland's *A Long Pull from*

Stavanger (Northfield, Minn., Nor.-Amer. Historical Assoc., 1945) are from pp. 15–16. Quotations on p. 178 are from Horn, *An English Colony in Iowa*, p. 66, and from Haugen, *Pioneer and Political Reminiscences*, p. 19.

XVIII: An Editor and His Friends

The major portion of this chapter is based on the Kristian Prestgard Correspondence in the Norwegian-American Historical Association archives. The quotation on p. 184 is from Henriette C. K. Naeseth, "Kristian Prestgard: An Appreciation," *Studies and Records*, XV, 132. Among Prestgard's better known writings are *En Sommer i Norge* (Minneapolis, 1928) and *Fjords and Faces* (Minneapolis, 1937), a translation of part of the former.

The Cities

XIX: Chicago

The story of the Offerdahls is from George Sessions Perry, "Your Neighbors: The Offerdahls," *Saturday Evening Post*, October 9, 1948, pp. 26–27, 164–166. The scene of the Norwegian Quartet Club ball is based largely on material from Osland's *A Long Pull from Stavanger;* I have also drawn extensively on his chapters, "Norwegian Clubs in Chicago," and "The Norwegian National League," for material on club life in the latter part of this chapter, as well as from Maurice B. Hansen and Norman Blessum, *Brief History of Normendenes Sangforening, Chicago, Illinois, 1870–1945* (Chicago, 1945). A detailed source of information on Norwegians in Chicago is A. E. Strand, *A History of the Norwegians of Illinois* (Chicago, 1905). I also used Albert O. Barton, "Norwegian-American Emigration Societies in the Forties and Fifties," *Studies and Records*, III, 23–42; Brynjolf J. Hovde (trans. and ed.), "Chicago as Viewed by a Norwegian Immigrant in 1864," *Studies and Records*, III, 65–72.

My sources for the discussion of Marcus Thrane were: Waldemar Westgaard (trans. and ed.), "Marcus Thrane in America, Some Unpublished Letters from 1880–1884," *Studies and Records*, IX, 67–76; Carl G. O. Hansen, "The Story of Marcus Thrane," *Sons of Norway*, January, 1949, pp. 17–19; Napier Wilt and Henriette C. Koren Naeseth, "Two Early Norwegian Dramatic Societies in Chicago," *Studies and Records*, X, 44–75; Marcus Thrane, *Den Gamle Wisconsin Bibelen*. The last appeared in 1881, was reprinted four times between then and 1912. Out of print for several years thereafter, it was finally reprinted in 1938 by the Scandia Publishing Company, Chicago. I have used the latter edition as the basis for my freely translated excerpts from it.

For an historical account of Bjørnson's visit see Arthur C. Paulson, "Bjørnson and the Norwegian-Americans, 1880–1881," *Studies and Records,* V, 84–109; Arthur C. Paulson, "The Norwegian-American Reaction to Ibsen and Bjørnson, 1850–1900," doctor's thesis, University of Iowa, 1932. Other publications referred to are: Blegen (I), 323–330; J. B. Wist, *"Pressen efter borgerkrigen,"* 91–93; K. Steenerson, "Recollections . . . ," p. 147. Quotations from Olaf Ray are taken from a letter of Ray's to J. Jörgen Thompson (April 30, 1943) in the Olaf Ray Correspondence in the Norwegian-American Historical Association archives.

XX: Minneapolis

Carl G. O. Hansen's *History of the Sons of Norway, 1895–1945* (Minneapolis, 1945) and the files of the monthly magazine, *Sons of Norway,* were the sources for all information on this organization. The best source for information about Kristofer Janson is his autobiography, *Hvad Jeg Har Oplevet.* My quotations from Andreas Ueland's *Recollections of an Immigrant* (New York, Minton, Balch & Co., 1929) are from pp. 48–49, 62–63, 164, 192–193, 194.

XXI & XXII: Brooklyn and The West Coast

The only single source of collected material on Brooklyn Norwegians is A. N. Rygg, *Norwegians in New York, 1825–1925* (Brooklyn, 1941). In addition I used files of the *Nordisk Tidende* and a pamphlet published by this newspaper, *Hvordan "Nordisk Tidende" blir til,* which includes an appendix, "An X-Ray Picture of a Norwegian-American Colony." The quotation about Julius Olsen was taken from *Nordisk Tidende,* May 27, 1948, p. 9. I have also used the *Annual Report, 1944,* of the Norwegian Lutheran Church of America, and material from Bjork's *Saga in Steel and Concrete,* pp. 456–458.

The quotation on p. 211 is from Osland's *A Long Pull from Stavanger,* p. 93. For the section on the West Coast I also used Stine's *Scandinavians on the Pacific, Puget Sound.*

Sailors

XXIII: In Great Waters

Knut Gjerset has written two comprehensive books on Norwegian sailors: *Norwegian Sailors on the Great Lakes: A Study in the History of American Inland Transportation* (Northfield, Minn., Nor.-Amer. Historical Assoc.,

1928); *Norwegian Sailors in American Waters: A Study in the History of Maritime Activity on the Eastern Seaboard* (Northfield, Minn., Nor.-Amer. Historical Assoc., 1933). I have quoted the remark of Capt. Robert Adams from this latter book, p. 63.

XXIV: STORY OF A RIVER CAPTAIN

The quotations on p. 219 are from Fred A. Bill, "Red River Steamboating," *North Dakota Historical Quarterly*, II, 212–213. Louis Nyhammer personally gave me an account of his life and experiences. In addition I had a typescript sketch of his life and work written by Dorothy Warren, river reporter for the *St. Paul Pioneer Press*, as well as articles by Dorothy Warren in the *St. Paul Pioneer Press*, August 24, 1941, and in *The Christian Science Monitor*, August 2, 1941. Quotations from Nyhammer's diary were taken from excerpts from it which he sent to me during a correspondence and which he kindly gave me permission to use.

XXV: A GREAT EMANCIPATOR

Grace Hadley Fuller of the division of bibliography, Library of Congress, in 1942 compiled a Furuseth bibliography containing 264 items, 221 of which are speeches, pamphlets, etc., by Furuseth himself, the rest articles about him. Professor Kenneth Bjork, who has a typescript of this bibliography, kindly made it available to me. The sources from which I have drawn most heavily in the writing of this chapter are: *Congressional Record* (vol. 50, 63rd Cong., 1st sess., pp. 5709 ff.) for the debate on Seamen's Bill led by Senator La Follette, October 21, 1913. The quotation from the Senator's speech is from p. 5716. The *Congressional Record* also has tributes to Furuseth by Senators Harold H. Burton (78th Cong., March 12, 1945) and Robert M. La Follette, Jr. (79th Cong., March 14, 1946); Arthur Emil Albrecht's *International Seamen's Union of America, A Study of its History and Problems* (Bulletin of the U. S. Bureau of Labor Statistics, No. 342, 1923, 120 pp.); "The Seamen's Act," *Sen. Doc. No. 694, 64th Cong., 2nd sess., 1917; "American Sea Power and the Seamen's Act," *Sen. Doc. No. 228, 65th Cong., 2nd sess., 1918; for material relating to President Woodrow Wilson I have used Ray Stannard Baker's *Woodrow Wilson, Life and Letters* (Garden City, N.Y., Doubleday, Page & Co., 1927–1939), I, 546; IV, 213, 364; VII, 537; VIII, 556; the quotation on p. 230 is from vol. IV, p. 364. Material relating to Samuel Gompers comes from Samuel Gompers, *Seventy Years of Life and Labor* (New York, E. P. Dutton & Co., 1925). The quotation is from vol. I, p. 348. A. N. Rygg in his article on Andrew Furuseth in *The American-Scandinavian Review*, XXVII, 123–133, quotes the passage from *La Follette's Magazine* which I have also used. President Wilson's alleged remark to

Tumulty I have taken from an article on Furuseth in the *Sons of Norway*, February, 1945. The letter about Andrew Furuseth from Olaf Ray to J. Jörgen Thompson (April 30, 1943) is in the Olaf Ray Correspondence in the Norwegian-American Historical Association archives. I have also used two articles by George P. West, "Andrew Furuseth and the Radicals," *Survey*, XLVII, 207–209; "Andrew Furuseth Stands Pat," *Survey*, LI, 86–90. Knut Gjerset has a good chapter on Furuseth in *Norwegian Sailors in American Waters*.

Outstanding Individuals

My sources for this section have been the standard biographical dictionaries and directories, chiefly *Who's Who in America, American Men of Science, Directory of American Scholars, Current Biography,* and *Dictionary of American Biography*. The latter has articles on the following Norwegian Americans: Hjalmar Hjorth Boyesen, Claus L. Clausen, Theodor H. Dahl, Johannes W. C. Dietrichson, Elling Eielsen, Gilbert N. Haugen, Nils P. Haugen, Elling Hove, Gjermund Hoyme, Kristofer Janson, Erik K. Johnsen, Johan N. Kildahl, John Koren, Ulrick Vilhelm Koren, Peter Laur. Larsen, Victor F. Lawson, Knute Nelson, Nelson O. Nelson, Sven Oftedal, Alfred Owre, Cleng Peerson, Christian K. Preus, Johan R. Reiersen, Knute K. Rockne, Ole Rynning, Ole E. Rölvaag, Friedrich A. Schmidt, Peer O. Strømme, Hans G. Stub, Georg Sverdrup, Bertha Feiring Tapper, Erik Tou, Thorstein B. Veblen, Agnes M. Wergeland. Of these Claus L. Clausen was born in Denmark and Friedrich A. Schmidt was born in Germany, but both belonged, sociologically, to the Norwegian American group.

Other frequently used sources of information were the files of *The American-Scandinavian Review, Sons of Norway, Nordmanns Forbundet,* and numerous newspapers, American and Norwegian American. References for figures like Boyesen, Veblen, and Rölvaag are numerous and easily accessible to the interested reader; I have cited merely a few that were particularly helpful to me.

XXVII: SCHOLARS AND SCIENTISTS

In Laurence M. Larson's *The Changing West* I drew heavily from two excellent essays, "The Norwegian Element in the Field of American Scholarship" and "Hjalmar Hjorth Boyesen." For material on Rasmus B. Anderson see his autobiography, *Life Story of Rasmus B. Anderson* (Madison, Wis., 1915) and Einar I. Haugen, "A Critique and a Bibliography of the Writings of Rasmus B. Anderson," *Wisconsin Magazine of History,* XX, 255–269. A sympathetic account of Agnes M. Wergeland's life is found in Maren Michelet, *Glimpses from Agnes Mathilde Wergeland's Life* (privately printed, 1916). The author of this book also came from a distinguished Norwegian family. Among the Michelets were several military and political leaders. Maren Michelet's father, a lawyer, emigrated to America after the Civil War. Most of his six children entered professions and married into old-stock American families. Maren Michelet graduated from the University of Minnesota, became a language teacher in a Minneapolis high school where she was instrumental in introducing, in 1910, the first course in Norwegian taught in any public high school in the United States; she published widely on the subject of modern language instruction, wrote a Norwegian grammar, and edited the works of Agnes M. Wergeland.

For material on Leonhard Stejneger see *Copeia,* October, 1931, which is a Leonhard Stejneger anniversary number with portraits, a biography by Albert K. Fisher, and other material related to Stejneger's work at the National Museum.

XXVIII: Medical Men

Sketches of Norwegian pioneer doctors are found in Knut Gjerset and Ludvig Hektoen, "Health Conditions and the Practice of Medicine among the Early Norwegian Settlers, 1825–1865," *Studies and Records,* I, 1–59. The most comprehensive source for material on Alfred Owre is Netta Wilson's *Alfred Owre: Dentistry's Militant Educator* (Minneapolis, 1937).

XXX: The Veblens

See Erling Ylvisaker's *Eminent Pioneers* for sketches of Thomas and Kari Veblen. Joseph Dorfman's *Thorstein Veblen and His America* (New York, 1934) is the only full-length treatment of Veblen's life and work. The quotation on p. 260 is from a letter in the A. A. Veblen Papers at the Minnesota State Historical Society, St. Paul, Minnesota. See Walter P. Metzger's "Ideology and the Intellectual: A Study of Thorstein Veblen," *Philosophy of Science,* XVI (1949), 125–133. In this refreshingly new approach the author analyzes Veblen's work "as it is representative of the response of 'intellectuals' to specific ideologies and to ideology in general." His main thesis is that while Veblen rejected the ideology of the dominant group (business) and did not defend the ideologies of the then aspiring groups (Progressives and Marxists), he himself constructed or produced—as a member of another group, the intelligentsia—an ideology that served the interests of this group, articulating its desire for rewards in a period when America's intellectuals were disillusioned and groped for an ideology of their own.

XXXI: Wars and Expeditions

The quotations from Colonel Heg's letters are from Theodore Blegen (ed.), *The Civil War Letters of Colonel Hans Christian Heg* (Northfield, Minn., Nor.-Amer. Historical Assoc., 1936), pp. 65, 79–80, 115, 246. Evans Carlson's story is told in Michael Blankfort, *The Big Yankee: The Life of Carlson of the Raiders* (Boston, 1947).

XXXII: Politics and Government Service

The best source for information about Knute Nelson is M. W. Odland's *The Life of Knute Nelson* (Minneapolis, 1926). The quotation on p. 268 is from a letter in the Nicolay Grevstad Correspondence in the Norwegian-American Historical Association archives. The statements by Floyd Olson are from Charles Rumford Walker's *An American City: A Rank-and-File History* (New York, Farrar & Rinehart, 1937), pp. 199–202. For further material on Olson see John S. McGrath and J. J. Delmont, *Floyd Bjornstjerne Olson, Minnesota's Greatest Liberal Governor* (St. Paul, 1937).

XXXIII: Newspapermen

The source for most of my material on Victor Lawson was Charles H. Dennis, *Victor Lawson: His Time and His Work* (Chicago, 1935). See Eric Sevareid's *Not So Wild a Dream* (New York, Alfred A. Knopf, Inc., 1946) for a noteworthy contribution in this field.

XXXIV: Business and Finance

My main sources for information on N. O. Nelson were his own numerous articles, particularly "My Business Life," *World's Work*, XIX, 12387–93, 12504–11, which deals with his childhood and youth as well as his later career. The following articles, all published in the magazine *Independent* over a period extending from 1901 to 1912 deal with his business and philanthropic activities: "One Manufacturer's Experiment," LIII, 423–427; "A Home for Consumptives," LVI, 414–416; "Leclaire's Progress," LVI, 1314; "Profit Sharing with the Customer," LVIII, 1179–1182; "Business Pure and Tainted," LX, 481–484; "My Latest Experiment," LXIV, 684–687; "The Remedy for City Congestion," LXV, 703–706; "Co-operation," LXXI, 643–645; "Profit Sharing," LXXI, 858–860; "Progressives," LXXIII, 123–124. See also George W. Eads, "N. O. Nelson, Practical Coöperator, and the Great Work He Is Accomplishing for Human Upliftment," *Arena*, XXXVI, 463–480, and Harry H. Dunn, "Fifty Shops Given to Clerks," *Technical World Magazine*, XXIII, 444–448.

Most of my material on Arthur Andersen I took from the files of his firm's publication, *The Arthur Andersen Chronicle,* for the years 1940–1944.

XXXVI: LITERATURE AND THE ARTS

The most important source of information on Rölvaag is Theodore Jorgenson and Nora O. Solum's *O. E. Rölvaag: A Biography* (New York, 1939). See also the following articles in *Studies and Records:* Einar I. Haugen, "O. E. Rölvaag: Norwegian-American," VII, 53–73; Kenneth Bjork, "The Unknown Rölvaag: Secretary in the Norwegian-American Historical Association," XI, 114–149; John Heitman, "Ole Edvart Rölvaag," XII, 144–166.

Luther Onerheim's work has been excellently portrayed in a booklet: *The Soldier Chorus: An Illustrated History of the Great A Cappella Choir Built by Luther M. Onerheim in the Fifth U.S. Infantry Regiment, Seventy-first Division* (Augsburg, Germany, J. P. Himmer, 1946). A. N. Rygg, *Norwegians in New York, 1825–1925* has information on numerous musicians, painters, and sculptors.

XXXVII: SPORTS

For material on Knute Rockne see *The Autobiography of Knute K. Rockne,* edited by Bonnie Skiles Rockne (Indianapolis, 1931) and Harry A. Stuhldreher, *Knute Rockne, Man Builder* (Philadelphia, 1931). For good material on skiing see Frank Elkins, "Norwegian Influence on American Skiing," *The American-Scandinavian Review,* XXXV, 335–340, from which I have quoted.

Index